Pieter Breughel, DANCING PEASANTS, Vienna Museum

THE ARTS AND HUMANITY

a Psychological Introduction to the Fine Arts

by

CHAS. W. COOPER, Ph.D.

Professor of English
Chairman, Fine Arts Committee
Whittier College

PHILOSOPHICAL LIBRARY
NEW YORK

68232

Preliminary edition, September 1947
Second printing, June 1948
Second offset edition, September 1949
(rewritten and enlarged)
PHILOSOPHICAL LIBRARY, April 1952
(third edition, revised)

PRINTED IN THE UNITED STATES OF AMERICA

To
V. S. C.
who loved all
the arts and humanity
and knew them
one

PREFACE AND ACKNOWLEDGMENTS

THE ARTS AND HUMANITY—a psychological introduction to the Fine Arts—is neither an academic treatise nor a popular guide. It is designed to be an instrument for General Education in the Humanities.

The point of view of this book is psychological and semantic, for it is concerned with human behavior both in creative art activity and in responsive art experience, and it considers works of art not only as beautiful (that is, valuable) but also as meaningful human phenomena.

In this introduction to the Fine Arts, more attention is given to Painting, Music, and Literature than to Architecture, Sculpture, Theater Art, and Dance, but they are all part of the synthesis; for the point of view of *The Arts and Humanity* is integrative, and the several different arts are looked upon as interrelated, forming a whole, an important area of human life, the World of Art.

Furthermore, it is the point of view of this book that art theory and art experience are also intimately interrelated, that a person's generalizations about art derive from his observation of particular works of art and that, in turn, such generalizations condition further art experiences.

Several purposes of *The Arts and Humanity* are stated or implied in the course of the book:

To help the reader clarify and enlarge his art theory.

To help him gain semantic control, through the techniques of definition and classification, of key terms useful in considering the arts.

To help him orient himself in the World of Art, and to suggest worthy goals for personal cultivation of taste.

To help him establish some basis for discussing beauty and meaning in art.

To help him appreciate the creative art activity that brings works of art into being.

To help him understand the physical make-up of works of art as they exist outside the mind of man.

To help him discriminate the several phases of his own complex responses to works of art and to make concrete suggestions that may lead to enriched art experiences.

To help him realize his human need for art, to provide him with a number of worth while and memorable art experiences, and to suggest standards for evaluation.

To help him see that the arts are inseparable from humanity, that they are ever-present in daily life, stretching back through the past to the very dawn of Man and reaching into the most intimate recesses of the human mind and spirit.

"No satisfaction," writes John Holmes of the poet's work, "equals the satisfaction of springing at last the obstinate words into the stubborn line." And, I might add, springing at long last the final words into the preface of a book. Such final words are, appropriately, the personal acknowledgment of various sorts of indebtedness.

First, it is a pleasure to thank the following persons:

I. A. Richards, university professor at Harvard University, for his generous encouragement and for the valued insights derived from his books on aesthetics and literary criticism; Albert W. Upton, long-time colleague at Whittier College, for his stimulating friendship in this and other ventures; William C. Jones and Harold F. Spencer, for making possible a sabbatical leave for rewriting this book and for the past years of freedom in developing the course in which it is rooted; Elnora Laughlin, Margaretha Lohmann, DeLisle Crawford, and (in past years) Herbert F. Evans, fellow members of the Fine Arts Committee, for their helpfulness and confidence; Anne M. Pierce, as well as other student assistants of these past years, and the students who made use of the first and second preliminary editions, for the questions they asked and suggestions they made.

Neff Cummings, Bill Eshelman, Celeste T. Wright, William A. Pullin, and Calvin S. Brown, for detailed comments on the preliminary edition; Millard P. Binyon, Hazel C. Schupp, and Richard N. Clark, Jr., for their various reports on the manuscript as rewritten; Benjamin G. Whitten and Madeline T. Wise, for help with the proofs of the present edition.

The staffs of the Harvard University libraries—the Widener, Houghton, Fogg Museum, Psychological Laboratory, and Music Department libraries —and of the Radcliffe College and the Whittier College libraries, for help in securing reference material; and William Tudhope, for a Greek translation.

Those who were especially helpful in preparation, production, and permissions for the first preliminary edition: Irving and Alva Cox, Murray Gregory and Commercial Offset Printers, University Prints, Cecilia Huntington, and Columbia Pictures; and those who prepared the master copy and manufactured the second offset edition, Edith K. Morrell and Edwards Brothers, Inc., Lithoprinters.

My school, college, and university instructors in art and music, literature and theater art: Nellie H. Geer, Bessie Ella Hazen; Herman Trutner, Ruth Grant; Herbert E. Harris, Herbert F. Allen, Percy H. Houston, Alfred Longueil, Willard Farnham, Guy Montgomery; Charles von Neumeyer, Evelyn Thomas, Tempe E. Allison.

My mother, Virginia S. Cooper, painter and sculptor; my father, Clarence Lincoln Cooper, student of architecture and literature; my elder sister Elizabeth, musician—indeed all my sisters and my cousins, and my uncles and my aunts, and kinsmen further removed, who have pursued the several arts and who have somehow taught or inspired me; my son, as one of those for whom this book was specifically written; and most especially my wife, Edris B. Cooper, companion in this undertaking, who has shared the tedious work on the manuscript and proof, discussing critical problems and giving heart to the project.

Second, it is a pleasant obligation to acknowledge indebtedness for permission to use certain photographs and copyrighted materials and for photo copy for the illustrations, and to give thanks to the following persons, firms, and institutions:

Elmer C. Aldrich, State of California, Division of Beaches and Parks, for the photo of California Redwoods, Bull Creek Flats, Humboldt State Park.

Art Institute of Chicago, for the contemporary copy by an unknown artist of *The Barque of Dante* by Delacroix.

Art Reference Bureau, Inc., and Fratelli Alinari, Florence, for photographs of *The Wrestlers, Pantheon, Perseus and Medusa* by Cellini, two models of the *Perseus* by Cellini, two copies of *Discobolus* by Myron, two views of *A Gaul and His Wife*.

(1902, renewal 1930) by Oliver Ditson Company. Words reprinted by permission.

Arthur Rothmann Fine Arts, Inc., sole agents for Anton Schroll & Co., Vienna (color prints), for *Dancing Peasants* by Pieter Breughel.

G. Schirmer, Inc., for the theme of *Adagio for Strings* by Samuel Barber.

Charles Scribner's Sons, see copyright page of this book.

Carroll S. Tyson, for *Sunflowers* by Vincent Van Gogh.

James K. Ufford, Fogg Museum of Art, for the photo of the *Discus Thrower* on the Harvard University Campus.

Duncan Wimpress, director of public relations, Whittier College, for the photo of The Plush Horror.

YALE REVIEW, copyright Yale University Press, and Celeste T. Wright, for *Grave in the Foothills,* and Celeste T. Wright for her memoranda relative to its creation.

Those who kindly provided photographs not finally included as illustrations in this edition: City Art Museum, St. Louis; National Park Service, Sequoia National Park; William Rockhill Nelson Gallery of Art, Kansas City, Missouri; Tate Gallery of London.

To all of the above named, again, sincere thanks.

C. W. C.

Cambridge, Massachusetts
    13 July, 1949
Westwood, Los Angeles, Calif.
    4 July, 1951

TABLE OF CONTENTS

TABLE OF ART WORKS

presented as illustrations

TABLE OF ART WORKS

THE ARTS AND HUMANITY

The Interrelation of Art Experience and Art Theory

> The one indispensable talent for creative art, whether of the
> theatre or literature or music or plastic representation, is the talent
> for experiencing.
>
> Mary Austin, *Everyman's Genius*

EXPERIENCING works of art and theorizing about art are two quite
different sorts of human activity.

Turn to the frontispiece, a reproduction of Pieter Breughel's *Dancing
Peasants,* and allow yourself a leisurely experience of it. Look at
it closely; let your eyes wander freely over the scene. Notice the expression
on the bagpiper's face, glance down to the jug handle and
nut shells on the ground, up to the bill posted on the tree, back to
the church tower, over to the flag hung from an upper window and
to the young man and woman at the door below it, farther over to
the kissing couple and down to the amazingly little folk by the bagpiper—and
then to the forward dancing couple (what is the position
of the man's legs? and what is stuck in his cap?) and back to
the other dancing couples.

Perhaps, as you look at this picture, you rather enjoy the rollicking
and rowdy activity that is represented, the care-free merry-making
and feeling of exhilaration, the free images of bousy laughter and
wheezy music, of hopping and swinging movement. Or it may be
the richness of detail and the activity of the forms that attract your
eye and attention. Or a sequence of reflective thoughts may be stirred
in you about folk art, about Flemish life in the dawning Renaissance,
about the values of social life and good fellowship. . . .

As you come back from the picture, remember that this one particular
art experience is to be considered as an *example* of art experience.
Other examples would be different in many ways—the listening
to a symphony, for instance, or the reading of *Alice in Wonderland*
or *Moby Dick.*

Now let us consider an example of art theory.

Give your close attention to the following italicized statement from Rhys Carpenter's discussion of 'the artistic function of pure form' in the art of painting: *"From the fusion of the two aspects of a line—its purely formal value with its representational quality—arises a new thing which I call the aesthetic or artistic emotion."*

The meaning of this statement will surely become clearer if we place it in its context in Rhys Carpenter's book, *The Aesthetic Basis of Greek Art.* "Suppose," he says of line, which he considers one of the most obvious pure forms—"Suppose that we isolate various lines by removing them from a picture and putting them by themselves. For lack of context, we have no notion of the objects which these lines helped to depict. We are treating them as unrepresentational lines, as lines that show nothing. Are they all emotionally alike? do we get the same feeling from every one?" he asks. "Not quite. . . . A straight line looks stiff; certain curves appeal to us as graceful; wavy lines have a restless effect. . . ." If lines are not alike in their effect, then, Carpenter says, "I have established the purely formal character of lines. But [he goes on] lines may also be representational. Such and such a combination of lines depicts such and such an object. . . . Does a line lose its formal value, the moment we see it represents a real object to us? Just here is the fundament and base of the contention. *From the fusion of the two aspects of a line—its purely formal value with its representational quality—arises a new thing which I call the aesthetic or artistic emotion."*

You may wish to pause for a moment to glance back over this paragraph to interpret more thoughtfully the last sentence here italicized. . . . Remember this is merely an *example* of art theory. It makes only one point of one limited sort. Other examples would be quite different in many ways—a definition of art or beauty, for instance, or a consideration of the relation of art to society, or the characteristics of the sonata form in music.

Experiencing Breughel's *Dancing Peasants* is one sort of thing. Thinking about Carpenter's statement of a point in his art theory is a very different sort of thing. The work-of-art experience is concrete and particular; the art-theory experience is abstract and general. The first may have involved rich sensations of line and form, lively free images, a variety of feelings and associations, as well as reflective thinking and evaluation. The second is strictly intellectual and critical, with perhaps limited images of line and form, certain thoughts of abstract concepts and relationships, and a calculated judgment of the validity of the statement. The work-of-art experience is thick and warm; the art-theory experience, thin and cool.

Perhaps, indeed, 'the fusion of the two aspects of a line' leaves you somewhat in a fog, and 'aesthetic or artistic emotion' just doesn't mean anything to you at all. Perhaps you ask a fearful or impatient question, "Does this mean that I have to see lines and triangles in everything?!" Be assured at this point that the present writer will not badger you, forcing you to 'see' anything at all. But the point of Carpenter's statement is that one can, and many people do, 'see' a particular line in a picture both as a curved line and as a man's shoulder and that this fused perception stirs a certain feeling that he calls 'aesthetic or artistic emotion.' You may deny that this accords with your experience, but you would have to admit—*he* sees double and likes it!

Your squaring this bit of art theory with your own experience is important to note, for it introduces our next point.

An abstract statement of art theory is ultimately derived from an observer's particular art experiences. That is, Carpenter's statement grew out of his thoughtful experience of many pictures, his noting the fusion of certain visual perceptions, his consciousness of feeling states, and his thinking about their cause-and-effect relation.

But it is also true that *a particular art experience is guided and controlled by the observer's art theory.* That is, if 'the fusion of the two aspects of a line causing an aesthetic emotion' is a part of a person's art theory, then he will probably experience such double perceptions and feeling when looking at a picture.

To illustrate this interplay of theory and experience, let us return to Breughel's *Dancing Peasants*, this time with Carpenter's bit of theory firmly in hand. Looking again at the bagpiper, you may note the lower line of his own right arm or the upper line of his right leg from groin to toe. . . . "That's right," you may say, "a line may indeed be thought of as having two aspects: that line *does* represent the bagpiper's leg, but it *is also* a line of a certain character and direction, an elongated double curve, not straight as I at first 'saw' it." And you may, in fact, realize a fusion of the somewhat irregular outline of the bagpiper's leg with a long free-sweeping double curve. "But," you may add, "this fusion does not give me anything that I personally could call 'aesthetic or artistic emotion.' "

As an experiment, trace freely the following lines on tracing paper pressed against the frontispiece: the straight line of the tall bagpipes over the player's shoulder, the curve of his back and the curve of his right arm, of his left knee, and that long sweeping line of his right leg—the two opposed straight lines of the arms of the distant dancer in the center of the picture, the curve of his back, the wavy lines of his upraised boot and of his partner's foot—the one crooked elbow and the other straight arm of the man dancing in the foreground, the line of his dagger, the straight line of the one leg and the angled line of the other—the forward leg of his fair partner, the line of her arm, and so on. . . . .

Hold the tracing paper away from the print, and just look at it! The stiff line, the full curve, the smooth glide, the sharp bend, the thrust and jump of the lines inclined at various angles, the wavy restlessness of the central lines! As these lines are abstracted from the picture, perhaps Carpenter's point becomes clear that 'lines are not alike in their effect.'

Now replace the tracing paper and let these abstracted lines fuse once more with the outlines of the human forms. If the individual fused lines do not give you certain distinctive feelings (call them what you will), perhaps the jamboree of fused lines (the abstracted lines on your tracing paper merged back into the active lines representing the dancing peasants) will evoke in you some sort of feeling that is exciting and expressive.

Perhaps this demonstration has made the statement in art theory clearer to you—perhaps it has also enlivened further your experience of the picture. It was intended primarily to do something else: to emphasize the fact that art experience and art theory go hand in hand. What you think about the arts and your gradually developed attitudes toward them will condition your looking at pictures, your listening to music, your reading of books. What your general art theory is will be a measure of your enjoyment, your understanding, your appreciation of the World of Art.

You may say, "But I don't have an art theory."

Everyone has some sort of art theory—not just artists or critics or teachers, but everyone. You may not have thought of it before, but everyone has some general notions of what is art and what isn't, of what he likes and dislikes, what he considers good, mediocre, and bad.

Indeed, the layman may never be conscious that he has an art theory; he may never put it into words; he may never work it out systematically; he may never call it 'aesthetics.' It may be vague and fragmentary; it may be inconsistent and contradictory. It may be a hodgepodge, pieced together from all manner of sources: tag ends of other persons' art theories, folk sayings and popular axioms, prejudices and preconceptions, and original observation.

One purpose of this book is to help you put your own art theory in order, to sharpen some of its outlines, fill in some of the gaps, and remove some of the inconsistencies. And this may seem to you to be worth doing when you see how directly your enlarged and clarified art theory may enrich your interest in art experiences.

On the World of Art and of People

One can, indeed, exist without art, but one cannot well *live* without it.

Eugen Neuhaus, *World of Art*

PIETER BREUGHEL depicted a lively scene in his *Dancing Peasants.* These Flemish folk of the Sixteenth Century are joyous and active, piping and dancing, drinking and love making. But if convivial delight is central in the picture, it is kept in perspective by the church on the horizon and by the abstracted expression of the bagpiper in the foreground. In this village street you may indeed see the world of people and the world of art as a fusion of two aspects of one world. Here, among the people are the arts—tavern flag and artful costume, homely dwelling and church architecture, strains of music and whirling dance. Wait but a moment and one of the tipplers will rise to sing or recite a contemporary or traditional ballad.

1. *Overture for this opera*

Since humanity is nowhere more vividly presented than in the theater, it is fitting to open this Prelude with Mozart's lively overture to his comic opera *The Marriage of Figaro.* There's really no need to know the opera itself or the circumstances of its composition in order to enjoy the music, but a bit of such background may be of interest to the curious.

Wolfgang Amadeus Mozart (1756-1791) was born in Salzburg, the son of a gifted musician. He showed signs of musical genius at three years of age when he absorbed the piano lessons given to his sister, four years older than he. At age six he was composing, his

7

father writing down his improvisations. The father, a practical man, took the child prodigy and his sister on tour. They performed before the ducal and regal courts of Europe. From childhood to youth, to manhood, Mozart's life, marked by personal ups and downs, was continuously creative. All in all, he wrote over forty symphonies, a wealth of chamber music, countless compositions for piano and various solo instruments, and a good handful of operas, several of which are still occasionally performed. He died tragically at thirty-five, while completing a great Requiem, and was buried in a pauper's grave.

The Marriage of Figaro was written in Vienna when Mozart was thirty. He saw the possibility for an opera in a then recent French comedy that, because of its incidental satire and certain of its scenes, had caused a stir and had been censored. One day he asked Lorenzo da Ponte whether he could turn Beaumarchais' Le Mariage de Figaro into the book for a musical comedy. Da Ponte reports in his Memoirs, "The idea was to my taste," and he set to work. "As fast as I wrote the words, Mozart wrote the music, and it was all finished in six weeks." The libretto, according to the conventions of the period, was written in Italian as the proper language for opera. It was not a mere translation, as da Ponte explained in a foreword, "but rather an imitation, or let us say an extract." The complicated intrigues of the original were simplified, some scenes omitted, the satirical elements made acceptable to the Austrian Emperor, who then gave his permission for its performance. Mozart himself coached the performers for the première at the Burgtheater in Vienna on May 1, 1786.

As you listen to a recording of Le Nozze di Figaro—a great many different recordings of it are available, some under the Italian title, some the English—imagine yourself seated in the theater, part of an audience, people in holiday mood, couples and groups as well as solitary persons off for an evening of entertainment. For this overture will set the mood of the performance to come, which promises adventure and love, intrigue and tenderness, piquant situations and good humor, wit and comedy, solo songs and ensembles. So, in the theatrical conventions of our own day, the lights are dimmed, the orchestral conductor is in the spotlight, a moment's pause, then the music. . . .

If music is all Greek to you, the following notation won't mean anything at all. But don't worry about it, just listen to the music and enjoy yourself. However, keep your ears open and your mind alert. Note the different tunes as they fly by you, as they are repeated, as they recur later in the overture. Perhaps you can whisper-whistle some of them along with the recording and so fix them more firmly in mind.

Themes of the Overture to
THE MARRIAGE OF FIGARO
by *Mozart*

If you are able to read music, even imperfectly, following the themes here noted may increase your enjoyment of this simple and straightforward composition. The *first* theme, played by the stringed instruments (violins, violas, 'cellos, basses) plus the bassoons, in unison and octaves, is a lively pattern of short trills and short runs.

The *second* theme follows at once. Oboes and flutes, alternating in the opening four measures, are then joined by the strings.

Now the *first* and *second* themes are repeated. Then comes a *third* group of themes and motifs, introduced in rapid succession principally by the strings. There are five of them, as here distinguished and lettered. Listen for the bass parts *b* and *e*.

Then follows the *fourth* and most lyrical theme, easy to sing or whistle. It is shared by the violins and woodwinds.

The *fourth* theme is repeated. Then comes a transition that leads back to the *first* theme, followed by the *second* and the *first* theme once again. This leads to the recurrence of *c, d,* and *e* of the *third* group of themes. Once more the *fourth* theme appears and is repeated. Then comes a violin passage something like the *first* theme followed by another passage that suggests the bass figure *b* of the *third.* With long descending runs in the strings, taken up by the woodwinds, the *fifth* and final theme is introduced and is repeated as the overture races to the goal.

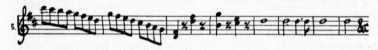

With this stirring conclusion to the overture the curtain should rise upon the first act of *The Marriage of Figaro,* a room in the castle of Count Almaviva. But the reader is to be unceremoniously hurried out of the theater at this point and into the next section of this discussion! If he resists such an interruption and wants to stay and hear the show, he may do so by listening to the recordings of the whole opera, available in many record collections, and by following the translated libretto to be found in most libraries. Very briefly, he would find the story to be this:

> Figaro, the popular barber of Seville, has become the valet of the Count Almaviva, whose courtship and marriage to Rosina form the intrigue of *The Barber of Seville* (Beaumarchais' earlier play made into a later opera by Rossini). Figaro is now in love with Susanna, Rosina's maid, and wants to marry her. But the Count, a restless spouse, has become interested in the maid, and therefore opposes Figaro's intention; and Figaro himself is pursued by Marcellina, whom he once promised to marry. With the help and interference of Cherubino, an attractive page, and after a complexity of concealments and discoveries, intrigues and assignations, disguises and overhearings, a jump from the window and the revelation that Figaro is the long-lost son of Marcellina, a token and a letter, a kiss and a boxed ear—the Countess subdues her fickle husband, and the way is cleared for the marriage of Figaro to Susanna!

Perhaps this story is not really sillier than the stories of popular musicals of our own day, but the living opera in the theater is much more than a mere synopsis of the plot would suggest. For in it a number of the arts co-operate, depicting the sequence of social scenes that make up its fuller substance. The literary and dramatic arts of dialogue and plot are given expressive enrichment by vocal and instrumental music; meaningful gesture and facial expression of the actors are supplemented by the costume and scenic design; the stage movement is amplified by the incidental dances; the whole performance is seen through the architectural picture frame of the proscenium arch complete with sculptural adornment! So, indeed, the separate arts of music and literature, of painting and dance, of architecture and sculpture are brought together in the art of theater—brought together to 'hold, as 'twere the mirror up to Nature,' to show man his own image, to please and to entertain people by presenting a moving picture of their princes and paupers, their problems and perplexities.

In this way the arts may be said to serve humanity.

2. Your world and mine

All of us live in a world of art. We live in many other worlds, too—the world of thought, the world of science, the world of social and political and economic relations, the world of nature, and so on. But we also live in a world of art. This world is by no means the special province of artists. They have, of course, contributed most significantly to it, for they have made many of the things that are about us to be enjoyed. But it is, all of it, your world and mine if we wish to experience it and thereby possess it.

When you warble in the shower or whistle at your work; when you doodle on the phone pad or draw in the margin of your notes; when you play with a lump of candle drippings or dream out the plan for a beach cottage; when you sing round a campfire or dance to moonlit music; when you arrange some flowers in a vase for the front hall or choose to wear a plain colored tie with a striped shirt; when you join with others in responsive reading and the hymn at public worship; when you take snapshots on your vacation or fix up the back yard—you are 'making' in the old sense in which poets were called 'makers'; you are creating; you are active in the world of art.

This world of art is all about you. The house or apartment in which you live, the interior arrangement of your own room and of the rooms you eat and lounge in, the furniture and draperies and pictures on the wall, the floor coverings and the tint and texture of the ceiling, the photographs and scarf on the dresser, the clothes upon your back and in your wardrobe, the nicknacks and books and magazines on the desk, the radio and record player—all of these are, or at least all of them may be, a part of this world of art.

And as you go outside of your home, your castle, as the saying goes, you by no means leave this world of art behind you. Down the steps and through the garden, along the tree-lined street, past public squares with their memorial statues, in view of towering office buildings and spiring churches, looking into shop windows, noting the passing cars and streaming people—there is still art, of one kind or another, all about you.

You may be quite unaware of much of it; you may be indifferent to most of it; it may be of no special interest to you—but it is here and there and everywhere, just the same, wherever man is or has been, across the land and through the ages.

If you are like most people, you are more or less conscious of much of this world of art, or you become conscious of it from time to time. You experience and enjoy some or many of such things as we have mentioned, but your art experiences are also of yet other kinds: You read short stories in the *Post* and novels condensed in the *Digest*. You listen to radio mysteries, go to the local cinema or watch television. You make up a party to go to a play or musical comedy. You tune in on the symphony hour or attend a concert. You enjoy a builders' exhibit or go through a model home. You look at the paintings reproduced in *Life* or stop for a moment to see the pictures in a hotel lobby. You go out of your way to visit our great public buildings and to see the national monuments. You note, not always with approval, the clothes people wear and the arrangement of their homes. You observe and comment on the color, lines, and fittings of the latest car models.

You do these things, or a good many things of the same sort, and we all do them. And so it has been since the dawn of Mankind. For primitive man made things and enjoyed them. The wall paintings in the caves of Southern France, the various artifacts of prehistoric man that are unearthed in ancient rubble to find their way into our museums, the many sorts of art works surviving from the ancient world and from the successive historic periods down to our own day—the world of art extends in depth back to the earliest times. No creature but man has made for himself such a world of things for his adornment and delight, for his pastime and his bodily comfort, for his peace of mind and soul's satisfaction.

3. For delight and worship

This Prelude 'On the World of Art and of People' may well be brought to a close by the presentation of a work of literary art, a short story by one of the great French writers of modern times, Jacques Anatole Thibault (1844-1924), who wrote under the name of Anatole France. Noted as a critic and novelist, he knew well the several arts and he understood humanity. Perhaps no further introduction is necessary to—

THE JUGGLER OF OUR LADY

by *Anatole France*

I.

In the time of King Louis there lived in France a poor juggler, native of Compiègne, named Barnabas, who went from town to town, performing tricks of strength and skill. On market days he put down an old worn-out carpet in the public square, and, after having attracted the children and loafers with the patter that he had learned from an old juggler, and of which he never changed a word, he assumed all sorts of unnatural postures and balanced a pewter plate on his nose. At first the crowd looked at him with indifference.

But when, with hands and head on the ground, he threw into the air six copper balls that shone in the sun and caught them again with his feet—or when, bending back till his neck touched his heels, he gave himself the form of a perfect wheel and in that posture juggled with twelve knives, a murmur of admiration arose from the crowd and coins rained on the carpet.

However, like all those who live by their wits, Barnabas of Compiègne found it hard to live at all.

Earning his bread by the sweat of his brow, he bore more than his share of the misery that derives from the sin of Adam our father.

Moreover, he could not work as much as he wished. To display his fine talents, he needed, as do the trees to flower and fruit, the heat of the sun and light of day. In winter he was no more than a leafless tree, as good as dead. The frozen ground was hard on the juggler. And, like the locust mentioned by Marie of France, he suffered from cold and hunger during the bad season. But, simple of heart, he endured with patience.

He had never given much thought to problems of wealth and human inequality. He firmly believed that, if this world is bad, the next must certainly be good, and this hope sustained him. He did not follow those who sell their souls to the devil. He never blasphemed the name of God; he lived honestly; and, although unmarried, he did not covet his neighbor's wife—for woman is the enemy of strong men, which is evident from the story of Samson as reported in the Scriptures.

Indeed, his mind was not bent toward carnal desires, and it would have bothered him more to give up wine than to give up women. For, although he was not intemperate, he liked to drink when the weather was warm. All in all, he was a good man, fearing God, and very devout to the Holy Virgin.

When he entered a church, he never failed to kneel down before the image of the Mother of God, and to address this prayer to her:

"Our Lady, watch over my life till it please God for me to die. And when I die, may the joys of paradise be mine."

II.

Now, one evening after a rainy day, walking along sad and bent, carrying his balls and his knives safely wrapped up in his old carpet, and looking for a barn where he might go supperless to bed, he came upon a monk who was going his way, and he addressed him respectfully. As they were proceeding at the same pace, they struck up a conversation.

"Friend," said the monk, "how does it happen that you are dressed in green? Perhaps you are going to play the part of a Fool in some mystery play."

"No, father," replied Barnabas. "You see, my name is Barnabas, and I'm a juggler by trade. It would be the best calling in the world—if one could eat regularly."

"Friend Barnabas," responded the monk, "take care what you say. There is no higher vocation than the monastic. In it one celebrates the praise of God, of the Virgin, and of the Saints, and the life of a religious is an endless hymn of praise to Our Lord."

Barnabas answered:

"Father, I confess that I have spoken in ignorance. Your trade is not to be compared with mine; and, although there may be some merit in dancing while holding a coin balanced on a stick on the end of one's nose, this merit is nothing as compared to yours. I would like, father, to sing the Office daily as you do, especially the Office of the Holy Virgin, for whom I have a special devotion. I would gladly give up the art for which I am known from Soissons to Beauvais, in more than six hundred towns and villages, in order to embrace the monastic life."

The monk was touched by the simplicity of the juggler, and, not lacking in discernment, he saw in Barnabas one of those men of good will of whom Our Lord has said: "Let peace be with them on earth." Therefore, he answered him thus:

"Friend Barnabas, come with me, and I will make it possible for you to enter the convent of which I am prior. He who led Mary through the Egyptian desert put me in your path to lead you to salvation."

In this way Barnabas became a monk. In the convent where he was received, the monks celebrated to perfection the cult of the Holy Virgin, and in her service each one made use of all such learning and talent as God had given him.

The prior, for his part, wrote treatises, in accord with the rules of scholasticism, on the virtues of the Mother of God.

Brother Maurice, in a clerkly hand, copied these treatises on parchment.

Brother Alexander illuminated them with delicate miniatures. He depicted the Queen of Heaven seated on the throne of Solomon, supported by four lions. Around Her haloed head flew seven doves, the seven gifts of the Holy Spirit: the gifts of fear, of piety, of knowledge, of fortitude, of counsel, of understanding, and of wisdom. As companions She had six virgins with golden hair: Humility, Prudence, Retirement, Respect, Virginity, and Obedience.

At Her feet were two little figures, naked and white, standing in suppliant attitudes. They were souls who implored, certainly not in vain Her all-powerful intercession for their salvation.

On another page Brother Alexander showed Eve facing Mary, so that one might see, at one and the same time, sin and redemption, Woman humiliated and the Virgin exalted. Elsewhere in this book one could see pictures of the Well of Living Waters, the Fountain, the Lily, the Moon, the Sun and the Closed Garden spoken of in the canticle, the Gate of Heaven and the City of God; and in each of these the Virgin was depicted.

Brother Marbode was likewise one of the most beloved children of Mary.

He carved statues with unceasing labor, so that his beard, his brows, and his hair were white with dust, and his eyes were perpetually swollen and full of tears; but he was strong and joyful in his old age, and it was clearly to be seen that the Queen of Paradise watched over Her child in his declining years. Marbode represented Her seated on a throne, Her brow encircled by a halo, with an orb of pearl. And he was careful that the folds of Her gown should cover the feet of the One of whom the prophet has said, "My beloved is like a closed garden."

Sometimes he represented Her with the features of a child full of grace, and She seemed to say, "Lord, Thou art my Lord!—Dixi de ventre matris meae: Deus meus es tu." (Psalms 21:11).

There were also in the convent poets, who composed Latin essays and hymns in honor of the Most Gracious Virgin Mary, and there was even a man from Picardy there among them who put the miracles of Our Lady into rimed couplets in French.

III.

With such competition in praise and such a rich harvest of creative work, Barnabas lamented his ignorance and his simplicity.

"Alas!" he sighed one day while walking alone in the little convent garden, "I am indeed unhappy because I cannot, like my brothers, praise worthily the Holy Mother of God, to whom I have given the devotion of my heart. Alas! alas! I am a rough and artless man, and I have for your service, My Lady the Virgin, neither edifying sermons nor treatises well turned according to the rules, no fine paintings, no statues neatly carved; no verses counted off by feet and marching in measure. I have nothing, alas!"

This is the way he carried on, abandoning himself to grief. One evening when the monks were conversing at their ease, he heard one of them tell the story of a simple brother who could recite only the 'Ave Maria.' This monk was scorned for his ignorance, but when he died five roses issued from his mouth in honor of the five letters of the name of Marie, and thus was his blessedness made manifest.

As he listened to this story, Barnabas again realized the bounteous goodness of the Virgin; but he was not consoled by the example of that miraculous death, for his heart was full of zeal and he wanted to serve and glorify his Lady in Heaven.

Unsuccessfully he sought the means of doing this, and his sense of affliction increased each day; but one morning he awoke joyfully, ran to the chapel, and stayed for more than an hour alone. After dinner he went there again.

And from that time on he went daily to the chapel whenever it was deserted, and he passed the greater part of the time there which the other monks devoted to the liberal and applied arts. He was no longer sad, and he no longer complained.

Conduct so singular excited the curiosity of the monks.

They asked themselves in their gatherings why Brother Barnabas went off by himself so frequently.

The prior, whose duty it is to ignore nothing as to the conduct of his monks, decided to observe Barnabas in his times of solitude. One day, therefore, when Barnabas was closeted as usual in the chapel, the prior came, accompanied by two elders of the convent, to observe through a grill in the door what was going on inside.

They saw Barnabas before the image and altar of the Holy Virgin, head down, feet in the air, juggling with six copper balls and twelve knives. In honor of the Holy Mother of God, he was performing the tricks which had earlier brought him the highest praises. Not understanding that this simple man thus placed his best talents and skill at the service of the Holy Virgin, the two elders cried out at the sacrilege.

The prior knew that Barnabas was innocent at heart, but believed him out of his mind. At once the three of them undertook to remove him from the chapel—when suddenly they saw the Holy Virgin descend the steps from the altar, to wipe with a fold of her blue mantle the sweat that bathed the brow of the juggler.

Then the prior prostrated himself, his face bowed down to the marble floor, and uttered these words:

"Blessed are the pure in heart, for they shall see God."

"Amen," responded the elders, kissing the ground.

PART ONE: INTRODUCTION TO ART, BEAUTY, AND MEANING

Chapter 1. Definition of Art

I don't believe any real artist cares whether what he does is 'art' or not. Who, after all, knows what art is?

Robert Henri, *The Art Spirit*

"But it appears to me to be no part of our business to dispute about a name, when we have proposed to ourselves the consideration of such important subjects."

Plato, *Republic*

'A work of art' means an expression of an artist's experience in a form which makes it communicable to many minds with only slight variations.

F. R. O'Neill, *The Social Value of Art*

THE WORLD OF ART, as described in the Prelude, comprises a world of different things that make up an important part of your environment. They are exciting, pleasurable, beautiful and significant objects and events and experiences—things that make life worth living, that make life richer and more abundant. You will want to look about you, examine some of these things, ask some questions, and get your bearings before we go forward together in further exploration. Such an orientation to the World of Art will involve more than spying out the land, locating and identifying its fixed points. Such an orientation will also involve your spying in upon yourself, studying your own responses to the many things about you. For the Kingdom of Art, also, is within you. To understand THE ARTS AND HUMANITY, you must heed the imperative: Know Thyself.

You will indeed know yourself better as you recognize more fully the relation of the inward Kingdom of Art to the outside World of

17

Art, the relation of your private experiences to those public objects and events that evoke them. You will know yourself better as you clarify your general thoughts about art, your art theory as it was called in the Foreword. Art experience and art theory, it was there asserted, are different one from the other, but intimately interrelated. Your art experiences are guided and formed by your art theory; and your art theory is generalized from your art experiences. Both theory and experience are part of that inward Kingdom; but it is your specific art experiences, your complex responses to works of art, that link your inward Kingdom to the outside World.

The first problem that arises as you begin to clarify and enlarge your own art theory is suggested by the question, What is art? It is an obvious and simple question. That is, it seems simple enough and unambiguous; but actually it is a complex question, and efforts to answer it have never been generally acceptable. Despite the hazards, this Chapter 1, 'Definition of Art,' will ask the question, What is art? and will proceed to answer it. As your present purpose is to enlarge your art experience and clarify your art theory, it is not important whether you agree with every particular point in the discussion as long as you keep clearly in mind the relation of the theory here presented to your own.

1. *Some existing definitions of art*

In a recent comprehensive book on the arts, 'a work of art' is defined as 'a type of aesthetic object.' The 'aesthetic object' is characterized by 'aesthetic quality.' 'Aesthetic quality' is specialized as 'artistic beauty.' And 'artistic beauty' is the sort of beauty one finds in the 'work of art.'

So this definition of art, perhaps not quite fairly summarized, comes full circle and a work of art turns out to be—a work of art. You may either get off the merry-go-round at the very spot where you got on, or take another ride. Such carousel definitions of art, whirling about in a cycle of abstractions, are not uncommon. If you find yourself riding one of them, jump off and get your feet on the concrete ground of art experiences. Only then can you make progress in clarifying your art theory.

In addition to these circular definitions there is another kind, yet more common, that will not prove very helpful. Without disparagement we shall call them literary definitions of art. Here are some quotable examples:

"Art is power."
"Art is a form of catharsis."

"Art is an instant arrested in eternity."

"Art is nothing more than the shadow of humanity."

"Art is that in which the hand, the head, and the heart go together."

"Art is a reaching out into the ugliness of the world for vagrant beauty and the imprisoning of it in a tangible dream."

So write Longfellow, Dorothy Parker, James Huneker, Henry James, John Ruskin, and George Jean Nathan.

It is quite unfair, again, to remove these definitions from their literary settings and to comment upon them in isolation. Perhaps that is the first thing to learn in regard to art theory: any single statement from a person's art theory is only to be fully understood in its relation to the whole system of which it is a part. But we shall, for our present purpose, look again at these definitions as given above out of context. Or listen to them, rather, for each of them, in its own way, has the orotund ring of high thought. But as you reread, think. Are not 'power' and 'catharsis' and 'instant in eternity' and 'shadow of humanity' and 'hand, head, and heart' and 'tangible dream' just as much in need of definition as 'art' itself? And are not these definitive terms just as abstract, as here given, as the aesthetic waypoints of the merry-go-round? Do not these definitions lead us, in apparently different directions, off into the unknown?

In fairness and truth it should be said that these literary definitions may suggest some relevant and profound thoughts about art, or evoke significant images or feelings, or establish valuable attitudes. You may say, "That's right, the artist has power to shape his material so as to express his creative ideas." Or you may think of Aristotle's definition of tragedy in terms of the purgation of the passions of pity and fear. Or you may glimpse an image of the Platonic shadows in the cave, or sense a feeling of personal fitness in the integration of hand, head, and heart. Or you may, by considering the contrasts of overwhelming urban ugliness and fleeting beauty, develop a new attitude toward art. However, to the extent that these quotations evoke in you responses of this kind, they are not cool bits of rational art theory, but warm bits of the very stuff that art is made of. They are emotive language and expressive metaphor; but they may leave you still asking the question, What is art?

Even though the literary definitions and the circular definitions do not provide very helpful answers, it is not necessary to despair with the artist Robert Henri, who exclaimed or asked, "Who, after all, knows what art is?" Perhaps most of those who have declared that art is indefinable have not sufficiently considered the nature of definition itself. For instance, it is always important to consider whether a given definition is of the word 'art' or of the mysterious thing *art*. Perhaps it is no longer necessary to insist that 'the word is not the thing,' but people still make the mistake at times of identifying a symbol with the thing symbolized. It is easy to forget that 'art' is but a word, a word used innumerable times by countless persons throughout the ages to refer to all manner of different items in their experience. There is nothing in the outer world that 'really is' *art*. When 'so-called modern art' was given prominent condemnation recently as 'merely the vaporizings of half-baked lazy people,' the implication was that the paintings in question were not really *art* at all, and that therefore the word 'art' should not be applied to them. We might well agree with Plato that 'it is no part of our business to dispute about a name,' and remember that 'a rose by any other name would smell as sweet,' that 'Romeo would, were he not Romeo called. . .,' and so on.

Definition is simply making clear the relation of words to the things they stand for. It is one of the most useful devices for controlling our thoughts whether we are writing or reading, speaking to be understood or listening to understand. Sometimes a speaker or writer carefully explains his use of key terms as he introduces them in his discussion. Or his listener, uncertain what the speaker is referring to, may ask him what he means by 'fusion'? Or the thoughtful reader may glance back over what he has read to see whether the author has indicated the special sense in which 'representational' is to be understood, or he may turn to his dictionary for a set of definitions, some one of which is likely to be helpful. In all such cases the question is, What is the meaning of the word right here in this sentence or in this chapter?

Each problem in definition is a miniature problem in navigation. You must determine your position by reference to certain fixed points and relationships. In definition one demonstrates the meaning of a word by pointing out its relationship to something that is known. With some common experience as the starting point, one proceeds from the known to the unknown by the statement of a relationship which also must be common knowledge. Definitions, which are important in any discussion of theory, must be in terms of commonly understood relationships and common experience—common, at least, to the persons involved.

If you asked me what I meant by 'figurine,' I might hold up a small bit of sculpture and by that very gesture say, "This is a figurine"—*this*, which we can both touch and see, *is*, in the sense of its being an example of, *a figurine*, the name commonly applied to things of this sort. Or I might draw a picture of one for you or point to the illustration in a dictionary. Or I might use words and say, "A figurine is a statuette" (using a common synonym) or "small statue" (using the known word 'statue' and the common relation word 'small'). Or I might provide a more complete logical definition with the formal genus-species-differentiae structure: "A figurine is a work of sculpture of a full human or animal figure in the round, smaller than a statue and characteristically carved from ivory or wood or cast in bronze, silver, or gold."

However, by no means are all attempts at definition successful. Sometimes the starting point is not really common ground as the writer and reader assume, or the notion of relationship is not made clear. Sometimes the process of definition becomes a verbal game, as we have seen, proceeding from one unknown to another or round a circle of abstraction.

2. Definition of 'work of art' by example

Let us begin our working definition by considering some examples of what I, for one, call 'works of art' or 'art works.'

When I use the phrase 'work of art,' I mean THIS sort of thing— and THIS and THIS. You will turn now to the first three illustrations on the next pages, but with an important warning: I cannot, alas, point in this book to the three actual works of art. You will have to imagine our walking into the nave of the *Reims Cathedral* and my glancing up and whispering, "*This* is a work of art!" And you will have to imagine our walking about the statue of *Wrestlers* and my saying, "*This* is a work of art"—or standing in the gallery before the painting of Van Gogh's *Sunflowers* and saying, "*This* is a work of art."

Now take a closer look at these three art works:

First, the great Church of Our Lady, the Notre Dame at Reims in northern France, usually called simply *Reims Cathedral*. It was planned as early as 1211 A.D., and was built later in the thirteenth century. If one faced this church from the street, one would notice the three wide doorways with high pointed arches, adorned with sculpture —above the central doorway, a large circular rose window of intricate design—to left and right the great towers. Entering by the central door, one would find himself within the nave—the word comes from the French for ship, and suggests the great open ribbed framework of a hull under construction. The nave is an extremely long enclosure of tremendous height, a forest of rising columns and interlacing branches of cross vaulting, with stained glass windows above, the clerestory, enclosing the nave and with broad side aisles flanking it to left and right. If you have worshipped in or visited any one of the great Gothic churches in our own country, such as the Cathedral of St. John the Divine or St. Patrick's in New York City, you will be better able to realize what the Reims Cathedral is like.

Second, the *Wrestlers,* an ancient statue by an unknown sculptor. It was found near the Lateran Church in Rome and is now to be seen in the Uffizi galleries in Florence. It has been copied many times, and indeed may itself be a copy of a more ancient Greek original. Marble reproductions of it may be seen in the Jonathan Club in Los Angeles and at Forest Lawn in nearby Glendale.

Third, *Sunflowers* by the Dutch artist Vincent Van Gogh (1853-1890). He seems to have been interested in this subject, for he painted a number of similar pictures. One is in an Amsterdam gallery; others are in the Tate Gallery and Soho Gallery in London. Still another is in the Collection of Carroll S. Tyson, and is to be seen at the Philadelphia Museum of Art.

But let us turn from these three examples of what I mean by 'work of art' to three other things, examples of what I do *not* mean.

You have perhaps visited the well-known groves of California Redwoods—the sequoia gigantea of the Sierra Nevada and the sequoia sempervirens of the Coast Range. You may have walked through one of the so-called Cathedral Groves in which the clean trunks rise like clusters of fluted columns to the high vaulting branches overhead, with shafts of golden sunlight coming in through the clerestory above the side aisles of shorter trees. The photograph reproduced on the fourth page of illustrations—taken at Bull Creek Flats, Humboldt Redwoods State Park by the State Division of Beaches and Parks— will serve as an example . . . I do *not* use 'work of art' to name such a thing as this grove of Redwoods.

You have perhaps attended a wrestling match in some gymnasium or sports arena—and have seen two men clutching each other in outlandish holds, straining and contorted in limb and body, sweating and gasping. Perhaps, for that is half the show in professional wrestling, they are herculean in muscular development, brutal and grimacing in aspect . . . I do *not* use 'work of art' to name this sort of thing!

You have perhaps seen one of those genuine-hand-painted flower pictures that occasionally adorned the front parlor of an earlier generation. The one I have in mind was recently rescued from an attic to be rechristened the Plush Horror. It is a sort of painting on velvet in which the pigment, mixed with metallic particles, seems to have been applied by means of a cake decorator. An amazing diversity of blooms, of uncertain botanical varieties, springs from common stems . . . I do *not* use 'work of art' to name this thing!!

photo by Braun

Interior of REIMS CATHEDRAL, the nave

photo by Alinari

Greek sculpture, THE WRESTLERS, Uffizi Gallery, Florence

Vincent Van Gogh, SUNFLOWERS, Collection of Carroll S. Tyson

photo by Mel Goldman

PROFESSIONAL WRESTLERS

Courtesy of State Div.
of Beaches and Parks

CALIFORNIA REDWOODS
Humboldt Redwoods State Park

Nessen Studio, N. Y. C.

Nessen TABLE LAMP   'THE PLUSH HORROR'

In looking at the illustrations on the fourth page of half-tones, again remember that I am not referring to the photographs here reproduced but to the things themselves, the actual Redwoods, the live wrestlers on the canvas mat, the picture itself. And while you are looking at these illustrations of three examples of not-art work, consider their relationship to the *Reims Cathedral,* the statue *Wrestlers,* and *Sunflowers,* the three examples of art work . . .

At this point you may indeed ask the question, "Why does the author choose to name the first three 'works of art' and not the second three?" Take a bit of scratch paper and make a few notes of such answers as occur to you . . .

But let us include another group of 'works of art,' as I call them, sufficiently different from the first three examples to warrant your attention.

The first of these examples is *the table lamp,* a photograph of which is reproduced on the fourth page of illustrations. You may have assumed that, because it was grouped with the Redwoods, live wrestlers, and Plush Horror, it was also an example of not-art work, and you may have thought up a good reason for so classifying it. But when I use the phrase 'work of art' I mean things like this lamp as well as things like the cathedral, the statue, and the painting.

For the second example in this group, let us cite *The Juggler of Our Lady,* the short story by Anatole France presented in the Prelude. You will notice that the story there reprinted is not just a reproduction of the story, like the photographs of the lamp or the statue. Even though it is an English translation of the French original, you would say that the story itself is here in this book; and this is what I now refer to as another example of art work.

The third of this group of examples, again from the Prelude, will be Mozart's overture to *The Marriage of Figaro.* For the present purpose, I am referring, not to the music on the page nor to the full score were it at hand, and not to the orchestra of musicians performing the music, but to the complex of sound waves that results from such a performance or that issues from your phonograph when you play a recording of the overture. It is the music that you can actually hear that I cite as this third example in the second group of what I call 'works of art.'

For comparison, here are three more examples of not-art work: a collection of brilliantly colored yarns, a newspaper report of current food prices, and the symphonic rhythmic sound of breaking surf along the Maine or Oregon Coast. Perhaps, again, you will question why I have said these are not works of art, and make a scratchpaper note of your answers . . .

As if these six examples, so different from one another, were not enough, I shall add two more, which will be yet more difficult to illustrate in a book. The first of these so-called works of art is *the dancing* of the peasants depicted in Breughel's painting, the frontispiece of this book. I mean the actual dancing of real persons, not just a picture entitled *Dancing Peasants,* not even a moving picture of such a scene, but the living breathing people, their bodily movements, the sound of the bagpipe and of their footfalls.

The second of this final pair of works of art is just as impossible to get into a book: a *stageplay* presentation of Beaumarchais' comedy *Le Mariage de Figaro*—I say this rather than a performance of the da Ponte-Mozart musical comedy, *Le Nozze di Figaro,* for then we can more easily distinguish the theatrical work of the stageplay from the musical work of the overture; the comic opera partakes of the character of both music and theater.

So let us add the dancing and the stageplay to bring our so-called works of art to eight in number. And with them let us couple two final examples of not-art work: first, a group of people playing bridge, and second, a game of basketball. Why, you may ask, do I exclude them from the world of art works? . . .

When I use the phrase 'work of art,' then, I mean things like the examples mentioned above: the stageplay, the dancing, the overture, the table lamp, the painting, the statue, and the cathedral. And I do not mean things like the basketball game, the bridge crowd, the sound of breaking surf, the news report, the colored yarn, the Plush Horror, the actual wrestlers, the giant Redwood grove.

But let us carry our working definition a step or two further.

3. Logical definition of 'work of art'

'Work of art,' then, is a phrase I am using to name things like these eight examples. Like them—yet how amazingly different they are from one another. You will at once ask why I lump them all together. And when I say that I do so because they all seem to me to be of the same general sort, you will ask what quality they have in common that justifies my saying they are of the same kind.

A logical definition may help to clarify your art theory at this point. You may recall from the paragraph defining 'figurine' that logical definition makes use of the genus-species-differentiae structure in expressing the relation of words to the things for which they stand. The formula is this: to place the thing to be defined (the species) within the class of things to which it belongs (the genus) and then to differentiate it from the other members of the class.

To start with, each of these eight so-called works of art exists, or is conceived as existing, as a separate and distinguishable entity, so we'll say that the generalization 'works of art' belongs to the larger class of 'entities' or 'things' as we shall call them. The word 'things,' then, is here used in a broad enough sense to include solid objects like the cathedral, statue, picture, lamp, and the pages of the book upon which the story is printed, but it also includes the pattern of musical sound waves, the complex of bodily movements and sound waves that comprise the dance and, with differences, the stageplay. The word 'things' also will serve to name the great Redwoods, the Plush Horror, and the complex activity of the wrestlers. The collection of colored yarns, the news items in the daily paper, the sound of rolling breakers, the assembled bridge players, and the game of basketball—these also are 'things.' Without going further, let us say that anything that can be identified and referred to as a unit will here be called a 'thing.'

The question now arises: How do the particular things we have called 'works of art' differ from all other things? Before reading further, glance at your scratch paper notes and consider further the differentiae that characterize works of art . . .

Let us say that there are three qualities that distinguish works of art as here conceived:

First, all eight of these so-called works of art are man-made. They are not creations of nature or things that God alone hath wrought, however you may wish to phrase it. Think back over the list of eight art works, and you will note that each of them resulted from creative human activity. All of them, furthermore, were 'made' in an objective material sense. They are not dreams or feeling states or thoughts; these art works were all created by hands and voices and bodily activities directed by the minds of men. They have a certain objective reality, these works of art, and can all be perceived by men other than their creators. Even the musical sound waves and the complex of body movements that comprise the dance can be said to exist as public objects, the result of human activity.

Second, all eight of these so-called works of art are beautiful. The quality of being man-made is easy to describe and identify; it can be observed and verified in a fairly objective way. On the other hand, the quality of being beautiful is most difficult to consider; it is essentially subjective and does not lend itself to objective verification. It is at this point that some theorists jump aboard the carousel or plunge us into the unknown. So important is 'beauty' to art theory and so often has the word been used to describe individual art experiences, that it will be discussed in some detail in sections of the next two chapters. Let us here simply say that 'beauty' is a value word used to name a wide variety of human responses to things. In common usage it often refers to a beautiful sunset as well as to a beautiful picture. Perhaps the very breadth of this usage makes the word a good one for our purpose. Certainly, the *Reims Cathedral,* the statue *Wrestlers,* the painting *Sunflowers,* the table lamp, the story of *The Juggler,* the overture to *Figaro,* the folk dancing in the street, and the stage comedy *Figaro*—certainly, if these are all called 'beautiful,' it is evident that no narrow or merely pretty or single-valued quality is designated. But more of this later.

Third, all eight of these so-called works of art are meaningful or significant. The quality of being meaningful is in some ways as subjective as the quality of being beautiful, and as difficult to deal with. There are some theorists who would strongly resist the inclusion of significance as one of the differentiae in a definition of art work. A fuller discussion of meaning in art will be found in Chapter 3, so one or two further remarks must suffice at this point. The word 'meaningful,' like the word 'beautiful,' is used in a number of different though related senses. As with beauty, the meaning of a work of art is not *in* the physical object, but is a part of human responses to it. Such meaning responses may be markedly different for different people even when they are experiencing one and the same work of art. However different their responses, most persons would agree that the cathedral has some sort of meaning for them, that the *Wrestlers* and *Sunflowers* (and the other art works we have listed) at least *make sense* in one way or another, though they may vary markedly in their significance. But, again, more of this later.

At this point let us develop a logical definition based upon the above discussion of the genus (thing) and the differentiae (man-made, beautiful, and meaningful); but it will have to be thought of as a tentative definition awaiting further discussion of the key terms 'beauty' and 'meaning.' And here's a good place for a warning, too: there is nothing absolute or ultimate about any such definition. Indeed you will not succeed in clarifying your own art theory and enriching your own art experiences until you finally answer for yourself the crucial question, What is art? But at this point, as a working definition for this book:

A work of art is a man-made thing generally evoking beauty and meaning responses.

Notice that word 'generally;' it provides a sort of safety valve. If you personally do not find the *Wrestlers* statue beautiful in any sense of the word, but if you discover that other persons for the most part do, then you might admit it to be a work of art despite your own lack of appreciation. One could, with fair objectivity, set up criteria for judging and measuring how generally persons have had responses of beauty and meaning evoked by certain man-made things. It would involve important decisions—what groups of persons to consider, how to select a fair sample of them, what data to collect relative to personal response, how to interpret such data, and what percentage to consider the equivalent of 'generally.' There are, of course, such objective data as the history of the publication, the record of reprints and sales reports for books, as well as critical reviews and the popular appraisal of film versions. Music publication, performance, applause, and recordings may also be useful data. So are gallery attendance and sale of reproductions—if you consider these relevant. This is enough to suggest, perhaps, that what is essentially subjective—for beauty and meaning are inward events in particular persons—is evidenced objectively in human behavior.

With this working definition in mind, let us return briefly to the examples of not-art work to see where they lie in relation to *man-made things generally evoking beauty and meaning responses.* You may well refer to the scratch paper notes you made when comparing these things with the art works paired with them.

The Redwoods were not considered art, for they are not man-made. Beautiful as they are and also meaningful to most persons who behold them, they are, after all, great works of nature. The sweating grunting wrestlers, whose postures and activity certainly are man-made, do not form a beautiful spectacle, in the opinion of most persons. The Plush Horror, undoubtedly man-made or woman-made, would not generally be considered beautiful or meaningful, though it doubtless had both of these qualities in the eyes of its maker and the neighbors, and you may rush to its defense as an American primitive!

The miscellaneous assortment of colored yarns, man-made and woman-gathered, is for many persons beautiful in itself, but without significance. The news report on food prices, man-made and meaningful for some, is not beautiful. Persons playing bridge are not engaged in an activity that is usually considered either beautiful or very meaningful. And that brings us down to the basketball game...

It is not necessary to comment on all eight works of art cited, but it may be helpful to consider one of them briefly in relation to the working definition.

Although history records the names of some of the successive architects who designed the great *Reims Cathedral,* we do not know the names of all those countless artists and artisans and laborers through whose efforts this great church was constructed and adorned. Though I have never entered this church either as a visitor or worshiper, I can reconstruct it in my mind from a close observation of photographs and reports of it, for I can call upon my actual experience of entering and viewing somewhat similar buildings. I can imagine myself within *Reims Cathedral* uplifted by its soaring shafts, transformed in spirit by the great sense of space, illuminated in a strange way by the light that filters through its stained-glass windows. Indeed, as I contemplate this experience, though but imagined, I unconsciously qualify it as beautiful. And my experience of this cathedral is also meaningful. My recognition of the pulpit, of the lectern, the bishop's throne, the choir stalls, the railing, the seats—their particular forms signify their special functions—is part of the meaning for me of this cathedral as a place for the worship of God and as the official church of a diocese. But my experience is also meaningful in other ways. This cathedral evokes thoughts of Gothic architecture and the Medieval way of life; it stands for the Church of Christ, on-going and universal; it symbolizes, in its vastness and transcendent illumination, the nature of God and the mysteries of Life. However differently other persons may phrase their comments, I believe they generally will agree that *Reims Cathedral,* as experienced directly or indirectly, is both beautiful and meaningful.

Let us close this section on logical definition by quoting one or two comparable statements from other books. In *The Arts and the Art of of Criticism,* Theodore M. Greene writes: "A work of art is here conceived of as a distinctive type of man-made object endowed with formal beauty." On first thought this definition may seem to you quite similar to the one herein developed. On second thought you may ask whether by 'endowed with' Greene means that beauty is actually in and a part of the work of art. On third thought, you may note that he refers to 'formal beauty,' apparently meaning beauty of form, and that he does not specify significance as a differentiating quality. Perhaps, then, Greene's definition and the one developed for this book are not as similar as they at first seemed.

Another statement comes from F. R. O'Neill's *The Social Value of Art:* " 'A work of art' means an expression of an artist's experience in a form which makes it communicable to many minds with only slight variations." This may seem to you very different from the definition developed above. But, however differently phrased, it is (except for the notable omission of beauty) really quite consistent with the point of view of this section and of this book.

4. *The art process and triad*

It will be apparent from F. R. O'Neill's statement that the work of art stands in a special relation both to the artist who creates it and to the many persons who experience it. D. W. Gotshalk, who defines art in *Art and the Social Order* as "the creation of objects for aesthetic experience," says that "the distinctive nature of art" is to be found "in the triadic pattern of creation-object-apprehension implied in the proposed definition of art. It rests upon the interrelation of process-object-process imbedded in the artistic transaction."

This relation of the work of art to the artist was implicit in our phrase 'man-made thing;' and the relation of the work of art to the persons who contemplate it was implicit in our phrase 'generally evoking beauty and meaning responses.' Something further, therefore, should be said about these relations. In this discussion we shall use the word 'artee' to refer to the listener, beholder, or reader, or to any person who experiences a work of art.

The Artist's *art activity* CREATES

a Work of Art that

EVOKES *art experiences* in Artees.

There are several observations to be made about this statement—beyond the fact that it is eccentric in typography. First, notice the chain of cause and effect in the art process that it describes: the artist's activity is the cause of the work of art that in turn is the cause of the art experiences in the artees. Second, notice that there are three members of the art triad: the artist — the art work — the artees. Third, notice that there are two sorts of activity involved: active creation of the art work and active responses to the art work.

It would be as easy to define 'artist' and 'creative art activity,' 'art experience' and 'artee' by example as it was to define 'work of art' in that way. All that would be necessary would be to point to a painter in the process of painting a picture, to an architect at his drafting board, to a poet at his desk, or to a singer singing, and to say, "What you see going on *there* is an example of what I shall call 'creative art activity.' And that person whom you see there engaged in creative activity, making a work of art, is an example of what I mean by 'artist'." It would be just as easy to define 'artee' and 'art experience' by example, pointing out a person gazing up at a great building, or absorbed in reading a novel, or listening to music with rapt attention. "What you see *there*," I might say, "is an artee, a person who is having an art experience. Since by its very nature an art experience is essentially within the person, it would be better simply to have you think of the complex goings-on within your own person while contemplating a work of art, and to say that *that* is an example of what is meant by 'art experience.'

Logical definitions of each of these additional terms may easily be developed in relation to the definition of 'work of art.' So, an artist is simply a man who creates works of art. Creative art activity is the activity by means of which an artist creates works of art. An artee is a person who perceives, responds to, contemplates a work of art. And an art experience is the whole complex response of an artee to a work of art. As creative activity and the work of art will be the subject of three chapters comprising Part Two of this book and as three phases of the art experience will be discussed in some detail in Part Three, they need not be defined further in this place.

It remains, however, to say a word about art in general—you may think of it as art with a capital A.

This 'Art,' or what we have called the World of Art, will be defined in broad enough terms to include all creative art activity, all works of art, and all art experiences. Phrased more formally: *Art consists of those man-made things generally evoking beauty and meaning responses, the human activity that creates such things, and the human responses to them.*

But if 'Art' is to be defined here in such sweeping terms, comprising creative activities and objective things and evoked responses, it is all the more necessary for you to be clear as to what you yourself mean by it. You must also be alert to the fact that other persons may be using the little word 'art' loosely or in definitely different senses. In daily conversation or reading concerning art, you should ask yourself constantly, "What do *I* mean by calling this thing art? . . . What does the other fellow refer to by his use of 'art'? . . . What part of the art process is he thinking of? . . . What seems to be *his* basic definition of 'work of art'? . . ."

If your mind is alert with such questions while reading or talking, eager to clarify the present relation of words to the things referred to, you need have no qualms about discussing with other persons your adventures in the World of Art. After all, a man is not a fool because he speaks of a beautiful sunset or an apple pie as a work of art; he is simply using 'art' in a different sense from the one developed in this chapter. Try to understand what he means. Try also to keep your own house in order, your own art theory consistent, your own use of the little word 'art' clearly related to whatever it is you may be referring to.

5. *Classification of art works*

Definition is the process by which man controls language and clarifies the relation of words and thoughts to the things they stand for or refer to. Classification is the related process of sorting and labelling the various items in his experience. Without such purposive and systematic sorting or classifying, the natural sciences could not exist, and the social sciences would be literally unthinkable. We have already made use of classification in working out a logical definition of 'work of art,' for we set up a genus-species-differentiae structure that established the large class of Things and two subclasses, Art Things (works of art) and Not-art Things. It was evident, when we formulated our definition, that works of art as a class were different from other things; they were all seen to be man-made, beautiful, and significant. It was equally evident that these works of art were amazingly different from one another. We shall now be concerned with their differences.

Noting differences and similarities is one way of responding to things. When we indicate the qualities of an object before us, we are really naming certain responses to it. Before me on my desk is an object, a small bust of Benjamin Franklin. One of my responses to it is that it is bronze in color. It is different, in the color scheme of things, from the green pencil, the yellow paper, and the red eraser. It is similar in this respect to the brown leather of my desk pad. Furthermore this bust is shiny. In the matter of surface reflection, it is different from the dull blotter and eraser; it is similar to the mucilage bottle. In considering the usefulness of my desk things, it has the quality of being useful as a paper weight, which differentiates it from the pencil, the paper, the blotter, and eraser; however, the mucilage bottle is also useful as a paperweight, though that is not its primary function. And so on we might go. The mere naming of qualities, then, involves more or less conscious sorting.

Sorting is the process of grouping things according to their differences and similarities. Assume that you are sorting the miscellaneous items and that it is your desk. If the sorting factor that you use is color-response, then items of similar hue will be grouped together and as many different groups or categories will be established as you see fit, for you will have to decide how many hues to differentiate. The green pencil, the dark green blotter, and bluish green book may fall into one category. The red pencil, the pink eraser, the red ink bottle top may fall into another. The yellow paper, the bronze Franklin, the gold pen, the tan mucilage bottle, the cream colored folder, may comprise a third group. The blue book may stand by itself. So much for that one sorting. But if you decide to re-sort the items, using as the sorting factor the nature of the material of which they are made, a new set of categories will be established—wood, paper, metal, and so on; and the things will fall into quite a different arrangement on your desk. The green pencil and red pencil will form one group; the gold pen and bronze paper weight and red ink bottle top will form another; etc. A third sorting, according to the cost of the articles, would bring the gold pen and the desk lamp together in the over-five-dollar group; the pencil, eraser, and blotter will fall into the five-cents-or-less group.

Purposive and systematic sorting is what we have called classification. If your purpose is, at last, to clear up the mess on your desk and put it in order, the sorting factor may be your convenience-response or your established-place-response. So, in no time at all, you stack books back on the shelf, pens and pencils on the base of the lamp, mucilage and Franklin to left and right; unanswered letters go into the drawer, waste paper into the basket. Indeed, in such schemes for bringing order out of chaos, there is "a place for everything, and everything in its place."

As a demonstration of the way in which we control the far-flung World of Art by means of classification, and as a means of exploring it further at the same time, let us manipulate the eight works of art earlier cited as examples:

1. *Reims Cathedral,* called 'Notre Dame'
2. *Wrestlers*
3. Van Gogh's *Sunflowers*
4. the table lamp
5. France's *The Juggler of Our Lady*
6. Mozart's Overture to *Le Nozze di Figaro*
7. the peasants' dancing [not the picture]
8. Beaumarchais' *Le Mariage de Figaro* [on stage]

You will find it helpful to make a 3 x 5 card for each one of them. The cards will then serve as tokens in the several sortings that we shall undertake. On them you can make brief notes of the categories into which these works fall in various classifications.

Perhaps you observed in making out the cards that some of the works of art have TITLES, and some do not. A classification on this basis would be important in identifying art works and in making a title index for a catalog. Did you also observe that for some of these works the ARTIST is known by name, for others unknown? A classification on this basis would be useful, again, for identifying works of art and in making an artist index.

If you were writing a history of art, you might classify these and other art works in several different ways:

First, you perhaps would arrange them by PERIODS or more exactly in chronological order. The sorting factor would be the date of creation; the categories would be the great historic periods: Ancient, Medieval, Renaissance, Baroque, Modern. In this classification, *Wrestlers*, *Reims Cathedral*, the dancing, the overture *Figaro*, the *Sunflowers* would fall respectively into these five successive categories. Beaumarchais' comedy would fall with Mozart's music in the Baroque category; *The Juggler* and the table lamp would be classified as Modern.

Or you might deal with these works of art on the basis of the COUNTRY of their origin. The native land of the artist would be the sorting factor, unless you decided to consider the country in which he was living when he did his work. So you would set up some such categories as these: Rome, France, Benelux, Austria, America. This would bring the Flemish peasants and Van Gogh's *Sunflowers* into the Benelux category; *Reims Cathedral*, Beaumarchais' *Figaro*, and Anatole France's story into the French category. Then there are the Roman *Wrestlers*, the Austrian overture to *Figaro*, and the American table lamp.

A third classification, and the commonest one of all, would sort these and other art works according to the several traditionally established ARTS: Architecture, Sculpture, Painting, Dance, Theater Art, Literature, Music—and the applied arts. And we have already taken this classification so much for granted that we have been using the conventional art labels in referring to these art works as the statue, the stageplay, and so on. You will notice that the first seven arts have been set off from the last one, for this classification differentiates the so-called Fine Arts from the so-called applied, practical, household, and industrial arts. Nor is the list of Fine Arts always the same. The seven here named, however, are the basis for this book on THE ARTS AND HUMANITY, with special emphasis on the arts of Music, Painting and Literature.

Among those classifications that are useful in considering art history, these three—by period, by country, and by established arts—will serve us as a beginning group. So far, then, your *Reims Cathedral* card has on it the title, *Notre Dame*, artist unknown, Medieval, French, Architecture. That doesn't tell you much, but it's a start.

A second group of three classifications is of a markedly different kind. They concern the physical nature of works of art, their relation to time and space, and how we perceive them. They are useful classifications to consider when art works are to be exhibited, seen or heard.

First, consider their PHYSICAL NATURE. As you shuffle through your eight cards, ask what sorts of sense stuff these art works are made of. You will at once note that some are made of *tangible and inanimate* material. Like the cathedral, the others too are relatively imperishable—the statue, the picture, the lamp, and the book containing the story. The music of the overture was described earlier as a complex pattern of sound waves; as such, it is *intangible*—it cannot be touched in the same way as stone, metal, paint, and paper. The dancing and the stageplay are different yet. They are tangible enough, but far from inanimate; they consist essentially of *human beings and activities*. But the stageplay, particularly, has inanimate components (scenery) and intangible components (speech sounds); and the dance includes the intangible sound waves of music and footfalls. Here then are three categories: tangible inanimate materials, intangible sound waves, and human beings in activity with sound. The first group of art works can be photographed, the second can be phonographed, the third can only be recorded on sound film. This classification may suggest some of the difficulties involved in illustrating a book on the arts. Further consideration of the physical nature of works of art will be found in Chapter 5.

Now think of the relation of these art works to TIME AND SPACE as you leaf through your cards again. Some of them—the ones whose material substance is tangible and inanimate—occupy three dimensions of measurable space and do not change or move. The established arts whose works are of this sort are often called the *space arts*: Architecture, Sculpture, Painting, and the applied arts. Literature, however, is not usually called a space art, though works of literature do occupy space. A second category comprises the *time arts*. These works—characteristically the intangible art works like the overture—do not exist in space in the usual sense, but only in the flux of time. Like music, as a time art, are the speech arts such as oratory and radio drama. Literature is usually called a time art because the reading of a work of literature is bound to a fairly fixed period of time, as is the listening to a work of music. A third category includes the *time-space arts*. To this class belong the peasants' dancing and the stageplay, whose complex materials we described as human beings in activity with sound. They occupy the three regular dimensions of space and the fourth dimension of time, for the spectator is bound to stay through the evening's performance if he wants to perceive the entire play. This classification is implicit whenever you hear the words spatial, temporal, and spaciotemporal used in relation to art.

Another common classification completes this group and may be called SENSORY. You may easily sort these eight works of art according to the five senses or such of them as are useful in the perception of art works. Again three convenient categories suggest themselves; and again the distribution of art works is similar to that in the physical-nature classification. Those works of art perceived through the sense of sight are the *visual arts*. Those perceived through the sense of hearing are the *auditory arts*. Those perceived through both sight and hearing are the *audiovisual arts*. Again, these terms are frequently used in the discussion of art, and you may have no trouble sorting the eight art works according to this scheme. No trouble, that is, unless you again puzzle the problem of Literature, which is not usually considered a visual art, though reading is of course a visual process. And you may question whether other senses, beyond sight and hearing, are not useful in the perception of art works. But the whole matter of sensory perception will be discussed in Chapter 7.

At this point, then, let us summarize by means of an example and reference to one of your cards: the *Wrestlers*, artist unknown, is Ancient, Roman, Sculpture. It is made of tangible inanimate material (specifically, marble); it exists in space (Florence, to be particular), and is perceived through the sense of sight. The word 'tangible' suggests an important addition to the sense of sight in this instance, for certain works of art are perceived through the sense of touch as well as sight. But more of this later.

A final pair of classifications will be no more than suggested. They are again quite different in kind. They are concerned with the interpretation and usefulness of works of art.

The first of these will be called a MEANING classification. If you glance through your cards thinking of these eight art works one by one, you will note that certain of them picture or represent persons or things. The statue is in the form of two men wrestling; the picture is recognizably one of sunflowers; the stageplay is performed by actors who portray characters. These works are *representational* works of art. The others are non-representational: The cathedral does not picture anything. This table lamp is not in the shape of a dog or a tree or a man. This music does not sound like a babbling brook or the screech of tires. Even the peasants' dancing does not, I assume, represent or picture or act out anything; that is, it is an abstract pattern of dance movements. These nonrepresentational works of art are all, in one way or another, *abstract*. They do not have a picture relationship to what they mean or stand for. The story of the juggler, also nonrepresentational, is a somewhat special case, and we shall for the moment simply call it *symbolic*. It consists of word signs that are abstract in their forms—they do not picture the things they mean or stand for—but they have the power to evoke in our minds pictures of persons and things as well as abstract relationships of thought. This classification introduces us to the words 'representation,' 'abstraction,' and 'symbolic' which are often used in the discussion of works of art. This important problem of meaning in art will be considered in Chapter 3.

The second of this final pair of classifications will be called FUNC-TIONAL. The sorting factor is the kind of usefulness attributed to the work of art. This will involve us in the problem of value, of which something more must be said later. It is enough at this time to suggest a classification for present use. Again it will have three categories: the cathedral and table lamp may be said to have *practical* use—the one housing worshipers, the other giving light. The overture and the dance have contributory use—the one preparing the audience for the opera to come, the other contributing to the social occasion. The statue and story have *terminal* or contemplative use—evoking experiences worthwhile as ends in themselves. Then what of Van Gogh's painting and the Beaumarchais comedy? Neither is of practical usefulness. But the picture may be considered either as an object of contemplation or as a picture of *instrumental* value making a useful contribution to the decoration of the room. Beaumarchais' satirical comedy, serving a social purpose in its own day, is now of largely terminal value, a thing to be contemplated and enjoyed as an end in itself. These three words 'practical,' 'instrumental,' and 'terminal' are of use in discussing the functional value of art works.

To summarize again with particular reference: The *Sunflowers* by Vincent Van Gogh is Modern, Dutch, Painting. It is made of tangible inanimate material (paint and canvas), occupies space in a gallery, and is perceived by the sense of sight. Furthermore, it is representational (it has as its subject a jug of yellow sunflowers); and it has terminal or instrumental value depending upon whether you think of it solely as an object of contemplation or as contributing to the decoration of a room.

6. *Art theory and application*

If you have followed closely this discussion of definition and classification of art, you may well be tired by this time. Discriminating various definitions of 'art' and describing the things referred to, setting up various classifications and sorting and re-sorting a group of art works—these are exacting processes of thought, fatiguing mental exercises. But they are certainly rewarding activities if you wish to control and clarify your general thoughts about art. William Blake, the artist and poet, once asked, "What has reasoning to do with Art or Painting?" Well, without doubt, logical processes of mind are essential to any development of theoretical knowledge; and your art

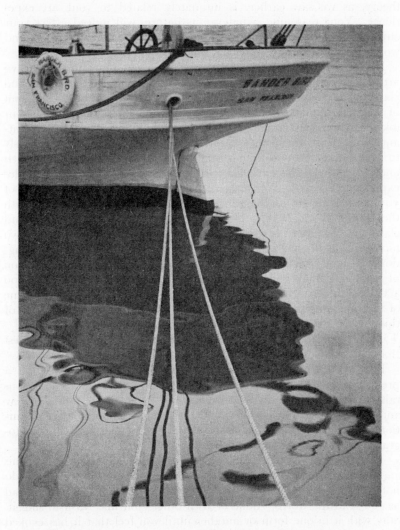

Arthur Hammond, F.R.P.S., WANDER BIRD, taken at Gloucester

theory, as we saw earlier, is intimately related to your art experiences. Your reasoning, whatever its nature, will indeed affect your enjoyment, understanding, and appreciation of music, pictures, and works of literature.

In addition to clarifying and enlarging in some measure your own art theory, this discussion and demonstration of art definition and classification should have had some other values. First, as a result of your manipulation of these eight works of art, by means of your token cards and note-taking, you have surely increased your acquaintance with them; for in the repeated sortings you were led consciously to assign them many different qualities, and your experience of each one of them was thus enriched with relevant detail. Second, the fuller experience of particular works of art serves to enrich the coffers of your own Kingdom of Art, and thus to enlarge your commerce with the outside World of Art. Third, this consideration of definition and classification may have given you added skill in the use of these two tools of thought that will continue to be useful in putting your Kingdom to rights, keeping your mind in order, controlling the relation of what you think and say about art to the art experiences that you actually have. And fourth, these pages have served to introduce some of the questions that will be taken up in later chapters and parts of this book.

There could be no better way to end this chapter than to suggest that you apply some of the ideas that we have been developing.

First, turn to the reproduction of a photograph reprinted on a preceding page. Considering it in relation to the various questions raised in this and the earlier sections will constitute a useful review and may serve to fix in your mind the related matters of art definition and classification. After all, what sort of thing is this photograph? and what qualities distinguish it from other things?

Then look at the following musical notation and song lyric. This anonymous American spiritual is so well known that, even if you do not read music, you will probably find the tune buzzing in your head as you read the words. Alone or with others you may wish to sing it. Stay with it in one form or another until you feel that it has evoked in you a full and appropriate response.

SWING LOW, SWEET CHARIOT
Artist Unknown

Swing low, sweet char-i-ot, Comin' for to carry me home!

Swing low, sweet char-i-ot, Comin' for to carry me home!

I looked over Jordan an' what did I see, Comin' for to carry me home!

A band of angels comin' after me, Comin' for to carry me home!

2.

If you get there before I do,
(Comin' for to carry me home),
Jus' tell my frien's I'm a'comin' too,
(Comin' for to carry me home).

3.

I'm sometimes up an' sometimes down
(Comin' for to carry me home),
But still my soul feel heavenly boun'
(Comin' for to carry me home).

Swing low, sweet chariot,
Comin' for to carry me home;
Swing low, sweet chariot,
Comin' for to carry me home.

Chapter 2. Orientation to Art and Aesthetics

Tell me what you like, and I'll tell you what you are.
Ruskin, *The Crown of Wild Olive*

Fine art is the creation of objects for aesthetic experience.
D. W. Gotshalk, *Art and the Social Order*

Beauty is pleasure regarded as the quality of a thing.
George Santayana, *The Sense of Beauty*

Swing Low, *Sweet Chariot*, with which we closed the last chapter, whether considered as the music and song lyric here in the book or as a complex pattern of sound waves resulting from its being sung, is a work of art as we defined the phrase. For in either case it is a man-made thing generally evoking beauty and meaning responses. The two key questions implicit in that definition—what is beauty? and what is meaning?—were answered only tentatively. They will be considered in some detail later in this chapter and in the next; for these three chapters together constitute Part One of this book under the title 'Introduction to Art, Beauty, and Meaning.'

These opening sections and chapters are introductory: they are intended to help you, each individual reader, to orient yourself to the World of Art. By 'orientation' we mean getting your bearings, seeing where you stand, plotting your position in relation to all of those things and activities and experiences and general ideas that make up the art phase of your life. So far we have distinguished art theory and art experience and have shown their interrelation; we have described the wide range of common things and daily events that come within the sphere of art; we have set up working definitions of 'artist,' 'creative art activity,' 'work of art,' 'responsive art experience,' and 'artee' as a step toward clearer thinking; and we have made use of classification as a device for discriminating and controlling the vast quantity of items within the general field. Now that some of these things have been brought into sharper focus, you are ready to look about you and determine what your own relation is to them.

This sort of stock taking and appraisal will surely be worth while if you are at all serious about developing the art phase of your life, clarifying your general ideas about it, and cultivating your taste. For you will have to start off on your course of self-development *from where you now are*. Whether you are impatient 'to see the distant scene,' the goal toward which a study of the fine arts may lead you, or whether you are content to see but 'one step' at a time, you will need to begin realistically by discovering and accepting your present position as a starting point.

1. Personal orientation to art

In making this personal orientation to the world of creative art activities and responsive art experiences, there are four questions for you to ask yourself: What is my aptitude for art activity? ... What sorts of art experiences have I had? ... What do I know about art history? ... What is my present art taste and art judgment?

To these questions you may give fairly definite answers, and in this way see where you stand in the world of art and in relation to the persons around you. Certainly the goals you set for yourself should take account of aptitudes, past experiences, accumulated knowledge, and present taste. You may be a person of unusually high aptitudes for various art activities, but very little experience or knowledge, yet with discriminating taste. Or you may be a person with only average art abilities, but a wide range of experiences, and a very considerable factual knowledge of art. Your goals should be adjusted to your needs and abilities.

The first question: *What is your aptitude for art activity?*

Let us consider aptitude in a broad sense including physical suitability, neuromuscular co-ordination, sensory discrimination, imaginative activity and insight, temperament, energy and self-mastery—personality traits that characterize the artist. As we shall suggest in Chapter 4, these are not different in kind from the traits of other men, but only in degree. This measuring of individual aptitudes is important, for instance, to those art schools and conservatories that are anxious to admit only students who have some chance to succeed; and it is of special use to persons who offer guidance and counseling. However, we are not thinking solely of aptitudes for creative art activity but also for responsive art experience. They are not necessarily the same, though often related.

Obviously the person who is stone deaf will not be able to hear musical sounds at all. However, a person who has had exceptional hearing and who then becomes deaf, as was the case with Beethoven, may be able to carry on creative work in music, for he may continue to have vivid auditory imagery. Persons who are tone deaf or who 'can't carry a tune in a bucket' will be limited in their various musical experiences. Individual differences in hearing ability are greater than you might suppose. Carl Seashore says in his book *In Search of Beauty in Music* that, of two equally intelligent persons, "one has more than a hundred times as fine a sense of pitch, sense of rhythm, sense of timbre as the other," and that these are relatively independent variables and that a person who stands high in one may be low in another.

As with hearing so with sight: everyone knows something about color blindness. It is generally said that about one man in twelve is somewhat color-blind, but only one woman in a hundred, for color blindness follows one of the laws of heredity. Few persons are really completely color-blind; but, even among persons of so-called normal vision, there are slight differences in sensitivity to color. There are also other individual differences in vision and eye-movements that will have some bearing upon creative and responsive art experience— extreme nearsightedness, for instance.

Individuals also differ in other significant ways that are relevant to art activities. Some persons have an unusually keen sense of balance. Some are naturally sensitive at their finger tips and clever with their hands. Some have superior muscular co-ordination in body and limbs. Some have especially resonant voices or superior articulation. Some are quicker to see the connections between words and things and to get the point. Some have a gift of tongue or an aptitude for verbal expression. And all people differ one from another in temperament. You can see that certain special abilities may make for success in the art of the dance, and that the possession of these aptitudes may make one better able to experience fully and appreciate a dance performance. But different special abilities will be necessary for the poet and for the fullest understanding and enjoyment of his art.

It is possible, within narrow limits, to find out where you stand as regards certain of these special abilities. For instance, there is a test devised by Carl Seashore that will measure certain factors involved in your musical activity. Another test, developed by Ishihara and widely used during the war, is useful in determining whether and in what way you may be color-blind. The Varnum test was developed to measure certain other factors involved in the visual arts. There are tests for measuring manual dexterity, or judging bodily agility and muscular co-ordination, for estimating vocal and articulatory ability, for determining your vocabulary, for calculating your general intelligence. Through the interpretation of the data from such tests, it is possible for you to see where you stand in relation to other persons as regards certain aptitudes for art activity. To place yourself in this way is, in a sense, to Know Thyself—to know what you can rightly expect of yourself, or what is apparently possible for you in the realm of creative and responsive art activities.

At one time or another you have probably been given a number of such tests. Before reading further, take a moment to think about your various aptitudes, abilities, special gifts and limitations and their relation to various sorts of art activity. If you have taken some such tests as those noted above, you might well summarize your relative aptitudes as measured by them. If not, you still may make some general notes on your various art skills and potentialities as you have observed them. . . .

The second question: *What sorts of art experience have you had?*

Again let us consider both the creative and the responsive phases of the whole art process and think of the various sorts of experiences that are possible within the different arts. Persons will differ markedly as regards the range of their art experience, and also as regards the intensity of their experiences or concentration upon particular activities. Some persons enjoy a wide range of responsive experiences —reading novels, listening to music, visiting art galleries, playgoing, and so on, and also play a musical instrument, take artful photographs, and from time to time try their hands at various other creative art activities. On the other hand, some persons do and have done very few of these different things, but have perhaps devoted themselves intensively to one of them.

Whereas a person's art aptitudes are inherited, though certain abilities are of course developed, the pattern of a person's art experience is largely the result of his environment—though persons of different aptitudes and temperaments are differently affected by their surroundings. The home and the community, the church and the school, all provide more or less opportunity and encouragement for creative art activity and for responsive art experiences.

As a first step in determining the range of your own art experiences, make use of the following list of questions, devised a few years ago by the author and Richard Harris, an artist and student. Cover the column of figures to the right, and check the questions to which your answer is 'Yes.' As this is a matter of range and not depth of experience, give yourself the benefit of the doubt.

INVENTORY
of creative and responsive art experiences

MUSIC	Check here	Yes-Responses
1. Have you taken a course in music appreciation?	☐	37%
2. Have you attended a performance of a symphony orchestra in recent years?	☐	67%
3. Do you listen to such radio programs as the Standard Symphony Hour?	☐	70%
4. Have you attended a concert by an instrumental or vocal soloist in recent years?	☐	62%
5. Have you attended an opera or light opera or listened to such on the radio	☐	82%
6. Do you play a musical instrument?	☐	53%
7. Have you ever played in a band or orchestra?	☐	32%
8. Have you ever sung before an audience either as soloist or with a group?	☐	66%
9. Are you studying music at the present time?	☐	16%
10. Have you ever directed group singing or playing?	☐	25%
11. Have you ever thought up an original tune or composed a piece of music?	☐	19%

Total

PAINTING and PHOTOGRAPHY

12. Have you ever taken a course in art appreciation?	☐	22%
13. Have you attended an art exhibit in recent years?	☐	80%
14. Do you follow the art features in *Life* or comparable journals?	☐	34%
15. Have you gone to a photographic exhibit recently?	☐	31%
16. Do you draw, cartoon, paint, model, or photograph?	☐	31%

17. Have you ever done art or photographic work for student organizations? ☐ 26%
18. Have you ever entered photographs in an exhibition? ☐ 2%
19. Are you taking any course in drawing, design, or painting? ☐ 11%
20. Have you shown an original drawing, painting, or piece of sculpture in an exhibit in recent years? ☐ 4%

Total

LITERATURE and THEATER ARTS

21. Have you taken a course in English or American literature? ☐ 85%
22. Have you taken a course in the literature of the drama? ☐ 20%
23. Have you seen any plays (outside of high school or college productions) in recent years? ☐ 78%
24. Do you enjoy reading dramas? ☐ 68%
25. Do you enjoy reading modern novels? ☐ 87%
26. Do you read magazine stories regularly? ☐ 48%
27. Do you ever read poetry? ☐ 77%
28. Have you acted in or helped produce high school or college plays? ☐ 50%
29. Are you taking dramatics in college? ☐ 11%
30. Have you ever written a story? ☐ 41%
31. Have you ever written any verse? ☐ 40%
32. Have you ever written a playscript? ☐ 17%

Total

ARCHITECTURE and APPLIED ARTS

33. Have you ever taken any course in applied art? ☐ 19%
34. Have you ever taken a course in the history of architecture? ☐ 5%
35. Have you attended an exhibit of building materials and house details? ☐ 45%
36. Do you enjoy visiting model homes? ☐ 91%
37. Do you enjoy exhibits of crafts work in textiles, metal, wood, etc.? ☐ 83%

38. Have you ever made your own Christ-
    mas cards?   ☐   37%
39. Have you ever made a fabric?   ☐   48%
40. Have you ever designed flower ar-
    rangements?   ☐   44%
41. Have you ever designed and made
    pottery?   ☐   23%
42. Have you ever sketched out plans for
    a house?   ☐   59%
                                      _____

                      Total
                                      _____

                   Grand total

This inventory was given over a number of years to students in a
required sophomore college course. The following percentages and
averages are based upon 435 individuals in the years 1940-45. The
numbers above to the right represent the percentage of persons who
answered in the affirmative. If you gave item No. 20 an affirmative
check, you can see that you are one of the very few individuals (4% as
represented by this study) who have exhibited a painting or work of
sculpture. If you failed to give item No. 36 an affirmative check, you
are one of those rare persons who do not like to visit model homes,
for 91% of the students here tabulated do. By noting the relation of
your check marks and unchecked items to the percentages in the margin, you can see to what extent your various sorts of art experience are
common or unusual.

Now add up the check marks for each of the four divisions of the
inventory. This will show you what the relative breadth of your experience has been in the different arts as here represented and grouped.
The averages for the 435 individuals, you may be interested to know,
are as follows: for music, 5.35; for painting, etc., 2.44; for literature
and theater art, 6.25; for architecture and applied arts, 4.59. If, for
instance, the total number of your yes-responses for music is 6, you
are just above average (5.35) in the breadth of your musical experience. If your painting, etc., total is 7, you are far above the average
in this field (2.44). You may also compare the grand total of your
yes-responses to the average grand total of 18.63. In this way you
may gain some idea of where you stand among your fellows in regard
to the general breadth of your art experiences and the pattern of concentration.

As you make a written memorandum of this survey of the range
of your various art experiences you might stress those items indicating
experiences of considerable or great depth—for instance, you may be

a really skilled violinist, or capable cartoonist, or wide reader, or devoted playgoer. . . .

The third question: *What do you know about art history?*

Knowledge of the arts from personal experience, both creating things and responding to them, is one thing; knowledge of the facts about art and art history is quite different. You may have picked up a good bit of general art information from enriched courses in history, from work in literature stressing cultural backgrounds, art and music appreciation. General reading in current periodicals and historical fiction and radio browsing may have added to the store of your factual knowledge about art. Or you may indeed have had separate courses on the history of English literature, or the history of art (usually in the sense of painting, sculpture, and architecture), or of music, or of the drama and theater. It will be obvious to you that people differ widely in this regard: Some seem to know all the answers, with the facts ready at hand, and any picture or piece of music or poem stimulates an Information-Please response—the artist's name, dates, period, country, style, most famous works, outstanding contribution, personal idiosyncrasies, and scandalous anecdotes!—while other persons remain silent or add an isolated fact.

Some estimate of your general art knowledge is an important part of your personal orientation to the world of art. A number of tests have been developed that may be useful in measuring your so-called general culture. Separate tests also are available for evaluating your fund of musical information, your knowledge of art history, and your literary acquaintance. A simple test of one narrow sort—the identification of titles of art works—is right at hand. Turn to the opening pages of this book, to the Table of Art Works presented as illustrations. Check lightly those with which you have had previous acquaintance; double check those that you have known well. Then add up the items that you checked (including those double-checked); then add up those that you double-checked. Comparison of your totals with the scores of others will be a crude measure of where you stand in this regard. . . .

The fourth question: *What is your present art taste and art judgment?*

Let us define 'taste' as the pattern of your likes and dislikes. Your art taste, then, is based upon the sum of your preferences and aversions. Taste is intuitive and irrational. On the other hand your judgment is a function of reason in the evaluation of things. Your art judgment, then, is based upon your thoughts of what is best and your conscious application of principles and standards. Your art taste and your art judgment are by no means the same. At times they are in opposition, and you find yourself 'liking' something that you really 'judge' to be inferior.

It is said there is no accounting for your taste. It would be better to say that the causes of your particular likes and dislikes are often obscure. The bases of your taste are to be found in your personal make-up and in your unique body of art experiences, factors that were suggested in answer to questions one and two above. Ruskin once said, "Tell me what you like and I'll tell you what you are." He might just as truthfully have said, Tell me what you are and I'll tell you what you like. The bases of your judgment, however, are to be found in your own art theory—those generalizations and principles and precepts, no matter how vague and fragmentary and contradictory they may be, that you have acquired and accumulated through the years. We have already seen that your art experience and art theory are definitely interrelated, so we may say that the bases of your taste and judgment in the arts are also interrelated.

There are a number of ways in which you may objectify your present taste and art judgment and thereby see where you stand in this regard. An entertaining and provocative book by Sanford E. Gerard, *How Good Is Your Taste*, is made up of a variety of test items calling for discrimination and choice in the field of the applied arts. Taken with a sense of humor and a grain of salt, these tests may prove to be a helpful index of your taste. However, there are tests more scientific in nature that are useful in measuring art, music, and poetry judgment and appreciation. These are really taste tests if the person taking them confines himself to simple preferences; but they become tests of art judgment (as we have defined it) if the individual becomes self-conscious and begins to use his head. Such tests as these will measure your taste in relation to standards established by the so-called experts!

A simple way to orient yourself to those about you as regards your taste and judgment is to consider, with a group of friends, a number of pairs of poems (comparable in theme but contrasted in treatment), a number of pairs of pictures (similar subjects treated by different artists in different styles), and a number of musical excerpts (again with some basis for comparison but notably different in effect). You may discover that your own personal preferences and conscious choices fall into a pattern: this over-all pattern is your present taste and judgment. Another simple device is to list your favorite musical compositions (with a set limit of, say, ten), your favorite pictures, your favorite literary works—perhaps also your favorite stageplays and moving pictures. Comparing your list with others may help you to characterize your art taste and judgment.

So much, then, for the four questions.

It is a good thing to know yourself in these ways: to recognize your own special aptitudes, abilities, gifts, and limitations as a person in relation to various sorts of art activity; to investigate and summarize the range as well as pattern and depth of your creative and responsive art experiences; to evaluate the extent of your factual knowledge about art; and to measure your taste or judgment objectively and to characterize the pattern of your present preferences among art works. This personal orientation to the World of Art will be extended by adding two more questions: What is the relation of your own to other art theories? and, What is the relation of your own to other ideas of beauty? But these two questions will require more extended treatment in the later sections of this chapter.

2. 'The Music Lesson' and your orientation

Let us, before asking these further questions, turn to *The Music Lesson* by Thomas Hart Benton. Take a good look at it. Let your eyes move over it as they please or as you will. Enjoy it for its own sake and respond to it as freely and fully as you wish. Think about it, too, along whatever lines of thought suggest themselves to you. Don't work too hard at it, but linger with it awhile. . . .

Now, without returning for another look at the picture, check down this list of questions. They are arranged in groups related to the four main questions of the above section, and in a rough way your ability to answer them is some indication of your art aptitude, range of experience, knowledge, and taste.

What object, if any, hangs on the wall?
What object, if any, lies on the floor?
In what posture is the little girl represented?
With what hand does the man pluck the strings?
Were you conscious of any rhythmic sensations?

Did you ever play the guitar?
Did you experience any feeling of balance or imbalance?
Did you as a child watch your father play an instrument?
Did you take music lessons as a child?
Were you raised in the country? or small town?
Did your father take time to teach or show you things?
Did you ever sit that way on a chair?
Did you ever draw a picture of a musician?
Were you ever taught 'how to look at a picture'?

Had you seen this picture before getting this book?
Did you know who painted it before reading it here?
Did you guess who painted it by recognizing the style?
Did you know that Benton was a Missourian?
Did you know that his father and uncle were statesmen?
Did you know that he is a modern American genre painter?
Have you seen reproductions of other Benton pictures?
Did you know this picture was voted a popular prize in 1945?

Is it a work of art according to our definition?
Do you like it? did you enjoy looking at it?
Do you especially like the subject matter?
Do you especially like the treatment?
Do you judge it to be 'good' art?
Do you judge it to be 'great' art?

Some of these questions may seem to you to be trivial, others
irrelevant. Asking them can have done no harm; answering them
may have brought your experience of *The Music Lesson* to bear
upon the general questions of personal orientation to art.

3. Orientation to established art theories

Before the fifth and sixth general questions can be asked and answered—*What is the relation of your own to other art theories?* and
What is the relation of your own to other ideas of beauty?—it will
be necessary to explore the general field known as Aesthetics.

The word 'aesthetics' is used to mean art theory; it is also used to
mean the theory of beauty. It is sometimes used to mean both of
these fields of study; or it may be used to name that overlapping
area of the two, the study of beauty in art. In a recent *Encyclopedia
of the Arts* Thomas Munro defines 'aesthetics' as traditionally meaning "that branch of philosophy dealing with beauty and the beautiful, especially in art, and with taste and standards of value in judging art; also a theory or consistent attitude in such matters." The
word itself was first used in this connection in the mid-eighteenth
century by Baumgarten, but philosophies of art and of beauty are
found all the way back to the Greeks.

Because many of the historic art theories have assumed that beauty
is a property of art, the philosophies of art and of beauty are closely
interrelated and comprise the general field of Aesthetics. You will
recall that our own definition of art is in terms of beauty and meaning. However, many important art theories are not based on a
consideration of beauty at all, and either minimize its importance or

photo by Colten

Thomas Hart Benton, THE MUSIC LESSON, Associated American Artists

reject it altogether. Indeed it is obvious that many well-known works of art are by no means beautiful in any usual sense of the word. And most theories recognize the beauties of Nature as well as of art. Therefore, we shall consider art theories and beauty theories separately, though we cannot avoid frequent cross-reference.

In order to see the relation of your own art theory to others, it will be necessary to survey a rather broad field. Many persons— including artists as well as philosophers—have set forth their general views about art and the separate arts. Although Robert Henri, the American artist, said, "I don't believe any real artist cares whether what he does is 'art' or not," he and many others have given expression to at least fragments of their art theories: da Vinci and Cellini, Hogarth and Reynolds, Coleridge and Wordsworth, Schumann and Wagner, Tolstoy and Stanislavski—to name a few successive pairs almost at random. But it is the philosophers who, from earliest times, have contributed the more systematic documents in art theory: Plato and Aristotle, Berkeley and Burke, Kant and Hegel, Santayana and Croce, Dewey and Richards—again to name examples in successive pairs.

In surveying the general field of art theory, two or three things are at once apparent: One kind of art theory is descriptive; it consists of generalizations upon creative art activity, works of art, and responsive art experiences, based upon the theorist's observation of things *as they are* and have been. On the contrary, another kind of art theory is prescriptive; it consists of generalizations of what, in the artist's or critic's view, an artist *should* do, what really constitutes a work of art, and what the artee should experience while responding to art work. We might expect the critics and philosophers to be more objective and descriptive in their theories, and we might expect the artists to be more subjective and dogmatic; but this is not necessarily so.

Some art theories are developed primarily from the creative point of view, the first phase of the art process, and generalize upon what the artist does or should do, what materials and techniques he uses or should use, what subjects and modes of treatment are used or are appropriate, what his relation to society is or ought to be, and so on. Other art theories are centered in the work of art itself: what it is or should be, and so on. Yet other art theories are developed from the point of view of the responsive art experience, the second phase of the art process, and generalize upon what the artee's sense perceptions are or should be, what his various naive responses are or should be (images, feeling states, emotions, attitudes), and what his interpretations and evaluations are or should be. We might expect the artist's theories to deal with the creative phase; but, again, this is not always the case.

It will be impossible here to examine the long line of art theories from Plato to the present or even to explore fully a number of representative specimens. We shall, rather, proceed by considering a series of six general art problems, each of them headed by a pair of contrasting or opposing terms. All art theories do not consider these problems, nor do the terms necessarily name irreconcilable ideas. But the scheme may be helpful to you in the process of seeing where you stand on the suggested issues. Our method of procedure will be to define each problem and then to quote brief statements from contrasting art theories. Again it must be said: any single statement from a person's art theory is only to be fully understood in its relation to the whole system of which it is a part. Some of the quotations here given may not indeed be fully representative of the artist's or critic's theories. However, as you read you may well check those quotations or statements that seem to express most adequately your own general views.

1. *The artist's imitation of nature or expression of self.*

This pair of contrasting ideas suggests a problem related to the first phase of the art process, creative art activity. Should the artist sketch from life, copy nature, imitate natural forms, represent the outer world in his work? *Or* should he look within himself, rely on imagination, or give expression to the inner world of his moods and feelings and private thoughts? There are many variations of these two generally contrasting theories. For Hulme there are 'two different kinds of art,' one of which he describes as realistic, the other abstract or geometric.

The idea that art should imitate nature, as for example in realistic art, is a widely held and popular view that goes back to Aristotle's *Poetics*, wherein he established the idea of imitation and stated: "The epic . . . and tragic poetry, and moreover comedy . . . and the greatest part of the art pertaining to the flute and the lyre, are entirely imitations," as are painting, sculpture, and the dance. According to his view, the artist should 'hold . . . the mirror up to nature,' as Hamlet said in regard to the art of acting. Leonardo da Vinci said, "That painting is most praiseworthy which is most like the thing represented." Certainly, whether by means of representation or language, the imitation of things, persons, and events has been widespread, not only in painting, but also in sculpture, theater art, and literature. Even music, characteristically the most abstract of the arts, is imitative in some degree in what is called program music. In many a person's art theory 'truth to life' is the central criterion in art judgment; and there are many varieties of realism involved in the imitation of nature, running from extreme naturalism on the one hand through impressionism on the other. The modern American artist Edward Hopper noted: "My aim has always been the most exact transcription possible of my most intimate impressions of nature."

On the other hand Clive Bell in his book *Art* (1913) wrote: "The representative element in a work of art . . . always . . . is irrelevant." Within the last century, particularly in regard to the art of painting, there have developed theories, strongly in opposition to the imitation theories, that we shall call expression theories. According to these views, the artist should express himself—his moods, his feelings, his visions, his abstract thoughts. There are many forms of expressionism, including such startling schools in modern painting as cubism, primitivism, surrealism, and abstractionism. It was Picasso who said, "There is no abstract art. You must always start with something. Afterwards you can remove all traces of reality." But while this is virtually true for most of the arts, it is not so for music, which by its very nature, is expressional rather than imitative. All music except so-called program music, which vaguely suggests natural scenes or events, is said to be abstract or absolute. This trend in painting, sculpture, and literature from realism toward expressionism is suggested in Walter Pater's remark, "All art constantly aspires to the condition of music."

But imitation of nature and self-expression are not irreconcilable opposites. Picasso's assertion that there is no abstract art, for the artist will 'always start with something,' gives a clue. The extreme realist tries to create in you the illusion that you are yourself looking out upon some bit of the actual world; the extreme expressionist, that you are looking in upon some corner of his mind or soul. But there are many intermediate points. Many an artist would have you see some bit of reality 'through his eyes,' as he sees it and feels about it; many another would express himself—his moods, feelings, emotions, attitudes—*by means of* imitating or representing or symbolizing some observation of life.

Now consider what your own views have been on this matter of the artist's imitation of nature vs. expression of self. The chances are that you have had fairly set opinions about subject matter in painting and about music that tells or at least suggests a story. Make a scratchpaper statement of your own art theory at this point. . . . With this in hand, turn to *The Music Lesson* and consider briefly the relation of your statement to your art experience. What, in your opinion, is Benton's position on the imitation vs. expression question? . . .

2. Pleasure or profit in the art experience.

Here the contrast is at the responsive end of the art process, and artists and critics alike have been interested in the ultimate purpose of art. Should the artist seek merely to please or entertain, divert or transport, amuse or delight those who experience his work of art? *Or* should he strive to instruct or uplift, enlighten or somehow profit those who behold or hear or read his work? Thinking of the other end of the art process: Should the artee expect merely pleasure of one kind or the other from his art experiences? *Or* should he expect some sort of benefit or profit as a result of his art experiences? Pleasure and profit are values, and we have already met the terms 'terminal' and 'instrumental,' which we used to mean 'valuable for its own sake' and 'valuable for some purpose.'

Pleasure theories of art are prominent in the history of aesthetics, and their outstanding expression is 'art for art's sake.' Walter Pater wrote that "art comes to you proposing frankly to give nothing but the highest quality to your moments as they pass, and simply for those moments' sake." And at about the same time Oscar Wilde, for whom "The artist is the creator of beautiful things," said, "All art is quite useless." A century earlier Sir Joshua Reynolds said, "The end of art is to produce a pleasing effect on the mind." In some cases such theories emphasize the sensuous pleasures, the delight of the senses in the mere perception of a work of art; in other cases, the higher pleasures of the mind in contemplation. In both, experiencing a work of art is viewed as an end in itself, as having terminal value.

The so-called profit theories have been quite as numerous. "The be all and the end all," wrote Bach of music, "should be to the Glory of God and for a recreation of the soul." The painter Overbeck: "Art is to me what the harp was to David. I use it on every occasion to utter psalms of praise of the Lord." And Tolstoy, for whom art was 'a spiritual blessing, essential for all man,' said, "The destiny of art in our time is to transmit from the realm of reason to the realm of feeling the truth that well-being for men consists in being united together; and to set up, in place of the existing reign of force, that kingdom of God, i.e. of love, which we all recognize to be the highest aim of life." Some instrumentalist art theories stress service to God, some stress service to humanity, and some (as we can witness in our own time) demand service to the state. Yet other such theories are concerned with the values of creative and responsive art experiences to the individual person: inspiration and uplift, enlightenment and moral guidance, vicarious experience and escape, the resolution of conflicts and tensions, or the development of understandings and appreciations and attitudes. Such are the 'art for humanity's sake' theories.

"It would be no little gain to us," wrote Plato, "if poetry [and we add 'all art'] can be shown to be profitable as well as pleasant." Indeed these contrasting points of view about the end of art need not be conflicting. The poet Horace declared: "Poets wish either to profit or to delight..." but he added, "He who joins the instructive with the agreeable, carries off every vote [for the prize], by delighting and at the same time admonishing the reader." So, many artists have consciously pleased in order to promote other ends, providing a sugarcoating for their pill of purpose; and many a person comes to art works for pleasure but remains to pray.

It remains for you to orient yourself to this problem of art theory, to determine where you stand, to clarify your own views. So you should again work out a one-sentence statement of your own art theory at this point. . . . By taking it with you as you return to *The Music Lesson*, you may not only apply it to your experience of that work but also speculate upon Benton's theory. Where do you think he stands on this question? . . .

3. The artist's following of tradition or experimentation.

With this pair of contrasting ideas we return to the first phase of the creative process. Should the artist, whether imitating nature or expressing himself or both, whether purposing to give the artee pleasure or profit or both—should the artist follow in the footsteps of his predecessors, using traditional art materials and techniques, subjects and forms, treatments and styles? *Or* should he strike out for himself, cast off the millstones of tradition, experiment with materials and techniques, subjects and styles, and create new forms and highly original works? Here, in truth, we have the eternal battle of age and youth, conservative and liberal, convention and revolt. Often it is a conflict of the art schools with the 'schools' of art. The music conservatories, art academies, and college departments of literature have tended to be on the side of tradition—the young musicians, painters, and writers (students or starvers in the Latin Quarters, Greenwich Villages, and art colonies) have championed the various modern 'schools' of art.

There is no need to examine here convention and revolt in the history of art theories, and the successive battles of the Ancients and the Moderns. The presence in our culture of bank buildings in the form of Greek temples standing beside cantilevered structures with glass fronts; of the string quartet beside the new electronic instruments; of realistic portraits beside surrealistic paintings; of love sonnets and laudatory odes beside free forms and abstract themes— these attest continuance of the eternal war between traditionalism and experimentalism in art theory.

Even here there are compromises between these seeming opposites, and most of the great artists have mastered the traditional forms and techniques before going off in their own more original ways. Furthermore, in many art theories, the traditions are respected but not slavishly followed, and the classical forms and techniques are adapted to present materials and purposes.

Here again you should pause to consider and set down your own attitude toward the question of tradition and experimentation in the arts. . . . What, again, of Benton's picture and his probable theory?. . . .

4. *Emotional or intellectual response to works of art.*

Although the emotional-intellectual contrast is applicable to both the creative and responsive phases of the art process, we shall give our attention to the latter. Should the artee be affected, have impulses aroused or satisfied, become conscious of mood or feeling-state, respond emotionally to the work of art? *Or* should the artee's response be thoughtful, contemplative, interpretative, critical, evaluative? In other words, should he use his heart or his head?

The theory that art speaks directly and essentially to the emotions is widely held, and is supported by many common observations. Aristotle defined tragedy not only as "an imitation of a worthy or illustrious and perfect action, possessing magnitude, in pleasing language, etc.," but "through pity and fear effecting a purification from such like passions." This is the emotional catharsis earlier referred to. Bonamy Dobrée, in our own time, says that "if a work of art succeeds through the measure in which it arouses appetencies in us [that is, impulses or desires], and satisfies them, the appetency and the satisfaction must not be in excess of each other; nor must each kind of art involve more impulses than it requires for its resultant emotion." One step away from the emotional view of art responses is that advanced by Bullough stressing the importance of 'psychical distance,' or a certain objectivity, if contemplation of an art work is to be achieved. And Jacques Maritain, in writing of art, says, "Beauty is essentially the object of intelligence."

Of course, responses to works of art may be both emotional *and* intellectual. Our definition of art in terms of 'beauty and meaning responses' suggests that there will be both feeling and thought phases of the responsive art experience.

Furthermore, some art theories are interested, not only in the emotional or intellectual nature of the response, but in the relation of the response to the thoughts and feelings of the artist, or at least to those that he tried to express or convey. "Art," says Curt Ducasse in a recent book, "is the language of feeling; and the works of the various arts are the expression and record, in communicable form, of the feelings with which their creators were inspired." Tolstoy says: "Art is a human activity, consisting of this, that one man consciously, by means of certain external signs, hands on to others feelings he has lived through, and that other people are infected by these feelings, and also experience them." F. R. O'Neill, whom we quoted at the head of Chapter 1, defines art as "the expression of an artist's experience in a form which makes it communicable to many minds." And John Dewey: "Art is the most effective mode of communication [of experience] that exists."

What, then, have been your views in regard to the emotional vs. intellectual problem and in regard to the communication of experience? . . . And what of *The Music Lesson* and the possible views of its creator? . . .

5. The artist's reliance on technical skill or inspiration.

This pair of contrasting ideas suggests the reverse side of the emotional-intellectual contrast in art responses. Should the artist develop and rely on technical skills, the knowledge and science of his craft, and intellectual powers of invention in his creative activity? *Or* should he develop and rely on inspiration, intuition, insights, and the *furor poeticus?*

Someone has defined a work of art as anything well done. Gotshalk says, ". . . art is the skilful use of instruments and materials to produce objects of value." Michelangelo once declared that "a man paints with his brains," and the artist Constable: "Painting is a science, and should be pursued as an enquiry into the laws of Nature." In our time Marriott has said, "Art is primarily the characteristic use of tools and materials." On the other hand, many art theories have scorned 'mere technique.' Ancient Plotinus said that "when artists falter, reasoning takes the reins." Sir Philip Sidney admonished himself and others to "look in thy heart and write," and Eugene Véron said that "art is the manifestation of emotion."

This apparent conflict of technique and inspiration is not, however, irreconcilable, for artists, while often emphasizing and honoring one or the other in their art theories, have always made use of both of them in their creative activity.

Again consider your own notion of where the artist should place his reliance, whether on skill or intuition, and try to formulate a brief statement. . . . And turn to *The Music Lesson,* with your bit of art theory in hand, to examine Benton's work and to reflect upon his possible views. . . .

6. *Beauty or significance in responsive art experiences.*

The last of these six pairs of contrasting ideas raises a problem that again is applicable both to the creative phase and to the responsive phase of the art process. But we shall at this time only concern ourselves with the latter. Should the artee experience the feeling of beauty as his essential response to a work of art? *Or* should he experience a system of thoughts or references or ideas as his essential response to the work of art? In view of our own definition of art as 'evoking beauty *and* meaning responses,' this either-or question may seem unnatural. However, many art theories include or emphasize only one of the two—beauty *or* significance, not both.

Oscar Wilde's statement, already quoted, defines art by implication as 'beautiful things,' and adds, "They are the elect to whom beautiful things mean only beauty." Coleridge, "The common essence of all [the fine arts] consists in the excitement of emotion for the immediate purposes of pleasure through the medium of beauty." Collingwood: "Art is to mean the special activity by which we apprehend beauty." On the other hand Tolstoy says, flatly: "People will come to understand the meaning of art only when they cease to consider that the aim of that activity is beauty, i.e. pleasure." For Delacroix beauty is not essential to art. Clive Bell rejects the word 'beauty' in favor of 'significant form' in defining art. Bosanquet points out that "among the moderns we find that more emphasis is laid on the idea of significance, expressiveness, the utterance of all that life contains." And Susanne Langer: "There is a strong tendency today to treat art as a *significant phenomenon* rather than as a pleasurable experience, a gratification of the senses." But beauty and meaning are in no way mutually exclusive.

What have been your own past views relative to beauty and significance in art? Make a note or two on your scratch pad. . . . Then turn yet again for a look at *The Music Lesson* to consider it in relation to this final pair of contrasting or complementary ideas, and to conjecture what Benton's views may have been. . . .

Now we are ready for the fifth general question proposed at the beginning of this section: *What is the relation of your own to other art theories?*

By summarizing your six memoranda relative to the problems discussed above, you will have a brief though necessarily incomplete statement of your own art theory. By noting your agreement or disagreement with the various artists, critics, and philosophers as quoted, you may achieve a tentative orientation to established art theories. But it may be interesting to see where you stand in relation to your friends. To effect such an orientation easily and objectively, check the following chart, using the center column to indicate equal emphasis or compromise, and leaving unmarked those pairs which you consider quite unimportant in your own art theory.

1.	self-expression	□	□	□	imitation
2.	pleasure	□	□	□	profit
3.	experimentation	□	□	□	tradition
4.	emotion	□	□	□	intellect
5.	inspiration	□	□	□	technique
6.	beauty	□	□	□	significance

Comparison of your check-list with others will suggest some of the ways in which your own art theory differs from, or is similar to, the theories of people about you. For a more particular orientation you may well read those other persons' fuller statements.

4. *Art theory and the 'Jefferson Memorial'*

Before proceeding to our next and last general question we shall introduce as an illustration the memorial in Washington, D.C., dedicated in 1943, the two hundredth anniversary of Thomas Jefferson's birth. During the seven years of planning and four years of construction, there was a considerable controversy between the Commission, created by Congress to develop the general plans and see them carried out, and the schools of architecture and the architectural journals; between the architect chosen by the Commission, and the self-appointed critics in the press. Different sorts of art theory came into sharp conflict.

The Commission selected the classical style of architecture without conducting a nation-wide contest as a means of exploring other possible styles of design; the Commission appointed the well-known John Russell Pope as architect without any show of democratic process; the Commission decided that the structure should not be a use-

photo by A. Rowe

John Russell Pope, JEFFERSON MEMORIAL, Washington, D. C.

Courtesy National Park Service

Courtesy Natl. Park Ser.   photo by A. Rowe

Rear view, JEFFERSON MEMORIAL
Washington, D. C.

Courtesy Natl. Park Ser.
photo by A. Rowe

Rudulph Evans,
THOMAS JEFFERSON

Thomas Jefferson, THE ROTUNDA
University of Virginia

photo by Alinari

Ancient PANTHEON, Rome

ful building but purely a memorial. There were sound reasons for these choices; there were also sound protests in opposition to them.

The place of Thomas Jefferson in American history is well established and well known. He is truly one of the founding fathers of Democracy, author of the Declaration of Independence, third President of the United States. He was a man of wide culture and interests, agriculturist and inventor, fiddler and architect. He designed not only his now-famous home at Monticello and the Rotunda for the University of Virginia at Charlottesville, but also submitted a model for the State Capitol at Richmond, Virginia. In these he was influenced by neo-classical theories and Græco-Roman architecture. The Pantheon, in Rome, for instance, is a rotunda with columned and pedimented portico.

The *Jefferson Memorial* designed by John Russell Pope consists of a rotunda whose dome, unlike that of the United States Capitol nearby, is rather low. Surrounding the rotunda that contains but one central and open chamber, is a colonnade giving way in front to a classical portico, a double row of eight columns supporting roof and pediment. The whole structure is mounted upon a wide foundation and is surrounded and approached by broad steps. The sculptural group high in the triangular pediment, the work of Adolph A. Weinman, depicts Jefferson reading his draft of the Declaration of Independence to a committee of the Continental Congress. Within the central high-domed chamber stands a nineteen-foot bronze statue of Jefferson by Rudulph Evans. The four great panels in this room are inscribed in large letters with those noble statements for which Jefferson is especially honored.

Perhaps you have visited the *Jefferson Memorial* and have experienced it at first hand in its landscaped setting on the Tidal Basin. If not, do your best to realize an imaginative experience of this work of art by close observation of the accompanying photographs. . . .

By recalling the six pairs of contrasts in matters of art theory and reviewing your own position as regards them, you may be able to appreciate the conflict of art theories that caused the controversy while this memorial was being planned and built. It is worth noting that 'imitation of nature,' as opposed to self-expression, may be correlated with 'imitation of the classics.' It has been pointed out in a recent study that a work of art may be looked upon either as a man-made thing or as a natural object. In Alexander Pope's consideration of poetry, "Nature and Homer were, he found, the same." So works of art, such as the ancient temples, may be imitated much as one would imitate a natural object. In considering the pleasure vs. profit contrast, bear in mind that, as regards the function of architecture, there are not only terminal and instrumental values possible, but also practical values. Consideration of your own art theory and the *Jefferson Memorial* may serve to advance a bit further your orientation. . . .

5. *Orientation to various conceptions of beauty*

There is a sixth and final question to be asked: *What is the relation of your own to other ideas of beauty?* Before you can answer it, you will have to explore the various theories of beauty.

We have already observed that beauty theories and art theories, which together constitute the field of Aesthetics, are in many cases interdependent. Indeed, Eugene Véron defined aesthetics as "the Science of Beauty in Art." But, as we have noted, some definitions of art either minimize the place of beauty or in certain cases deny it. Theories and isolated definitions of beauty differ both in character and scope. Susanne Langer says, "Artistic value *is* beauty in the broadest sense." And George Boas: "Let us for the sake of simplicity and regardless of common usage, call whatever positive value a critic finds in a work of art 'beauty,' " and he proceeds to analyze the possible meanings of 'This is beautiful' as used in various situations by artists and critics. As suggested in the preceding chapter, 'beauty' is used in this book with a broad-gauged meaning to be explored further in the next chapter.

Not only do persons differ widely in their verbal definitions of the word 'beauty,' they also differ widely in what things they regard as beautiful. Even when in agreement as to a verbal definition of the word, two persons may disagree sharply as to its application to a particular thing. On the other hand, when they both say that a certain work of art or natural object is beautiful, they may be unaware that, using the word in different senses, they are really meaning quite different things; or they may discover the ambiguity of the word when they become particular as to exactly what aspect of the work, or their responses to it, is beautiful.

As the basis for your orientation to various conceptions of beauty, we shall consider a number of established senses of the word. Observing what quite different things persons mean by 'beauty' may help you to clarify your own usage of it and materially help you in understanding the varied usage of other persons.

In *The Foundations of Aesthetics*, by C. K. Ogden, I. A. Richards, and James Wood, (first published in 1922 and reprinted as recently as 1948), a multiple definition of beauty is developed. With one modification in order, our classification of the senses of 'beauty' follows their scheme. The definitions here given are theirs, and the order is theirs also except in one case, but illustrative quotations are added from a variety of sources. Again the warning: such isolated quotations do not always represent fairly the full thought of their authors. Yet the excerpts from various theories of beauty here given may be useful for our present purpose. The sixteen senses of beauty are as follows:

Sense 1. *"Anything is beautiful—which possesses the simple quality of Beauty."*

Marcus Aurelius wrote: "Whatever is Beautiful, has that Quality from itself." In our own times, John Laird writes, "If colour, sound, and similar properties really do belong to physical things, it seems unnecessary to deny that beauty also may exist in the things themselves," and he asserts elsewhere that "the values of beauty or its opposite belong to certain things in certain connections, just as objectively as other qualities." Theodore Greene, for whom 'formal aesthetic quality' is synonymous with 'beauty,' says, "Aesthetic quality is . . . *as* objective as the secondary qualities of color and sound, and may (following G. E. Moore) be called a tertiary quality." Some of the theorists who say that beauty is a simple unanalyzable property of certain things, assert (with Thomas Reid) that man has an 'instinctive sense of beauty' by means of which he apprehends it.

Sense 2. *"Anything is beautiful—which has a specified Form."*

Aristotle said, "The essential characters composing beauty are order, symmetry, and definiteness." For the painter Hogarth there was "but one precise line ['the serpentine line'] properly to be called the line of beauty," and he thought that the triangular form and the serpentine line were "the two most expressive figures that can be thought of to signify not only beauty and grace, but the whole order of form." Michelangelo is reported by Lomazzo to have had similar views. Roger Fry, in our time, declared that "the aesthetic emotion is an emotion about form," and speaks of the "pleasure in the recognition of order, of inevitability in relations, and that the more complex the relations of which we are able to recognize the inevitable interdependence and correspondence, the greater the pleasure. . . ." Efforts have been made since ancient times to isolate the formal relationships which are beautiful per se. 'The golden sector' of the Greeks and 'dynamic symmetry' of Hambridge, Bragdon, and others in our own century have been attempts to define beauty in geometric terms. A recent elaborate effort by Birkhoff is called *Aesthetic Measure.*

These first two definitions of beauty are concerned with the central member of the art triad, the work of art as a public object, its inherent quality and essential form. The next four definitions are related to the artist and the nature of his creative activity.

Sense 3. *"Anything is beautiful—which is an imitation of Nature."*

This is certainly one of the most popular conceptions. It is, of course, directly related to the imitation theory of art, which we discussed at some length. Many persons will say that the beauty of a work of art is really in the representation of beautiful things of nature—persons, things, or scenes—or in the presentation of events or themes that are somehow beautiful in themselves, which really takes us back to 'beauty' in sense No. 1 or ahead to, say, the pleasure theory, No. 10. On the other hand, many persons will say that the beauty of a work of art is in the skill of representation, without regard to the beauty of the subject matter; and that is the sense that we shall consider here. When the emphasis shifts, and beauty is seen in the illusion of reality in the artee's response, we are really using the word in our sense No. 8 below. If a person held strictly to this one definition of beauty—manifest in the artist's skill in the imitation of nature—he would see no beauty in nonrepresentational works of art, which includes not only abstract painting but furniture and absolute music.

Sense 4. *"Anything is beautiful—which results from successful exploitation of a Medium."*

In this sense the ground is shifted from the artist's choice of subject matter and skill in representation to technique and manipulation of materials. Austin Dobson, in his poem *Ars Victrix* advises the poet, the sculptor, and the painter to forego 'the loosely-sandaled verse,' 'the yielding clay,' and 'the transient tints,' so as to devote themselves to creative work in the more exacting media; for if the artist's work is to be of enduring and surpassing beauty, it must evidence real craftsmanship. Bosanquet, who defines all beauty as being "in perception or imagination," says that it is "subject to the conditions of abstract or general expressiveness in the medium." Beauty, in this conception, is defined in terms of successful techniques and appropriate utilization of the artist's physical materials.

Sense 5. *"Anything is beautiful—which is a work of Genius."*

Kant said that "the beauties of art by their nature must be considered as products not of scientific understanding but of genius." Eugene Véron: "Aesthetics [which, you will recall, he defined as 'the Science of Beauty in Art'] is the science whose object is the study and elucidation of the manifestations of artistic genius." And Külpe, in our century: "Art is the product of genius—according to Kant and Schopenhauer." This is not an uncommon view. Many persons will say of a work of art, 'If Beethoven [or Keats or Michelangelo—all recognized geniuses] created it, of course it's beautiful.'

Sense 6. [In the original scheme this was No. 9.] *"Anything is beautiful—which is an Expression."*

For Croce, "nature is only beautiful for the man who sees it *with the eyes of an artist*," and he defines art in terms of intuition and expression. Carritt asserts: "All beauty is the expression of what may be generally called emotion, and all such expression is beautiful." The Rev. S. A. McDowell: "Beauty is the expression of an understanding of that relationship," i.e. 'God is Love; Reality is Love. Love is relationship.'

These four definitions have been pinned to the first member of the art triad; the next three, with which we shall deal more rapidly, are affixed to the third of the triad—the artee and his art experience.

Sense 7. *"Anything is beautiful—which reveals* (1) *Truth,* (2) *the Spirit of Nature,* (3) *the Ideal,* (4) *the Universal,* (5) *the Typical."* Such definitions are various and to be found throughout the history of criticism related to the art-for-profit theories. Classical theories emphasized the typical and ideal. Keats wrote enigmatically, "Beauty is truth, truth beauty." Pater said that "all beauty is in the long run only *fineness* of truth, or what we call expression." For Robert Bridges beauty "awakeneth new ideas that advance the spirit /in the life of Reason to the wisdom of God."

Sense 8. *"Anything is beautiful—which produces Illusion."* We noted this definition in relation to No. 3 above. Schiller said, "Beauty is the common object . . .of the play impulse." Lange and Groos developed theories of 'Art as Play' based upon illusion games and make-believe.

Sense 9. *"Anything is beautiful—which leads to desirable Social effects."* This definition is also related to certain of the art-for-profit theories, such as Tolstoy's, discussed earlier in this chapter.

So much, then, for these three definitions which see beauty as affecting the artee in certain ways—revealing truth, producing illusion, promoting the social good. The final seven definitions, all psychological, are also concerned with responsive art experiences.

Sense 10. *"Anything is beautiful—which causes Pleasure."* This, we saw earlier, is the basis of very popular art theories. Plato defined beauty in terms of 'profitable pleasure.' Wolff, in the eighteenth century: "What pleases is called beautiful; what displeases ugly." And Santayana, early in this century, "Beauty is pleasure regarded as the quality of a thing."

Sense 11. *"Anything is beautiful—which excites Emotions."* Muratori (1706) defined the beautiful as "whatever, when seen, heard, or understood, delights, pleases, and ravishes us by causing within us agreeable sensations and love." Burke speaks of "the passion caused by beauty." Ducasse, in our time, "Any object is to be called beautiful when . . .the feelings which one obtains from the aesthetic contemplation of it are pleasurable feelings."

Sense 12. *"Anything is beautiful—which promotes a Specific emotion."* Clive Bell, who avoids the word beauty because of its common usage, says that "there is a peculiar ['aesthetic'] emotion provoked by works of art." The quality common and peculiar to all objects that provoke this aesthetic emotion he calls 'significant form.' And we have already quoted Roger Fry: ". . .the aesthetic emotion is an emotion about form."

Sense 13. *"Anything is beautiful—which involves the processes of Empathy."* The word 'empathy,' of which more will be said in Chapter 8, is defined by Lipps to mean, "not a sensation in one's body, but feeling something, namely oneself, into the aesthetic object." Vernon Lee says that, when we have thus projected our consciousness into the object being contemplated, "we welcome the form thus animated by ourselves as 'beautiful.' "

Sense 14. *"Anything is beautiful—which heightens Vitality."* Nietzsche said, ". . .the feeling of power utters the judgment 'beautiful' concerning things and conditions which the instinct of importance can only value as hateful and ugly. . . . 'This is beautiful' is an affirmation."

Sense 15. *"Anything is beautiful—which brings us in touch with exceptional Personalities."* The definition of beauty as a work of Genius, sense No. 5 above, prepared the way for this one, in which beauty is conceived as communion with the artist through his work of art, or the communication of the artist's thoughts and emotions to the artee. We suggested briefly, in our discussion of the emotional-intellectual contrast, some art theories that stress communication.

Sense 16, the final definition in *The Foundations of Aesthetics* and the one developed by Ogden, Richards, and Wood: *"Anything is beautiful—which induces Synaesthesis."* The key word here, 'synaesthesis,' they define in terms of the impulses aroused in what we call the artee. If these impulses are harmonious, so that each has free play without frustration, there results a kind of balance. "In any equilibrium of this kind, however momentary, we are experiencing beauty. . . The ultimate value of equilibrium is that it is better to be fully than partially alive." This definition they derive in part from the Confucian doctrine of equilibrium and harmony. It is suggested in Schiller's definition of beauty as resulting from the reciprocity of two opposite impulses, and in Ethel Puffer's *Psychology of Beau-*

ty wherein the aesthetic experience is described in terms of 'tension, equilibrium, or balance of forces.' Stites, who discusses these sixteen definitions in *The Arts and Man*, says: "Synaesthesis means simply a union of all the contributing aesthetic factors in a work of art."

So much, then, for these sixteen senses of the word 'beauty.' There is no need to remember them all or to fix in mind the many artists, critics, and philosophers from whom the illustrative quotations have been drawn. Our treatment of them has necessarily been incomplete. Statements could have been gathered from quite as authoritative sources disputing these individual definitions. Of the first one, for instance, Hume once wrote: "Beauty is no quality of things themselves; it exists only in the mind which contemplates it." And of the last definition, Stites says, "If synaesthesis is that which describes or explains Beauty, one still has to explain the more universal term 'the Sublime,' which has overtones of the dynamic inspirational element of art."

Certainly the sixteen categories would not be enough for the classification of all the uses of the word. For instance, we might need such an additional definition as this: *Anything is beautiful—which evokes vivid perceptions.* "Beauty in its very nature," says Lord Kames, "refers to a percipient." William D. Ross speaks of "how beauty is bound up with sense perception." And D. W. Gotshalk, who avoids the word 'beauty' to name it, says that "aesthetic experience is simply alert perception allowed intrinsic scope" and that "Sensation might be described as the core around which intuition and intellect and feeling and imagination operate to complete the perceptual apprehension of the object." Rupert Brooke once wrote: "It is, possibly, true that when men say, 'This is beautiful' they do not mean 'this is lovely.' ... [But] as a matter of fact, they are wrong." In the same discussion he said: "One of the perils attending on those who ask 'What is Art?' is that they tend, as all men do, to find what they are looking for: a common quality in Art." And this may well be a warning to all of us.

Now we are ready for the sixth and final question: *What is the relation of your own to other ideas of beauty?*

Before you can answer this question, you will need to clarify your own thoughts on the matter of beauty. As an aid in doing this, jot down a list of some dozen or more things of different kinds that you personally consider beautiful. Then think about them, their creation and your response to them. What, in each case, is the apparent cause of your beauty response? You need not, heeding Brooke's warning, seek a common quality in all of these things, activities, or experiences;

but there is no doubt that you will tend to generalize upon the nature of your beauty responses. Now add to your list the *Jefferson Memorial*, Benton's *The Music Lesson*, and *Swing Low, Sweet Chariot*, and reflect upon your experiences with them. Upon the basis of these reflections and generalizations, work out a brief statement of your idea of beauty—a definition based on your own use or uses of the word 'beautiful.' . . .

With this statement in hand, glance back at the definitions explored above in this section so as to see the relation of your own to other ideas of beauty. With plus and minus marks check the definitions that are most like and those which are quite opposed to yours. This will serve as an orientation to the established conceptions of beauty. But it may also be of interest to note where you stand among your fellows in this regard. It will be easy enough now to compare your own brief statement with others, and to see which numbered statements are generally approved and rejected.

Such, then, is the final step in your Orientation to Art and Aesthetics.

6. *For delight and reflection*

The following page of music may serve you in a number of ways. It was chosen because of its simplicity and brevity and familiarity. If a piano is available and you can play at all, you will probably enjoy playing it. The right hand almost plays itself, so you can give your chief attention to the left hand chords; perhaps you will develop sufficient confidence to stumble through the tricky measures toward the end. Or, if you don't play at all, get someone to play it for you several times. Sit at the piano with your companion, and follow along as best as you can. You may also wish to hear a recording of this *Prelude*, Op. 28, no. 4 in E minor, of which there are several generally available. Or perhaps you know it so well that you can simply read the music, feeling the rhythm and hearing in your mind's ear every note of the melody and each harmonic change. In any case, allow yourself ample opportunity to have a full-blown experience of this work of art.

It may be of interest to you to know that Frederic Chopin (1809-1849), born in Warsaw, was a Polish revolutionary who spent a good bit of his short and romantic life in France as a political refugee. His career, especially his love for Mme. Dudevant, the eminent French authoress 'George Sand,' has been the subject of both drama and film. He was a brilliant pianist, and is known especially for his many short compositions for the piano. He composed the set of Preludes, of which this is one, while staying at Palma on the island of Majorca. . . .

PRELUDE, Opus 28, No. 4
by *Frederic Chopin*

A pair of poems, both by recent English poets, will serve to close this chapter.

THE GREAT LOVER

by *Rupert Brooke*

I have been so great a lover: filled my days
So proudly with the splendour of Love's praise,
The pain, the calm, and the astonishment,
Desire illimitable, and still content,
And all dear names men use, to cheat despair,
For the perplexed and viewless streams that bear
Our hearts at random down the dark of life.
Now, ere the unthinking silence on that strife
Steals down, I would cheat drowsy Death so far,
My night shall be remembered for a star
That outshone all the suns of all men's days.
Shall I not crown them with immortal praise
Whom I have loved, who have given me, dared with me
High secrets, and in darkness knelt to see
The inenarrable godhead of delight?
Love is a flame;—we have beaconed the world's night.
A city:—and we have built it, these and I.
An emperor:—we have taught the world to die.
So, for their sakes I loved, ere I go hence,
And to keep loyalties young, I'll write those names
Golden for ever, eagles, crying flames,
And set them as a banner, that men may know,
To dare the generations, burn, and blow
Out on the wind of Time, shining and streaming. . . .

These I have loved:
          White plates and cups, clean-gleaming,
Ringed with blue lines; and feathery, faery dust;
Wet roofs, beneath the lamp-light; the strong crust
Of friendly bread; and many-tasting food;
Rainbows; and the blue bitter smoke of wood;
And radiant raindrops couching in cool flowers;
And flowers themselves, that sway through sunny hours,
Dreaming of moths that drink them under the moon;
Then, the cool kindliness of sheets, that soon
Smooth away trouble; and the rough male kiss
Of blankets; grainy wood; live hair that is
Shining and free; blue-massing clouds; the keen
Unpassioned beauty of a great machine;
The benison of hot water; furs to touch;

The good smell of old clothes; and other such—
The comfortable smell of friendly fingers,
Hair's fragrance, and the musty reek that lingers
About dead leaves and last year's ferns. . . .
                                    Dear names,
And thousand others throng to me! Royal flames;
Sweet water's dimpling laugh from tap or spring;
Holes in the ground; and voices that do sing:
Voices in laughter, too; and body's pain,
Soon turned to peace; and the deep-panting train;
Firm sands; the little dulling edge of foam
That browns and dwindles as the wave goes home;
And washen stones, gay for an hour; the cold
Graveness of iron; moist black earthen mould;
Sleep; and high places; footprints in the dew;
And oaks; and brown horse-chestnuts, glossy-new;
And new-peeled sticks; and shining pools on grass;—
All these have been my loves. And these shall pass.
Whatever passes not, in the great hour,
Nor all my passion, all my prayers, have power
To hold them with me through the gate of Death.
They'll play deserter, turn with traitor breath,
Break the high bond we made, and sell Love's trust
And sacramented covenant to the dust.

—Oh, never a doubt but, somewhere, I shall wake,
And give what's left of love again, and make
New friends, now strangers. . . .
                                    But the best I've known,
Stays here, and changes, breaks, grows old, is blown
About the winds of the world, and fades from brains
Of living men, and dies.
                    Nothing remains.

O dear my loves, O faithless, once again
This one last gift I give: that after men
Shall know, and later lovers, far-removed
Praise you, "All these were lovely"; say, "He loved."

A BALLADE

CATALOGUE OF LOVELY THINGS

by *Richard Le Gallienne*

I would make a list against the evil days
    Of lovely things to hold in memory:
First, I would set down my lady's lovely face,

For earth has no such lovely things as she;
And next I add, to bear her company,
The great-eyed virgin star that morning brings;
Then the wild rose upon its little tree—
So runs my catalogue of lovely things.

The enchanted dogwood, with its ivory trays,
The water lily in its sanctuary
Of reeded pools, and dew-drenched lilac sprays,
For thee, of all fair flowers, the fairest be;
Next write I down the great name of the sea,
Lonely in greatness as the names of kings;
Then the young moon that hath us all in fee—
So runs my catalogue of lovely things.

Imperial sunsets that in crimson blaze
Along the hills, and, fairer still to me,
The fireflies dancing in a netted maze
Woven of twilight and tranquility;
Shakespeare and Virgil, their high poesy;
Then a great ship, splendid with snowy wings,
Voyaging on into eternity—
So runs my catalogue of lovely things.

ENVOI

Prince, not the gold bars of thy treasury,
Not all thy jeweled scepters, crowns, and rings,
Are worth the honeycomb of the wild bee—
So runs my catalogue of lovely things.

Chapter 3. Beauty and Meaning in Art

To the beautiful belongs an endless variety.
George C. Bingham, *Art, the Ideal of Art...*

They are the elect to whom beautiful things mean only Beauty.
Oscar Wilde, *The Picture of Dorian Gray*

A work of art means to us whatever effects (not necessarily emotions) it evokes in us.
John Hospers, *Meaning and Truth in the Arts*

BEFORE it was possible for you to orient yourself to the World of Art, it was necessary to bring that World into focus, settle its boundaries, and box the compass by means of definition and classification. Now we are ready to go back to the two key questions left virtually unanswered in Chapter 1 when we defined a work of art as 'a man-made thing generally evoking beauty and meaning responses,' and to develop working definitions of *beauty* and *meaning* for this book.

1. Beauty in art

Despite the fact that the word 'beauty' has so many established senses, as we saw in Chapter 2, and is so often ambiguous or vague in meaning, there are two very good reasons for using it here in this book. One reason is that the word is both historically and popularly associated with the arts and art theories, and we could therefore not avoid some consideration of it. A second reason is that its very ambiguity and the wide range of established senses are advantageous in framing a definition that is intended to be comprehensive.

As already suggested, ours will be a broad-gauged definition of beauty. George C. Bingham, an American professor of art and artist of the last century, said, "To the beautiful belongs an endless variety," and Robert Frost, poet of our day, once said, "I hope I have some

79

range in the appreciation of Beauty. I can see it all the way from exquisite through homely and mean, even to vile." Our own tentative definition of the word as used in Chapter 1 was that *beauty is a value word used to name a wide variety of human responses to things*. It remains now to clarify and develop that statement.

What do we mean by calling 'beauty' a value word? The answer will take us back to our earlier discussion of definition and classification, wherein it was pointed out that we respond to things selectively. By means of varying responses we differentiate one thing from another. We give names to these responses, and we use them like labels in sorting and controlling the divers items of our experience. But, although it is attributed to the thing that causes it, the named-response or quality is really *in the mind of man*.

Beauty is a quality, a named-response to certain things; and it is, according to our own and many other definitions of art, one of the distinguishing qualities or properties of the work of art.

Several sorts of qualities have been discriminated. The so-called primary qualities of substance (e.g., zinc oxide), size, shape, and movement, which may be described as objective or public; and the so-called secondary qualities of color (e.g., redness), sound, and touch, which are less objective yet somewhat public, as we shall see in Chapters 5 and 7. However, certain qualities of quite another kind may be attributed to things—such as goodness, usefulness, rarity, desirability; and these may be called tertiary qualities. They are not objective in the sense that substance (e.g., zinc oxide) is; and they are not the direct result of sensation, like color (e.g., redness). They involve subjective responses, evaluative feelings and thoughts about the object to which they are attributed. Beauty has been considered by some philosophers as a quality of this third kind.

What, then, is the particular tertiary quality that we call 'beauty' and attribute to things of nature and works of art?

Beauty names a positive value of a special sort. Usefulness is attributed to an object because of its potential practical use. Goodness, because of its relation to some moral standard, or in common speech, because it is good *for* something. Desirability, because it is an object of desire; it is wanted for possession. But beauty is a positive value without regard to use, moral standards, desire for possession. A thing of beauty, as the word is here used, is of positive value just to be perceived, to be experienced, to be contemplated.

Most works of art and beauties of nature have other positive values as well; they are also useful or good or desirable. Oscar Wilde's saying, "All art is quite useless," is not so in our view, but all beauty as such is quite useless. We have already noted, as a possible definition of 'beautiful,' the evoking of vivid perceptions. Gotshalk says that "aesthetic experience is simply alert perception allowed intrinsic scope." We may now add that beauty is a positive value—in perception, intuitive response, and contemplation—without reference to use or the serving of other ends. Earlier the word terminal was used to name such values. But if beauty is a tertiary, positive, and terminal value, we must not forget that a work of art may be more useful because it is beautiful; its beauty may contribute to its serving a good cause; and its beauty will make it desirable. So, paradoxically, beauty is a terminal value that may also serve instrumental ends.

Furthermore, beauty as a tertiary quality, positive and terminal, is, according to our view, intuitive rather than rational. Albert W. Upton, in his *Design for Thinking,* considering the psychology of qualification, distinguishes three sorts of qualities by reference to the parts of the nervous system dominant in making the response: "sensory, emotional or affective, and logical or rational." He cites 'the quality of loveliness' as an example of affective quality, a felt-response; it does not involve the higher processes of the mind. You can reason yourself into thinking that something ought to be beautiful, but no one can argue you into really feeling that it is so. When Shakespeare's songster sang, "Tell me where is Fancy bred, /Or in the heart or in the head," he was thinking of love; he might as well have been thinking of beauty. Kant once said that "beauty, apart from relation to our feeling, is itself nothing."

George Santayana, earlier quoted, defines beauty as "pleasure regarded as the quality of a thing." Leaving 'pleasure' aside for the moment, we may well underscore his phrase '*regarded* [that is, looked upon] as the quality of a thing.' We know, as he knows, that the value really is not *in* the thing that is called beautiful; our discussion of qualification has made that clear; but we do attribute qualities *to* things. We do look upon works of art, for instance, as actually possessing the values that, as we think about it, we know are only attributions. Our heads know that the beauty really is not *in* the picture, or *in* the complex of musical sound waves, or *on* the page of poetry; but our hearts go their own old way and feel that the beauty is out there to be apprehended by anyone with eyes to see or read and ears to hear.

It is perhaps unnecessary to add that though beauty is a positive felt-value, with ugliness as its opposite, there are many degrees of positive value. If one is faced with a number of works of art, the least beautiful will perhaps be shunned and the most beautiful will receive the greater part of our attention—as though there were a scale of beauty; most, more, medium, less, and least beautiful. But most persons' vocabularies have an odd assortment of value phrases such as these: 'by no means ugly,' 'pretty,' 'really beautiful,' 'exquisite,' and 'out of this world,' which last is a popular equivalent of 'sublime,' a word of great importance in the history of Aesthetics from Longinus through Burke to A. C. Bradley. There is a middle ground between beauty and ugliness that we may call indifference. Then come the various degrees of the ugly, for most persons also attribute this negative value in terms of more or less. Again there is a graduated scale, of a rough sort, descending, in the vernacular, from the 'by-no-means-beautiful,' through the 'plain' and 'really-ugly' to the 'horrible' and 'hideous.' Let each person choose his own words and his own order to name the various degrees of positive (or indeed negative) felt value attributed to works of art.

To summarize this discussion, let us attempt a more complete definition of beauty than that proposed earlier—which was, 'a value word used to name a wide variety of human responses to things.' For our present purpose, then: *Beauty is a tertiary felt-quality, of some degree of positive and terminal value, regarded as possessed by the thing to which it is attributed.* But a briefer definition may be more serviceable: BEAUTY IS A POSITIVE VALUE REGARDED AS INHERENT. As an aid to understanding this conception of beauty, the following comments are enumerated:

1. 'Beauty' is but a word. There is no such thing as Beauty in the outer world. Beauty exists in human experience as a felt response to some things.

2. Beauty is attributed to things of nature as well as to works of art.

3. The artist may 'see' beauty in nature, or in what he is creating, or in his completed work of art.

4. The artee may recognize beauty as a part of his response to things, or 'see' beauty in nature or works of art, or 'see' beauty in the creative activity of the artist, or in the objects that the artist represents, or in the work of art itself.

5. If the artist tries to 'put' the beauty that he 'sees' in nature into his work of art, he is really trying to create a work of art that will evoke in him—and in future artees, he hopes—the same sort of beauty response evoked in him by that view of nature. That is, he tries to give adequate expression to his original beauty response. If artees generally do respond as he expects, we may say that beauty has been communicated from the artist to the artee by way of the work of art.

6. But beauty is a subjective and highly individual sort of response. It differs markedly among persons even of so-called good taste in the

same culture. It differs radically among persons of different cultures and historic periods. It also differs in a single person who will not respond consistently to similar works of art or to the same work of art under different circumstances.

7. Two persons who agree that something 'is beautiful' may only be in verbal agreement. Actually they may be using widely different senses of the word 'beauty.' Or, if they are in verbal agreement as to a definition, they may discover that they are applying their criterion of beauty to quite different aspects of their complex art experiences. On the other hand two persons who disagree that something is beautiful may really only be in 'dispute about a name' rather than about the 'phenomena it describes,' to use Plato's words.

8. For two persons to discuss beauty in art calls for more than usual semantic control. You yourself should try to make clear your own use of the word 'beauty' and the particular subjective responses or effects to which you refer, and the particular causes of those effects in so far as you can point them out. You should also try to understand the other person's theory of beauty and the nature of his response to particular items in the work of art.

9. Certain works of art, man-made things generally evoking beauty and meaning responses, may leave you cold. Your response is perhaps one of indifference or definite ugliness. Considering the diversity of subjective felt-responses, this is bound to be true. Indeed, if you find everything to be beautiful indiscriminately, or if everything that is generally considered beautiful is really beautiful to you—you should have your head examined; your definition needs surgery! On the other hand, if none or only few of the recognized works of art, as you know them, are beautiful to you, then—you should have your heart examined. "Unhappy will be the man who is so completely out of touch with his fellows and his human ancestry that he can find no pleasure in the things that have pleasured them," as the author has written elsewhere, in his *Preface to Poetry*.

10. As beauty is a felt-quality, there is no rational means of 'seeing beauty' in things that for you are not beautiful. You cannot be taught to 'see' beauty in things, but you can be encouraged to have deeper and richer experiences of things that are generally considered beautiful. You can consciously stay with a work of art, enrich your own experience of it by continued sensory exploration of it, by renewed or repeated perceptions. You can consciously allow time for full and various naive responses to it, giving the imaginative and empathic and emotive phases of your experience free play, 'living with' the music, picture, or work of literature. Furthermore, you can bring to bear all manner of relevant data and your best critical powers to effect a full and enlivened interpretation of it. In the process of doing this, your value response

to the work of art may indeed change or be intensified. No work of art is likely to be beautiful for you if your total response to it is momentary, fleeting, and casual.

With these warnings and admonitions in mind, let us place our own definition—briefly, that *beauty is a positive value regarded as inherent*—in relation to the conceptions of beauty enumerated in the preceding chapter. We shall confine ourselves to a few general observations.

First, all seventeen of the definitions may be interpreted as attributing positive value to the things called beautiful, or to the effects they have on people. There is an implication of positive value in the first 'simple quality' definition, in the 'specified form,' in the (skillful) 'imitation of nature,' in 'successful exploitation of a medium,' in 'work of genius,' in intuition and 'expression,' in 'Truth' and 'the Ideal,' in 'illusion,' in 'pleasure,' and so on down to 'synaesthesis' and 'vivid perceptions.' These are, or may be viewed as, positive value concepts of one sort or another. They are preferable qualifications, desirable attributes or states of mind.

Second, however, many of these definitions are really quite different from our own, when you look at them more closely. It is apparent, for instance, that we have rejected the 'simple quality' and 'specified form' definitions as, from our point of view, untenable. It may be less apparent that, from the point of view of this book, we do not 'see' beauty in imitation as such, or in exploitation of a medium or in any work of a genius or in expression as such; that the revelation of Truth and the furtherance of social ends are other values, different from beauty as here defined; that excitation of emotion, involvement of empathy, heightened vitality are often concomitant but not essential to beauty; that pleasure is too narrow, significant form too nebulous, and synaesthesis too rare to define the positive value for a conception of beauty as comprehensive as the one we propose.

Third, on the basis of 'positive value' it is possible, however, to rationalize the differences in these various definitions and see their relations to each other and to the broad-gauged definition that we have proposed, for we wish to consider 'beauty' as a value word used to name a wide variety of human responses to things. Our previous discussion has limited the field of human responses, as the following phrases suggest: tertiary quality, positive value, terminal value, felt response, regarded as in the thing, relative value. But there is still room for a wide range of human responses to a wide variety of things.

It is natural to ask the question at this point as elsewhere, What do you call those man-made things—pictures, musical scores, verses—

that do not evoke positive value responses of the sort we have called beauty? In Chapter 1, with the Plush Horror as an example, we simply called them not-art. In art schools, conservatories and writing courses, the creative work submitted by students is generally looked upon as projects, problems, exercises, studies, compositions, with careful avoidance of the designation 'works of art.' Similarly the studies, sketches, and rough drafts of recognized artists are not usually considered works of art, for the values attributed to them are of a different kind, often instrumental rather than terminal. But it must be remembered that there are varying degrees of beauty, and some student works and master drawings and drafts *are* beautiful in the eyes of many who experience them, indeed *are* works of art according to our definition.

Our own definition is similar to Susanne Langer's, "Artistic quality is beauty in the broadest sense," and to George Boas's, "Let us . . . call whatever positive value a critic finds in a work of art 'beauty.' " Accepting the general phrasing of George Santayana's definition—"Beauty is pleasure regarded as the quality of a thing"—our own definition would broaden the positive value implicit in the word 'pleasure' so as to include a vivid object-centered perception at one end of the responsive experience and, at the other end, that synaesthesis, already referred to, that equilibrium and harmony that 'brings into play all our faculties.'

If the thing of beauty itself is a 'joy forever'—or at least for the moment—any mere discussion of beauty is likely to make the reader rather unhappy. Such a discussion promises to make everything simple and clear; but, when all is said and done, there remains a certain . . . inexplicable . . . ineffable . . . indescribable something—the *je ne sais quoi* of beauty, as Leibnitz and Burke and others of their times put it. And you may be inclined to say with Socrates: "Upon my word, Hippias, beauty has given us the slip." But will you not add with him: "I still have hopes that the mysterious nature of beauty will be revealed."

2. *Particular beauty responses*

Before proceeding to the next major consideration, meaning in art, let us put to use the theory of beauty developed in the above section. To do this we shall apply what has been said about beauty to the three works of art presented at the end of the preceding chapter. We shall ask the reader to make the application by answering some relevant questions.

Turn back to Chopin's *Prelude*, hum through it and revive your earlier experience of it. Think of the music as actually heard by you, whether from a recording or directly from a piano ... Can you distinguish the secondary qualities of the sounds actually heard from the primary qualities of sound-waves measurable in so-and-so many vibrations per second? Can you distinguish the secondary qualities of the sounds actually heard—the changes of pitch, the length of the notes, the varying loudness—from tertiary qualities such as might be suggested by, 'It's melancholy,' 'It's worth getting a record of,' 'Good background music,' 'Better than the *Nocturne* in E flat,' and so on? Can you distinguish between your felt responses and rational responses to it, such as: 'It's a bit too sweet and dreamy for me' and 'It is in the key of E minor?' ... Does it have positive value for you which you designate as 'beauty' using the definition here proposed? Does it seem to you to have terminal value? Does it seem also to have instrumental value? If so, what end does it serve? Do you see what is meant by knowing that the beauty is not really in the music out there, but nevertheless feeling that it is? In what degree do you attribute beauty to Chopin's *Prelude*? ... If such a catechism has not proved sufficient exercise and demonstration of this theory of beauty, it may be repeated with another work or two, say a picture and a poem.

For a somewhat different application of this discussion of beauty, reconsider Rupert Brooke's *The Great Lover*, particularly the central portion beginning, 'These I have loved ...' Glance back to reread Brooke's remark on beauty and loveliness near the end of section 5 in the preceding chapter. Now turn to the enumerated comments on beauty in the first section of this present chapter, especially Nos. 3 — 5 and No. 9 ... What seems to have been Brooke's conception of beauty or loveliness as exemplified here? Do you personally have a beauty-response to Brooke's poem? to the things that he loved?

In what way does Brooke's idea of beauty seem to you to differ from Richard LeGallienne's? Do you find the *Ballade* beautiful? the 'lovely things' that it catalogues? In your general scale of positive values, neutrality, and negative values, where would you place your felt-responses to these two poems? Which of the two do you feel to be the more beautiful? ...

3. *The importance of meaning in art*

Works of art, we said, generally evoke beauty and meaning responses. Would it have been safer to say 'beauty and/or meaning'? For you will recall the contrast of beauty or significance in our exploration of established art theories. Some of these, we saw, were based on the idea of beauty, whereas others denied it. This conflict of opinion may well serve as a transition to the fuller discussion of meaning in art, which will occupy the remaining part of this chapter.

"Every one wants to understand art!" cries Picasso. "Why not try to understand the song of a bird?" J. F. Herbart, a philosopher writing early in the last century, said, "People visit picture galleries with catalogues, and operas with librettos; if they can get none, they complain of not understanding the pictures or the music. And for like reasons poetry is often accompanied by commentary. Works of art are expected to have a meaning! . . . But music is *music* and to be beautiful need mean nothing!" Archibald MacLeish wrote: "A poem should not mean/But be." Bonamy Dobrée wrote of *The Waste Land*: "To try to explain the poem would be fruitless; every good poem is its own only possible explanation."

Upon hearing the poem read by the White Rabbit in evidence against the Knave, Alice said, near the end of her *Adventures in Wonderland*: " 'I don't believe there's an atom of meaning in it.' . . . 'If there's no meaning in it,' said the King, 'that saves a world of trouble, you know, as we needn't try to find any. And yet I don't know,' he went on, spreading out the verses on his knee, and looking at them with one eye: 'I seem to see some meaning in them, after all . . .' "

With many artists and critics there is indeed no question that works of art do have significance or meaning in some sense, but they add: such meaning as they have cannot be put into words—or, in the case of literature, into other words. Hanslick, wrote, a hundred years ago: "The ideas which a composer expresses are mainly and primarily of a *purely musical* nature . . . [Music] is a language we speak and understand, but which we are unable to translate." Susanne Langer, in our day, has said that "we are inclined to credit works of art with *significance,* although . . . we can never say what they signify." Tolstoy wrote: "The artist's work cannot be interpreted. Had it been possible to explain in words what he wished to convey, the artist would have expressed himself in words." A. C. Bradley said of 'pure poetry' that "if we insist on asking for the meaning of such a poem, we can only be answered, 'It means itself' !" And in the same vein, Oscar Wilde said, "They are the elect to whom beautiful things mean only Beauty."

But there seems to be no doubt that, for the most part, people do believe that works of art have significance—not only importance or value, but also some sort of thought meaning. As human beings we try to 'make sense' of all the data sent up by our various 'senses.' It is natural that the phenomena of art should be expected to make sense, just as the phenomena of nature make sense to the naturalist. But works of art are man-made. Most persons assume that they are not the result of random daubing or strumming or scrawling, but of purpose and design, skill and foresight, knowledge and intuition. As the products of human design and activity, works of art would be expected to make sense.

However, because of the air of mystery with which some prominent artists and critics have surrounded the arts in our own century, many persons develop an unnatural feeling of insecurity in regard to the meaning of art works. In our own time, besides the original and strong work that is being created by many artists in the several arts, there is indeed much that is exotic and outlandish, extravagant and ostentatious, experimental and otiose. And these efforts, too, are exhibited as works of art, performed as music, printed as literature, and then reviewed by pretentious critics in esoteric terms that leave the layman—and often the serious student of art as well—wondering what it's all about. It is not strange, then, that many people seek gallery catalogues, program notes, and explanatory reviews of books, hoping to find relevant clues to the meanings of these works of art.

Aldous Huxley has said: "Some critics have written that music and painting signify nothing but themselves: that the only things they 'say' are things, for example, about modulations and fugues, about colour-values and three-dimensional forms. That they say anything about human destiny or the universe at large is a notion which these purists dismiss as merely nonsensical. If the purists were right, then we should have to regard painters and musicians as monsters. For it is strictly impossible to be a human being and not to have views of some sort about the universe at large, very difficult to be a human being and not to express those views, at any rate by implication." Again in *Music at Night* Huxley wrote: "We are grateful to the artist . . . for 'saying' clearly what we have always felt but never been able to express."

So far, then, art has been described (1) as meaningless, (2) as meaning something that cannot be explained, (3) as meaning something that only the experts can interpret, and (4) as meaning something that can be understood generally. These are four quite different views; they reflect markedly different art theories.

If indeed art is stuff and nonsense, with rime but without reason; a tale, not indeed told by an idiot, but signifying nothing—if, as the King said, "there's no meaning in it . . . that saves a world of trouble, you know, as we needn't try to find any.' . . . If, on the other hand, art has meaning but of a sort that cannot be explained, then we should be content to realize or intuitively sense the meanings of works of art but without trying to verbalize our responses or explain them to others . . . If, however, the high priests of Art—the critics, scholars, lecturers—are able and alone able to put these mysterious meanings into words, then, of course, we should take out our notebooks and prepare for dictation . . . If, finally, works of art have meaning of one sort or another open to you and to me—and to persons generally who are willing to stop, look, listen, and think—then it will be worth while to explore what is meant by the phrase 'to have meaning,' what relevant sorts of meaning there are in art, what can be done by way of understanding such meanings, and which sorts of such meanings may be put in words or explained.

In the hope that this last condition may prove generally true, we shall proceed with our discussion of meaning in art.

4. Art works are signs of meaning

Let us say simply: *a work of art is a sign.*

When we say that something is a sign, we merely mean that it stands for something other than itself; that is, it expresses or evokes a thought of something else. The thought it was intended to express may be different from the thought that it actually evokes in the interpreter; and the thoughts that a sign evokes in two or more interpreters may be somewhat or quite different one from another. For instance, you and I are looking across a canyon; we hear and see a boy calling and waving his arms. 'He's in some sort of trouble,' you say. 'Oh, no, he just wants to say hello,' I rejoin. And we are both unconscious that he is really trying to call our attention to a mountain lion (or deer, if you'd rather) in the underbrush just above us.

A thought that is expressed or evoked by a sign is called a reference; and the thing that the thought is of, that is, what it points to or refers to, is the referent. The referent is what the sign stands for. This relationship of sign, reference, and referent was first pointed out by Ogden and Richards in *The Meaning of Meaning,* and, following that book, it is usually diagrammed as an equilateral triangle whose base is a dotted rather than a solid line.

To further your understanding of the theory of signs as it applies to meaning in art, you should take a bit of scratch paper—the back of an old envelop will do—and draw such a triangle with its base a dotted, not a solid, line. Write the word 'sign' just outside the left corner, the word 'thought' just above the top corner, and the word 'referent' down by the right corner. In thinking of the second phase of the art process, the artee's response, you can now say, looking at the triangle and pointing with your pencil: the sign *evokes* a thought that is *of* a referent. So, label the left side of your triangle 'evokes,' with an arrow slanting up toward the thought corner of the triangle, and label the right side 'of,' with an arrow slanting down toward the referent corner. A work of art is, of course, a complex sign, consisting of many simple signs. However, the work as a whole may evoke a general thought of a referent, which referent may be a complex abstraction; and each of the signs that you may identify as making up the complex whole work of art will evoke a thought of a referent. Your diagram represents the artee's triangle of reference, so, to keep things straight, print 'ARTEE' just above the word 'thought' on your diagram.

But let us consider the artist's point of view. To do so, sketch another triangle, beginning half an inch below the first one; but stand this triangle on its head, with the horizontal dotted side at the top and the point at the bottom. This time the upper left point will be the work of art; so, once more write the word 'sign.' Label the lower corner 'thought' and the upper right corner 'referent.' Notice that, in this second triangle: the referent *calls up* the thought that *is expressed by* the sign. So you may label the right side of the artist's triangle 'calls up,' with an arrow slanting down to the thought corner; and label the left side 'is expressed by,' with an arrow slanting up toward the sign corner. Below this, the artist's triangle of reference, you may well print 'ARTIST.' Notice that the artist's thought is expressed by the sign; or, looked at the other way, the sign expresses the artist's thought.

Now look at the two triangular diagrams. If, as suggested, you sketched one just below the other, you will note that the word 'sign' appears twice on the left; and you may now print 'THE WORK OF ART' to the left and in between the two words 'sign.' You will note now that the art triad—artist, work of art, artee—stands out in printed letters.

You have probably also noted that the word 'referent' appears twice over to the right. Referents, you will recall, are whatever things the thoughts are of or refer to; so you may wish to print the phrase 'THE WORLD OF THINGS' between and to the right of the two words 'referent.' If you are in a graphic mood, you may wish to draw a circle around 'THE WORLD OF THINGS' and the two words 'referent.' If you wish to sketch in lightly a couple of continents within this circle—the concrete material things of this world—the surrounding space will then suggest the oceans of love and other less tangible things that are just as much a part of this world, and a bit of misty atmosphere about your globe may indicate the abstractions and other thoughts that may also serve as referents.

Then draw a rectangular picture frame about 'THE WORK OF ART' and the two words 'sign'—just to join them in a common framework. Now you may surround the 'ARTIST' and his 'thought' with an outline of a human brain, or head if you'd rather. (Remember, Michelangelo said that 'a man paints with his brains.') And supply the 'ARTEE' and his 'thought' with the same sort of outline symbol for his mind.

So, except for a touch or two, your diagram is complete—though perhaps a bit surrealistic in appearance. Like any complex sign, such as a work of art, this diagram has meaning. But your drawing and marks might not mean anything at all, say, to a Fiji Islander—for him, then, it wouldn't be a sign. And it might not mean very much to some friend of yours who hasn't read these paragraphs, or its meaning might be somewhat different for him from its present meaning for you. However, there are a few observations now to be offered that, it is hoped, will make it still more meaningful even to you:

First, notice that there is no line directly connecting the mind of the ARTIST with the mind of the ARTEE. The only route from mind to mind is via signs. You may say, 'But the artist could tell the artee what he had in mind.' Yes, in a sense, and some artists have tried to explain their meanings in words. But words are themselves signs, and what the artist has then done is merely to substitute one set of signs for another. The result may be a mediocre paragraph of explanation for a really good poem, picture, or piece of music. It is true that some thoughts cannot be adequately symbolized in words or in words other than those already chosen by the poet. This, you will recall, is the contention of many artists and critics who, admitting that art works have meaning, say that such meaning cannot be translated or explained in other words. There is no *direct* thought transference from the mind of the artist to the mind of the artee—we can believe this without denying the miracle of human insights and intuitions. Therefore there is no direct line connecting the top and bottom points on our diagram. You may wish to put in a faint dotted line just as a reminder that there is no solid line between those points.

Second, notice that there is no direct line from THE WORK OF ART to THE WORLD OF THINGS. Dotted lines connect the sign and referent in each of the separate triangles. Using Ogden and Richards' phrase again: a sign 'stands for' a referent; this is an imputed relation, not a direct connection, except as we shall later observe in commenting on so-called projections and natural signs. The only solid route from sign to referent in the upper (the artee's) triangle is via the mind of the artee; the only solid route from referent to sign in the lower (the artist's) triangle is via the mind of the artist. There is (usually) no direct connection between sign and referent—between the work of art and the world of things. But the imputed relation, represented by the dotted line, is very important, for that is essentially what we mean by 'having meaning.' There are a number of different sorts of imputed relation between signs and referents, three or four of which will be explored later in the next section.

Third, notice that if you think of the whole diagram as roughly circular, the little arrows all point around in a clockwise direction, from the artist's referent down by way of the artist's thought, up to the work of art, on up to the artee's thought, and down again to the artee's referent, once more in THE WORLD OF THINGS. This is intended to show the general drift, to indicate only the principal direction of the activities suggested. However, thought is more like the electric spark of an alternating current, jumping back and forth, than like a steady and direct flow. The artist's thoughts are an interaction of mind and referents—things call up thoughts that then refer back to the things; and the artist's thoughts and signs also interact—he creates signs to express his thoughts, but the signs he creates also evoke further thoughts in him. So, too, with the artee: signs evoke his thoughts because he reads them, refers to them, goes to them; and his thoughts refer to referents that in some cases were his thoughts of a moment ago. But, however much interaction is implied in the alternating currents of thought, the general clockwise direction of the little arrows may well stand in our general picture.

Fourth, notice that the word 'referent' appears twice within the WORLD OF THINGS. It would have been better to draw two worlds instead of one, overlapping, it is true, but separate. We would then have labeled one of these worlds 'The Artist's World of Experience,' and the other, 'The Artee's World of Experience.' These *two* 'worlds of things' are not really out there in the cold world at all, but within the warm minds of artist and artee. Even the most objective and material 'things' are 'things as experienced,' and that means as seen, heard, felt, perceived, and conceived of.

Fifth, notice likewise that the word 'sign' appears twice within the framed WORK OF ART. We have already said that a work of art is a complex sign, compounded of many interrelated simple signs. But the word 'sign' appears twice in your diagram, not to suggest that a work of art consists of many separate signs, but rather to suggest that each separate sign—a single note or chord or sequence of sounds, a single line or form or configuration, a single word or phrase or unit of discourse—each separate sign will, in a sense, be a different sign for the artist who created it and for the artee who perceives it. As we said, what is a sign for one person (what has meaning for him) may not be a sign for some other person (may not mean anything to him, may evoke no reference or thought in him).

The work of art *as the artist sees it* with his eyes, or hears it or reads it over, *is* the sign for him. The work of art *as the artee sees it with* HIS *eyes,* or hears it or reads it, *is* the sign for him. Their perceptions of the public work of art may be very similar, but they will certainly be slightly different.

Sixth, it may have occurred to you that THE WORK OF ART with such signs as it may include is really a part of THE WORLD OF THINGS. This is very true, and the globe which you outlined, with its continents of objective things, might indeed be thought of as enlarged so as to envelop or include *all* the other points in the diagram. The fact that the sign is really a part of the larger world of things, and that it means or signifies whatever it stands for (that is, its referent), may lead to the question: Can a sign mean itself? Can a sign evoke a thought that refers to itself alone and not to anything else? Looked at from the artist's viewpoint, can an artist create a sign that expresses only the artist's thought of the sign itself? This question in its various forms may sound like unprofitable hairsplitting, but it is exactly the question discussed in §3 above on 'The importance of meaning in art.' For it, there is no simple answer. If by 'meaning' we signify the thoughts evoked by a work of art, these evoked thoughts may refer to objective referents, or to quite subjective referents like formal feeling states and beauty, or to logical referents like abstractions and evaluations; or the thoughts evoked by a work of art may refer back to the perception of the sign itself or to its various emotive effects, or to that abstraction based upon the whole responsive experience. There need be no quarrel, then, with those whom we quoted as saying, of a poem or painting or musical composition, 'It means itself.' In the case of some works of art as intended by some artists and interpreted by some artees, this may indeed be true. But most works of art for most people are signs that have meaning in a more usual sense: they signify something other than themselves; they express or evoke thoughts pointing to referents outside themselves.

5. *Evocations, contexts, and signs*

A broad definition of meaning in art by John Hospers has been quoted at the head of this chapter: "A work of art means to us whatever effects (not necessarily emotions) it evokes in us." Our own definition of 'meaning' is not at all in terms of emotions but of thoughts, references to referents, which are one, but only one, of the effects evoked by a work of art. It may be well, then, to consider briefly the range of different effects evoked by a work of art and what relation they may have to one another.

The first kind of effect evoked as part of a responsive art experience is vivid perception, already referred to in our discussion of the various definitions of beauty in Chapter 2. Second, comes a group of somewhat different effects which we have already called affective qualifications and other naive responses—visual and other images, empathic and other feeling states, simple liking, moods and emotions, attitudes and the special effect which we call beauty. Third, as a general sort of effect, are the thoughts that are evoked by the work of art, that is, the response to it as a sign, its meaning. This includes, not only the interpretation of the various simple signs that make up the work of art, but the more elaborate interpretation of the work as a whole, and the rationalization of the various naive effects just referred to. And it includes various critical judgments as well.

All of these are effects that may be evoked in a person as he listens to music, looks at a picture, or reads a novel. But they are not isolated effects; they form a complex of intricately interrelated effects, and taken all together they comprise the responsive art experience, which will be explored in detail in Part Three of this book.

Following Upton's threefold classification of qualities earlier referred to—'sensory, emotional or affective, and logical or rational'—we have, then, divided these effects into three groups: (1) perception of the work of art or sign itself, (2) the various intuitive or naive responses—images, empathic and other feeling responses, simple liking, moods and emotions, attitudes and beauty; and (3) the meaning—that is, the various logical or rational responses, simple thoughts, more complex interpretations—and critical judgments.

The question now arises: What is the relation of these various effects one to another?

A single mark (such as *a* below) may serve as an example. The

a.   b.   c.

first effect evoked by it is simply seeing it. Second, it may—even without regard to its signification—evoke certain feelings or affective responses, though these may not be very strong. But looked at in an inverted or oblique position (such as *b* and *c*), I think you will see that the form itself has some effect upon you. The nature of such evocations we shall consider further in Chapter 8. Third, without doubt, the mark (*a* above) also is a sign for you; that is, it has meaning, it evokes a thought or thoughts that point to certain things in your world of experience. It means a cross, or the Cross, or the Church, or Christ. It stands for or signifies one or all of these things, which are its referents.

Because of the rich emotional associations that these referents may have for you, your thought evoked by the sign (*a* above) may in its turn evoke a whole group of secondary emotional or affective responses. The thought of the Cross may evoke an image of a certain crucifix or an image of organ sounds, or a simple affection for the things symbolized, or a mood of reverence, and so on. Furthermore, the images or mood evoked by the thought of the Church may in turn evoke additional thoughts—perhaps a thought of the meaning of the crucifixion or a thought of a certain Bach chorale or a thought naming the evoked mood as 'reverence.' So the effects evoked by even a single mark will be a complex of interacting effects, perceptual, affective, and referential; and we shall consider the thoughts evoked by the image of the crucifixion and by the mood as part of the meaning of the outward sign.

What, for you, is the somewhat different set of effects evoked by *b* and by *c* above? There is the obvious perceptual difference—they look different one from another. Do they evoke in you any affective or emotional effects without regard to their possible meanings? any feelings of balance or imbalance, for instance? Are they just black marks or are they also signs for you; that is, do they have meaning, evoke thoughts of things? If so, what different sets of thoughts do they evoke? Do these thoughts in turn evoke any further affective responses? . . .

Now turn once again to your diagram of the triangles of reference. You will note that it is only concerned with the work of art as a complex sign or group of signs. Those shapes or colors in a picture that are signs (that is, evoke thoughts) may also evoke other effects as we have seen; but there may be many shapes and colors in a picture that are not signs, and evoke only non-referential effects. So, with music: some sounds or groups of sounds may evoke meanings—thoughts of referents—as well as other effects; but many sounds or groups of sounds do not directly evoke thoughts. In a poem, the words and groups of words evoke thoughts primarily, but these thoughts in turn evoke other effects that may be of more value than the mere sense of the words. Though your diagram does not show the non-referential evocations, you may think of some way to indicate that the artist and the artee have hearts as well as heads, that their brains are the centers of imagination as well as reference, and that the work of art may include evocative elements—pure forms and sounds—that are not necessarily signs of meaning. . . .

But let us turn from these various evocations to a second question, What causes a sign to mean one thing rather than another? and proceed by way of another example.

Let's take this mark, ∼ . Does it mean anything to you? If it doesn't refer to anything in your experience, then it isn't a sign at all, it's just a shape. However, when this shape is provided with a context, it will perhaps have some meaning for you: cañon. At once you may say, 'Oh yes, the Spanish tilde, indicating a special pronunciation of the n sound in the word usually spelled c a n y o n.' But appearing in another setting, as here given to the right, the ∼ mark will signify something quite different to you, if it means anything to you at all. Perhaps you know that ∼ indicates a musical turn, and means the sequence of notes as here written out. Notice that it is the surrounding marks that tell you what sort of meaning to make of it.

In the language field of experience, it means one thing; in the musical field or universe of discourse, it means something quite different. In this next context, $5 \sim 9 = 4$, what does the ∼ mark mean? . . . Perhaps if you have never seen the mark used in this way, it may still become a sign for you. You may be able to figure out its meaning by taking account of various clues in the mathematical context, for the meaning of a sign is relative to its context.

A third general question for consideration in this section is this: What are the several different relations, the imputed relations already referred to, that may exist between the sign and the referent? There are four sorts of imputed relation between sign and referent that are relevant to our discussion of art: the symbolic relation, the resemblative relation, the projectional relation, and the natural relation. These will be considered in turn.

In the first of these, the *symbolic* relation, the sign has an arbitrary or conventional relation to that which it signifies. Signs that stand in this relation to their referents are called symbols. Words and punctuation marks, musical notes and marks, numbers and arithmetic signs are all common examples. Language, consisting of so many signs, is a symbol system. Musical notation is a symbol system. Mathematics also is, or makes use of, a symbol system. By saying that symbols are conventional or arbitrary signs, we mean that there is no natural relation between them and their referents, the things they stand for. In certain social groups people simply have come to agree that 'butter' stands for a certain yellow dairy product or, in many families, oleomargarine. Neither the printed or written word 'butter' nor the sound for it has any natural cause-and-effect relation to the thing named. Everyone learns the word by being taught its arbitrary relationship to what it names, or by observing its usage by others in his family or social group. The ∿ mark, as we observed, is a sign. It is a symbolic sign, or symbol, with different meanings as used in the language, musical, and mathematical symbol systems.

The second sort of imputed relation between sign and referent we said was *resemblative*. In this case the sign looks like or sounds like the thing it stands for. Signs that are imitative, that resemble their referents, we shall call resemblative signs, or resemblants, for want of a better word. The bow-wow theory of the origins of language holds that all words were originally sounds that imitated what they stood for, but that they gradually became conventionalized as people lost sight of the resemblance between the sign and its referent. So it may not have occurred to you that Bowzer's name vaguely sounds like his bark. Similarly the ∿ sign, now you think of it, does look a bit like the configuration of the notes it represents, particularly in context, and suggests the musical turn as sounded on an instrument. If you interpret the sign as imitative, it is a resemblant. If you had not noted the resemblance or have forgotten it, the sign will be arbitrary and conventional for you, a symbol. If you are sensitive to the pitch and placement of speech sounds, the ∿ mark in 'cañon' may have had a certain similarity to the sound of tilde *n,* though here also the ∿ is not a resemblant but a pure symbol for most persons. Although cross mark *a* (above) is a symbol in the religious universe of discourse—it means Christ, a Christian, the Church, or the Catholic Church, or a chaplain by convention depending upon its context—yet it is first of all a resemblative sign; that is, it is a small representation of the sort of wooden cross used in crucifixion. A tiny silver or gold or ivory cross is, first of all, a resemblant standing for the Cross; its further meanings are symbolic.

The third sort of imputed relation between sign and referent we noted as a *projectional* relation. Signs of this sort are called projections. A projection has a point for point, cause-and-effect relation to what it stands for. A map of, say, Pennsylvania will serve as an example, for the outline bounding the state and the meandering lines signifying the Ohio, Allegheny, and Monongahela Rivers have a point for point relation to the area and geographic features mapped. The map means Pennsylvania with its rivers, etc. By foreknowledge of the system of projection, you can interpret a map, for instance a map of the Northern Hemisphere, and take account of distortion. Another example of projectional sign, again useful in illustrating distortion, is a person's shadow. A photograph also is a projection. Notice that with the map and the photograph there will be a direct connection between the referent and sign, but only in the *lower triangle* of your complex diagram. That is, though the map-maker or photographer expresses his thoughts (interpretation) of the referents in creating the sign, still there is a direct and objective relation between the territory mapped or subject photographed and the map or photograph. In the case of the photographer, the more he becomes an artist—the more he selects, poses, or arranges his subjects, the more he manipulates the lighting, the more he uses color filters and special film and exposures, the more he controls development, sharpness, enlargement, cutting, and contrasts in printing— the less the finished photo is a pure projection and the more it becomes a resemblative sign. Similarly a phonograph recording and the music that results from playing it are projections of the music originally performed. Except in photography and phonography—and the cinema, radio, and television arts dependent upon them—projectional signs are seldom found in the arts.

The fourth sort of imputed relation between sign and referent we said was *natural*. Signs of this sort are called natural signs. You might expect natural signs to be only such signs as are things of nature. In this case natural signs would not fall within the scope of art at all. This is true, however, of such natural signs as those usually cited: clouds may be interpreted as a sign of rain; a light in the house is interpreted as a sign someone is home; a narrow hard ring in the crosscut of a tree is interpreted as a sign that the winter in, say, 1642 was severe; a shadow on the hall wall may be interpreted as a sign that the postman is at the door—though in this last case notice that the sign is also a projection of the postman's figure, and this is interpreted as resemblative of the postman. In these cases— all remote from the world of art—the sign has an imputed direct relation to the referent; it is interpreted as being the cause or the effect of the referent.

In the same way a work of art may be seen as a natural sign of what caused it. Robert Henri said, "The picture ... may be ... interesting as a sign of what has passed." To the extent that a work of art signifies the creative activity of the artist, it is a natural sign.

In such a case the referent is the activity that caused the work of art. When you as an observer are interested in the painter's technique, for instance, a little blob of paint may signify brush stroke or pallet knife or finger smear. It's as though you were looking at the picture as if it were a thing of nature—the sign and your referent are related causally, without regard to what the artist may have intended to signify. Still, this is, after all, only an imputed causal relation and does not call for a solid line in your diagram.

A work of art may be a natural sign or consist of natural signs in a slightly different sense. We spoke, earlier in this and in the preceding section, about the various sorts of effect evoked by a work of art, sign meaning being only one kind of effect. Others were perception, image, feeling, beauty, mood, etc. These were described as intricately interrelated effects, and together comprising the full art experience. It was pointed out that you may have a certain image evoked as an effect, but that this image may in turn evoke a thought. That is, you see the cross mark (a) and an image of the crucifixion is evoked by it. As you think about it, the cross mark becomes a sign that stands for that fleeting image. A natural, cause-and-effect relation exists between the sign (the cross mark) and the referent of your thought (the image effect); and in this case we may assume that it is not merely an imputed relation but an actual direct relation—and would justify *in such instances* a solid line as the base of the upper triangle in your diagram.

If the ∼ mark evokes in you a feeling of gracefulness or beauty —it is the serpentine line of grace or line of beauty of which Hogarth spoke—and if you therefore think of ∼ as standing for the felt-response of beauty, it is indeed a sign of beauty; the feeling of beauty is its meaning for you. And this is the sort of meaning which we shall refer to as emotive meaning, a term widely and variously used in semantic theory.

Such, then, are the *four sorts of sign*: symbols, resemblants, projections, and natural signs. We have pointed out that their meanings are always relative to contexts, the circumstance of their use, for they have no inherent meanings. Only in certain cases is there any direct relation between sign and referent; in all cases the meaning, the reference to or thought of a referent, is in the mind. As we have seen, anything such as a mark or sound, or a complex work of art, may evoke images, moods, feelings, or emotions, and then it may become a sign of these effects.

A work of art, then, may have meaning for you in two important ways: first, as evoking thoughts that point to things in the so-called outer world of your experience; second, as evoking thoughts that point to the various sensory, affective, and logical effects that make up your total responsive art experience.

6. *Three works of art as signs*

Let us proceed to an application of this theory of meaning to three particular works of art: a work of literature, a picture, and a musical composition. We shall find that they will serve to illustrate three of the four kinds of sign—symbolic, resemblative, and natural—omitting only the third, projectional sign, which we noted as having but limited relation to the Fine Arts.

The first work of art that we shall consider as a sign of meaning comes from *The Gospel According to Saint Matthew* 13: 3-9.

PARABLE OF THE SOWER
related by *Jesus*

Behold, a sower went forth to sow.

And when he sowed, some seeds fell by the way side, and the fowls came and devoured them up.

Some fell upon stony places, where they had not much earth; and forthwith they sprung up, because they had no deepness of earth. And when the sun was up, they were scorched; and because they had no root, they withered away.

And some fell among thorns; and the thorns sprung up, and choked them.

But other fell into good ground, and brought forth fruit, some an hundredfold, some sixtyfold, some thirtyfold.

Who hath ears to hear, let him hear.

This is certainly a work of art as we have defined it. You can readily see that it is a man-made thing, though we might not be in agreement as to whether Matthew is the author or Jesus and whether it represents human wisdom or divine inspiration. Perhaps we would agree that, for our purposes, it is a man-made thing of a kind that generally evokes beauty responses, and you may yourself attribute to it positive and terminal value of high degree. But this man-made thing of beauty is also, for you who have eyes to read, a thing of meaning. In so far as this set of black marks on the page does have meaning for you, it is a sign. Taken as a whole, it is a sign of that meaning. But it is a complex sign made up of many simple signs. These signs are essentially the words—also the punctuation marks, indentations, and spacing. Each of these signs evokes a thought or thoughts that refer to things in your experience; but groups of words, phrases and clauses and whole statements, are also signs and, as we have said, the entire parable may be looked upon as a complex sign evoking a complex thought of a complex referent. These words are not natural signs; there is no simple cause-and-effect relation between the word 'thorn' and the sort of plant that it names. Nor are these words resemblative signs; the word 'sower' does not look like a farmer planting seed. These words are, rather, symbols; their relation to what they stand for is conventional and arbitrary, and they are a part of that symbol system, the English language. It is because we have been conditioned to them through our experience with words and events that the marks 'went forth' are a symbolic sign that evokes a thought referring to an abstraction of our experiences of 'bodily movement away from some point,' in other words our experience of 'going out to do something.'

The thoughts evoked in the interpreter by these word symbols are likely to be of several kinds: the plain sense of the words and statements, the wider meaning of the statements, and the value of the whole experience—its significance or beauty or importance for you. But it is important to note that these thoughts of various sorts are not the only evocations that you as reader are likely to experience. As you read you may be conscious of clear pictures in your mind's eye of a particular farmer or Millet's French peasant sowing grain; you may become conscious of the bodily movements of sowing. You may read the parable in a mood of reverence and solemnity, as this is Holy Writ, or you may be provoked by what you consider an intrusion of irrelevant religion in a book on art! These images and feelings are not thoughts, they are not part of the meaning; but you may discover that they do, in their turn, evoke a second group of thoughts—that is, you may think about such feelings and images. However, it is the running stream of the plain sense of the words as you read them and the interpretative thoughts of the larger meaning, intention and implication, that are the two principal kinds of thoughts evoked in most readers by this parable.

The plain sense of these words is simple enough, and readers are not likely to disagree in the main, even though their experience with farm life is limited. You might well put your understanding of the literal meaning of this parable into other words. . . and then compare your paraphrase with the similar interpretation of others. . . .

The main thought of the first verse will doubtless be similar for all or most readers: 'A farmer went out to plant grain,' or words to that effect. But what of 'Behold'? Is the sense of it, 'Picture in your mind's eye,' or 'Give attention to this,' or 'Listen, now'? and is 'the way side' merely the edge of the field or a boundary path or road? And are 'the fowls' black birds or chickens? And does 'no root' mean no roots at all, or shallow roots, or roots not rooted in the ground? And does 'among thorns' mean among existing brambles or hedgerow or simply weed-sown ground? Yet, even with all such possibilities, the plain sense of this simple narrative is certainly clear enough.

But what of the over-all thought? 'Who hath ears to hear, let him hear.' The word 'parable' in the title as here given—it is also in the introductory phrase in Matthew—suggests, and the 'Behold' emphasizes, that here is a little story with a special significance and signification, a bit of moral truth. It's a sort of extended metaphor or simple allegory. The sower and the seed—the referents of these symbols are in themselves intended to be interpreted as symbols evoking thoughts of yet other referents. What is the sower and what the seed? what the wayside and the stony places? the thorns and good ground? fruit and an hundredfold? You may well commit yourself to a penciled note and so objectify your own conception of the meaning of the parable. . . . Is the sower, for you, God Himself, and the seed his children? Is the sower Jesus, and the seed his teachings? Is the sower any man who would do anything, and the seed his deeds? Are you yourself the sower, and the seed your own best efforts to do good? . . . And beyond the parallel streams of thought, what is the theme of this parable, if indeed its meaning for you can be stated in succinct terms? Is it: 'Environment conditions growth,' or 'The readiness is all,' or, 'Do not expect all seed to yield harvest,' or, 'Who shall say what efforts will bring results'?

The disciples themselves came and said to Jesus, when he spoke to the multitude in parable, "Why speakest thou to them in parables?" He answered that he spoke in parables "Because it is given unto you to know the mysteries of the kingdom of heaven, but to them it is not given." So, for all hearers his simple farm story of the sower made plain sense and carried its direct and truthful observation of life, but only those with keener insight were able to catch his spiritual message. And Jesus proceeded to explain to his disciples the metaphorical meaning (Matthew 13: 18-23):

Hear ye therefore the parable of the sower.

When any one heareth the word of the kingdom, and understandeth it not, then cometh the wicked one, and catcheth away that which was sown in his heart. This is he which received seed by the way side.

But he that received the seed into stony places, the same is he that heareth the word, and anon with joy receiveth it;

Yet hath he not root in himself, but dureth for a while: for when tribulation or persecution ariseth because of the word, by and by he is offended.

He also that received seed among the thorns is he that heareth the word; and the care of this world, and the deceitfulness of riches, choke the word, and he becometh unfruitful.

But he that received seed into the good ground is he that heareth the word and understandeth it; which also beareth fruit, and bringeth forth, some an hundredfold, some sixty, some thirty.

But let us turn from the *Parable of the Sower*—works of art too are seed scattered amongst us to wither away or to bring forth fruit—and consider the meaning of a second example.

On an accompanying page you will find a reproduction of a painting by Hans Holbein the Younger (1497-1543). It may be of interest to note that Holbein, the son and grandson of painters, was born in Bavaria, left his father's workshop to travel and study in Switzerland and probably Italy, became a guild member in Switzerland at 23. He drew the title page for an early edition (1521) of Luther's translation of the New Testament; he painted the portrait of Erasmus, the great Dutch humanist, shortly thereafter, and brought a letter of introduction from him to Sir Thomas More when he came to England a few years later. By the year 1532 he was settled as court painter to the rotund monarch Henry VIII, and has left memorable portraits of the King himself, his successive wives, and courtiers. Holbein died of the plague in 1543.

The present portrait is of Edward, only son of Henry VIII by his third wife, Jane Seymour. Born in 1537, Prince Edward became King Edward VI of England upon his father's death in 1547, but he himself died in 1553 to be succeeded first by his elder half-sister Mary Tudor (1516-1558) and then by his other half-sister, the red-haired Elizabeth, born in 1533, the daughter of Henry VIII and Anne Boleyn. Holbein painted two well-known portraits of Edward, one of the baby prince at the age of two, which is part of the Mellon Collection in the National Gallery of Art in Washington, D. C., and the portrait here reproduced which is in the Bache Col-

Courtesy Metropolitan Museum of Art

Hans Holbein, EDWARD, Metropolitan Museum of Art, New York

lection in the Metropolitan Museum, in New York City. . . . How old do you judge Edward to have been at the time this picture of him was painted? . . . How old does he look? How old was Edward when Holbein died? What does the lettering 'AETATIS SUAE VI' mean? . . . Is this, then, a portrait of King Edward VI or of Prince Edward?

Some or all of these data and questions may seem irrelevant to you for a consideration of the meaning of the painting under consideration. But if this picture has meaning—and it hardly seems necessary to re-argue that point—it is a sign; and its meaning, in our sense, is the stream or system of thoughts that it expresses or evokes. For you and for me as artees, the meaning of this portrait consists of the thoughts that are a part of our total response to it, and these thoughts are references to various things, items in the somewhat different worlds of our experience. Now it was earlier pointed out that the meaning of a sign is relative to its context. The context in which a sign is found and which gives it meaning consists of two parts: all the surrounding signs and also all the relevant items in the interpreter's experience. So, I perceive that certain shape of a certain size and color and texture as below the hat and behind and above the face, which are elements in the visual context; and that same shape I furthermore perceive in relation to my own vital experience of human heads of hair. It means (for I have seen the original and color prints) red-headed! And the symbol 'VI' in the visual context of an apparent portrait and in the verbal context 'AETATIS SUAE' (being Latin for 'in the —th year of his life'), means six. The richer the interpreter's discrimination and observation of relationships among the sensory data that come to him from a work of art, and the richer his store of relevant data accumulated through past experiences, the more meaningful will be his present art experience.

This picture is what we called a resemblative sign. It means 'a boy' because it looks like a boy. To persons in the Court of Henry VIII it meant 'Edward' because it looked like the prince. The words on the canvas are, however, symbolic signs; theirs is a purely conventional relation to what they mean, 'painted in the sixth year of his life.' Sometimes such pictures include the name of the subject, more often the name of the artist; but portraits are essentially resemblative signs. A portrait may be said to mean the person whom it resembles. But, just as the parable was meaningful at two levels, so this portrait may evoke thoughts of several sorts. The plain sense of it is 'Prince Edward at age six.' In some persons, however, there may be evoked thoughts of the far-off look in the eye of a pale and sensitive child, frail hope of an indulgent father, and the pawn of powerful family interests.

There are yet other sorts of thoughts that may be evoked by this painting. Some observers, even without being told, would have recognized it as the work of Hans Holbein. The evidence of simplified realism, the nature of the costume, the Latin phrase, the formal design all serve as signs whose meaning for such observers would be 'a portrait by Holbein.' Similarly this picture might mean, to some others, 'the height of German Renaissance art,' or, 'naturalism.' It must be remembered that the meaning of a work of art for a particular person is whatever relevant thoughts it may evoke in him.

But let us introduce our third example.

It is not necessary here to reproduce in full the musical notation for Claude Debussy's *Clair de lune*, though the two principal themes are here given. Debussy, who was born in 1862 and died in 1918, is known as one of the greatest of modern French composers. As a young man he was trained in the Paris Conservatory of Music and won its outstanding prize at the age of 22. He turned his back upon the academic traditions in music, went to Rome where he began his independent and revolutionary work in composition. He was greatly influenced by his contemporary French painters and poets and by Balinese and Russian music. He experimented with new musical forms and the whole-tone scale. He is recognized today as one of the greatest of the impressionists; and though his works were subjected to much contemporary scorn and ridicule, certain of them have won a wide and even popular audience.

Clair de lune, for piano, is one of a group which Debussy called 'La Suite bergamasque,' composed in 1890 and consisting of a Prelude, a Menuet, Clair de Lune, and Passepied. It is available in many different recordings and is in the repertoire of many performers. The following notation may be of help to you in your listening, and may serve to fix the principal themes in mind. The first is the well-known and, for many people, haunting melody. It moves in thirds—with an alto voice, as it were, two notes below it—and the simple bass, also in thirds, only an octave underneath.

Thematic Notation

CLAIR DE LUNE

by *Claude Debussy*

(Permission for reprint granted by Jean Jobert, Paris, France and Elkan-Vogel Company, Inc., Philadelphia, copyright owners.)

A six-measure development of this initial theme leads to a twelve-measure animated passage that increases in volume and closes in high arpeggio chords. Then, above a harp-like bass, comes the second theme:

Some fourteen measures of further development of this second theme lead back to the initial melody, now heard above the harp-like bass and then with a bass of solid chords, concluding with an arpeggio passage and high chord.

It is now time to ask the question, What is the meaning, if any, of *Clair de lune*?

In asking this question I do not refer to the musical notation but to the live music, the complex of sound-waves coming from piano or radio. There is no doubt that the black marks on the page are signs, with meaning for those persons who can read musical notation. Such marks are essentially symbolic signs, like words. To read music one must learn its special conventions: what the arbitrary signs stand for, the clefs, sharps and flats, staff, time signature, rests, dynamic directions, notes, slurs, bars, etc. But it is also true that musical notation is somewhat resemblative: the higher the note is on the staff, the higher the sound in pitch; the lower on the staff, the lower in pitch. When one catches on to this and several similar matters of convention, then it is true that the music on the page has a certain resemblance to the melody that one hears. In any case, the music on the page means the music as sound, and it is the latter that we are now concerned with.

In answering the question, What is the meaning, if any, of *Clair de lune* as sound? it is necessary to observe that musical tones and phrases are not like speech sounds, words and phrases. Musical tones and phrases are not usually symbols; they do not acquire conventional and arbitrary meanings except in rare cases. The opening notes of Beethoven's *Fifth Symphony* are indeed symbolic for many music lovers, and are often called the 'Fate motif.' 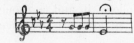 During World War II, they acquired a special meaning and became widely known as symbolizing 'V for Victory.' As is sometimes the case, their symbolic meaning was an outgrowth of a stage in which this sequence of sounds was a resemblative sign; but the resemblance of the sound sequence to someone's (Fate's) knocking at the door and the resemblance of the sound sequence to the V symbol in the International Morse Code (. . .—) were never recognized or were forgotten by many persons for whom the musical phrase continued to be a meaningful symbolic sign. 'Clair de lune' does not seem to include any such symbolic signs. Nor, except for the melodic accompaniment and chords that resemble the characteristic arpeggios and broken chords of the harp, does it include resemblative signs. That is, there are no musical phrases in it that sound like cuckoo birds or purling brooks or rifle fire.

If *Clair de lune* has meaning, then, and since it is neither symbolic nor resemblative, it must be a complex natural sign or be made up of simple natural signs. (The fourth sort of sign, you will recall, was projectional. The phonographic recording of *Clair de lune* is a projection of the original musical performance by the interpretative artist.) Remembering that by 'meaning' here we mean such thought as may be evoked, the question is, Does this music evoke any thoughts at all, any references to things in the world of your experience, or does it only evoke non-referential effects: images, moods, feeling states, etc.? It will not be enough to say that the title *Clair de lune* means moonshine. If the music itself, because of the suggestion in the title, evokes thoughts that point to your experience of moonlit nights, that is a different thing. There is no doubt that, for some persons, the title does point the way for visual imagery and related moods that are then evoked by the music itself as it unfolds. To the extent that one has thoughts of these non-referential effects, whether it directly evokes thoughts or not of things in the outside world, *Clair de lune* may be said to have meaning. And that almost brings us back to the artists' and critics' phrase, "It means itself."

There is another way in which *Clair de lune* has meaning, and I am indebted to my colleague for the suggestion. As one becomes acquainted with this composition so that, when he hears it played, he knows what comes next, every part of the complex pattern comes to mean the parts that precede and follow it. That is, this phrase evokes the auditory image of the phrase that follows it and a thought of that succession as previously experienced.

Similarly the repetition of a musical phrase or theme puts the hearer in mind of the earlier occurrences of that phrase or theme. Just as the plain sense of the words and statements was the first and most obvious sort of meaning of the *Parable of the Sower,* so this recognition of the musical motifs, phrases, themes and their recurrences, modifications, and development may be looked upon as the plain sense of musical thought. But if music 'makes sense' to the listener—or in some cases fails to make sense to him—we must not expect it to make sense in terms of words or in terms of visual images. It is important to remember that, characteristically, musical sounds are not symbolic signs or resemblative signs, but natural signs of a special sort.

So much, then, for our application of this theory of meaning to these three particular works of art.

7. *Final comment and example*

Let us return once more to the complex diagram that you sketched while reading §5 on 'Art works as signs of meaning,' and make a final comment on the communication of meaning through art. You will recall that there was no direct connection, no solid line, between the thought in the mind of the artist and the thought in the mind of the artee. Yet, somehow, we do often feel that we, as readers or observers or listeners, have gotten the artist's meaning as part of our total experience of a work of art. And when there is good reason to believe that the artee's thoughts evoked by the work of art are similar to the artist's thoughts to which he tried to give expression in creating the work of art, then we may say that communication of thought has taken place.

Such thoughts in the mind of the artist and artee will be similar if they refer to similar items in the artist's and artee's worlds of experience. Therefore the communication of thought through works of art will really depend upon the extent to which these two individual worlds of experience may be overlapping or somewhat alike. But such communication will also depend upon the skill of the artist in so fashioning his work of art that it will actually evoke in the artee the same sort of thoughts that it expresses; and it will also depend upon the skill of the artee in the interpretation of works of art as signs of meaning. As Jesus well knew in commenting upon the *Parable of the Sower,* there are wide differences in interpretative ability, for some persons 'seeing see not; and hearing they hear not, neither do they understand.' He did not expect more than partial communication with them, but he had hoped that others, such as his disciples, with ears to hear and eyes to see, would receive the seed into the good ground, hear the word and understand it.

But a work of art may communicate much more than thought alone.

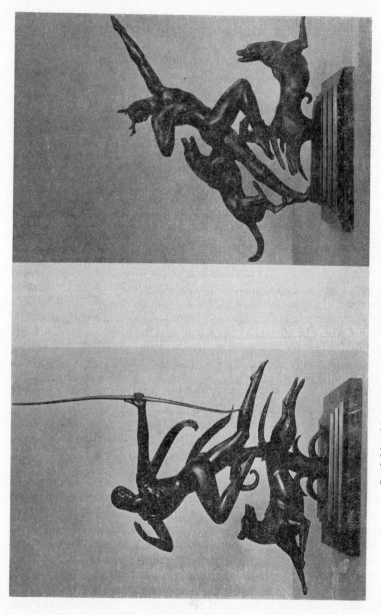

Paul Manship, DIANA and ACTEON, Carnegie Institute, Pittsburgh

To the extent that the images, moods, feeling states, and emotions evoked by the work of art are similar to the images, moods, feeling states, and emotions of the artist or that the artist tried to give expression to in creating the work of art, we may say that communication of these things also has been effected. There is no chance of knowing, of course, whether such communication has really occurred; but the feeling is sometimes very strong in the artee that he indeed does feel just what the poet or painter or composer felt. And the communication of moods, images, formal feelings, emotions may in many works of art be more important than the communication of thought. Who shall say whether the fleeting imagery, the eerie mood, and the other non-referential effects evoked in me as I listen to *Clair de lune* are reasonably similar to those to which Claude Debussy gave expression when he created this work of art? or whether such effects are more important than the complex of my thoughts evoked by the music itself and by my feelings about it? No one, I presume.

Let us bring this chapter to a close by presenting photographic reproductions of a pair of bronze statues by the contemporary American sculptor Paul Manship. They are entitled *Diana* and *Acteon*. They are to be found at Carnegie Institute in Pittsburgh. Other examples of the same works are in the Addison Gallery in Andover and in the Gardner Museum in Boston. In observing them closely—it is unfortunate that replicas of the actual statues cannot be at hand—you may consider such beauty and meaning responses as they evoke as a part of your total art experience. You would find it convenient, no doubt, to be presented with a set of leading questions to guide your thinking about the beauty and meaning of these statues, but would not your own preparation of a set of relevant questions about the *Diana* and *Acteon* serve as some measure of your understanding of the theoretical considerations of this chapter? On the chance that it will, you may well glance back through the preceding sections and then jot down a few questions to be asked about the beauty of these works of sculpture and a dozen or so questions about them as signs of meaning. . . . And you may now find it profitable to answer your own questions.

On the Personal Cultivation of Taste

> We apply the term taste to that act of the mind by which we like or dislike whatever be the subject.
>
> Sir Joshua Reynolds, *Discourses,* VII.

YOU CAN HARDLY have considered Manship's statues *Diana* and *Acteon*, interpreting them thoughtfully and reflecting upon the beauty and meaning responses evoked in you as a part of your art experience, without becoming conscious that you liked or disliked one or both of them. If you enjoyed observing them and thinking about them, well and good. If you really did not care for them, there is no reason why you should feel upset or disturbed. There will be many things in the World of Art that, frankly, are not to your taste. As a part of your personal orientation to art in Chapter 2, you made some effort to Know Thyself the better by investigating your present art taste and art judgment.

As stated in the Foreword, one of the purposes of this book is to help to clarify and develop further your art theory, and a second purpose is to provide you with a variety of enriched art experiences. But there is a third purpose: to encourage personal self-cultivation of your taste in the arts. It has already been said that you will have to start off on such a course of self-cultivation from where you are. It was also said that the goals you set for yourself should take account of your aptitudes, past experience, accumulated knowledge and present taste. This interlude will presently consider what such goals may well be. But first let us take time out for comedy.

1. *Preference and aversion*

It is quite impossible, as already suggested, to bring a stageplay within the compass of a book. Scenery, actors, gestures, stage movement, and living tones of voice are quite as important to the work of theater art as the characters' words, which alone (supplemented by scanty stage directions) form the substance of the playbook or work of dramatic literature. But the reader who has some experience as a playgoer may, with little more than the dialog to guide him, produce a lively comedy in the theater of his imagination.

There follows here a scene from that famous English drama *The Rivals,* written by Richard Brinsley Sheridan (1751-1816) and first produced in Covent Garden. Like most of the great writers of English comedy, Sheridan was an Irishman. He was a man of action as well as conversation, and lived such wit, intrigues, and romance as he depicted in his plays. His short and brilliant career as dramatist was followed by years of theater management and a distinguished service as a member of Parliament.

In *The Rivals* Lydia Languish is in love with a handsome man called Beverley, who is really Capt. Jack Absolute in romantic disguise. She must gain her aunt's consent to marry; but her aunt, Mrs. Malaprop, decides to marry her off to Sir Anthony Absolute's son (Jack). So the rivals for her hand really are one and the same person. In scene 2 of Act I, Lydia is reading as Mrs. Malaprop and Sir Anthony enter:

from THE RIVALS, I, ii

by *Richard Brinsley Sheridan*

MRS. MALAPROP. There, Sir Anthony, there sits the deliberate Simpleton, who wants to disgrace her family, and lavish herself on a fellow not worth a shilling!

LYDIA. Madam, I thought you once—

MRS. MAL. You thought, Miss!—I don't know any business you have to think at all—thought does not become a young woman; the point we would request of you is, that you will promise to forget this fellow—to illiterate him, I say, quite from your memory.

LYD. Ah, Madam! our memories are independent of our wills. It is not so easy to forget.

MRS. MAL. But I say it is, Miss; there is nothing on earth so easy as to *forget,* if a person chooses to set about it. I'm sure I have as much forgot your poor dear uncle as if he had never existed—and I thought it a duty to do so. And let me tell you, Lydia, these violent memories don't become a young woman.

SIR ANTHONY. Why, sure, she won't pretend to remember what she's order'd not! Aye, this comes of her reading!

Lyd. What crime, Madam, have I committed to be treated thus?

Mrs. Mal. Now don't attempt to extirpate yourself from the matter; you know I have proof controvertible of it.—But tell me, will you promise to do as you're bid? Will you take a husband of your friends' choosing?

Lyd. Madam, I must tell you plainly, that had I no preference for anyone else, the choice you have made would be my aversion.

Mrs. Mal. What business have you, Miss, with *preference* and *aversion*? They don't become a young woman; and you ought to know, that as both always wear off, 'tis safest in matrimony to begin with a little *aversion*. I am sure I hated your poor dear uncle before marriage as if he'd been a blackamoor—and yet, Miss, you are sensible what a wife I made! And when it pleas'd Heav'n to release me from him, 'tis unknown what tears I shed!—But suppose we were going to give you another choice, will you promise us to give up this Beverley?

Lyd. Could I belie my thoughts so far, as to give that promise, my actions would certainly as far belie my words.

Mrs. Mal. Take yourself to your room. You are fit company for nothing but your own ill humours.

Lyd. Willingly, Ma'am—I cannot change for the worse.

(*Exit.*)

Mrs. Mal. There's a little intricate hussy for you!

Sir Anth. It is not to be wondered at, Ma'am—all this is the natural consequence of teaching girls to read. Had I a thousand daughters, by Heavens, I'd as soon have them taught the black art as their alphabet!

Mrs. Mal. Nay, nay, Sir Anthony, you are an absolute misanthropy.

Sir Anth. In my way hither, Mrs. Malaprop, I observed your niece's maid coming forth from a circulating library! She had a book in each hand—! . . .

Mrs. Mal. These are vile places, indeed!

Sir Anth. Madam, a circulating library in a town is an evergreen tree of diabolical knowledge! It blossoms through the year! And depend on it, Mrs. Malaprop, that they who are so fond of handling the leaves, will long for the fruit at last.

Mrs. Mal. Well, but Sir Anthony, your wife, Lady Absolute, was fond of books.

Sir Anth. Aye—and injury sufficient they were to her, Madam. But were I to choose another helpmate, the extent of her erudition should consist in her knowing her simple letters, without their mischievous combinations; and the summit of her science be—her ability to count as far as twenty. . . .

MRS. MAL. Fie, fie, Sir Anthony, you surely speak laconically.

SIR ANTH. Why Mrs. Malaprop, in moderation, now what would you have a woman know?

MRS. MAL. Observe me, Sir Anthony: I would by no means wish a daughter of mine to be a progeny of learning; I don't think so much learning becomes a young woman. For instance, I would never let her meddle with Greek, or Hebrew, or Algebra, or Simony, or Fluxions, or Paradoxes, or such inflammatory branches of learning. Neither would it be necessary for her to handle any of your mathematical, astronomical, diabolical instruments. But, Sir Anthony, I would send her, at nine years old, to a boarding school in order to learn a little ingenuity and artifice. Then, Sir, she should have a supercilious knowledge in accounts. And as she grew up, I would have her instructed in geometry that she might know something of the contagious countries. But above all, Sir Anthony, she should be mistress of orthodoxy that she might not misspell and mispronounce words so shamefully as girls usually do; and likewise that she might reprehend the true meaning of what she is saying.—This, Sir Anthony, is what I would have a woman know; and I don't think there's a superstitious article in it.

SIR ANTH. Well, well, Mrs. Malaprop, I will dispute the point no further with you; though I must confess that you are a truly moderate and polite arguer, for almost every third word you say is on my side of the question. . . .

(1775)

2. A goal for self-cultivation of taste

With all of her malapropisms Lydia's aunt succeeds in saying a number of thought-provoking and quotable things, but the preferences and aversions of our present interest refer to taste, not in matrimony, but in art.

Taste was defined in Chapter 2 as the pattern of your likes and dislikes. Your taste in art, it was then said, is based upon the sum of your preferences and aversions. As a heading for this Interlude, Sir Joshua Reynolds was quoted, defining taste as "that act of the mind by which we like or dislike whatever be the subject." Ruskin said taste was "the instinctive and instant preferring of one material object to another." Sanford Gerard, in his recent book on the subject: "Your taste is simply what you like." A person's taste, then, is his individual pattern of likes and dislikes.

It is hardly necessary to add that each person's art taste is somewhat different from the taste of others. "What's one man's meat is another man's poison," as the saying goes. "Chacun à son gout," as the French put it; or "Every man to their own taste, as the farmer said when he kissed the cow," which is an American version of an old English proverb already in print when obese Henry VIII was displaying his eclectic taste in wives. As David Hume wrote in 1757, "the great variety of Taste, as well as of opinion, which prevails in the world, is too obvious not to have fallen under every one's observation." Your own taste, then, is unique and differs at least somewhat from the taste of others.

The causes of your taste in art, it was pointed out in the previous discussion, are often obscure. Some say indeed that there is no accounting for your taste. Let us rather say that it is hard to isolate the complex causes for your liking or disliking particular things. In general it may be said that your taste is relative to your structure and conditioning. As you discovered in your personal orientation to art, the kind of person you are, measured in terms of your aptitude for art activity, and the various art experiences that you have had are the bases of your art preferences. The French painter Ingres said, "Fine and delicate taste is the fruit of education and experience. All we receive at birth is the faculty for creating such taste in ourselves and for cultivating it. . . . It is up to this point, and no further, that one may say that taste is natural to us." But the 'faculty' that we receive at birth—visual acuity, color sensitivity, auditory discrimination, equilibrial sense, and so on—does differ for each of us; and this, together with 'the fruit of education and experience' determines our individual and unique taste.

Your art taste—the kind of art works you really like—is irrational. Ruskin speaks of taste as preferences "without any obvious reason." And George Boas says, "There is no arguing about taste. You either like a thing or you don't. Nor can most of us give the reason why we like it." That is, not the 'real reason.' When cornered with the demand to state your reasons, you are usually resourceful in thinking up reasons and explanations. But these turn out to be rationalizations, as James Harvey Robinson called them—good enough reasons for continuing to like what you like anyway! Reynolds pointed out that, if one could teach taste by rule and reason, it would no longer be taste at all. Indeed the essentially irrational nature of taste was recognized in the ancient proverb: *De gustibus non est disputandum,* and indeed there is no disputing a person's taste.

It might seem, then, that your art taste—comprising your intuitive preferences and aversions, and resulting from your inherited and developed bodily and neural and mental structure and from your irrevocable past experiences—is set and settled once and for all. But this is not so.

The pattern of your likes and dislikes in the World of Art is ever-changing. What you once liked may now bore you. What you once disliked intensely, you may now actually view with affection. And such changes of taste are to be explained in terms, again, of structure and conditioning as affected by life processes and experience. Some changes in your art taste are short range in character and result from satiety and fatigue. You simply get fed up with, let us say, Brahms, or you become tired of the Romantic lyrics. The processes of digestion and rest will restore your taste. But the long range changes are different in character and are like the slow process of growth. You may be quite conscious that certain works of art which were once to your taste—perhaps *Black Beauty*, or *Melody in F*, or *The Horse Fair*—no longer fit into the pattern of your current preferences. In art, as Mrs. Malaprop observed about matrimony, preference and aversion both may wear off, and she added cynically that " 'tis safest in matrimony to begin with a little aversion!"

Not only does your taste change, it may consciously be changed either by you yourself or by other persons. Such changes in the pattern of your likes and dislikes do not result from argument or dispute, from the advice of well-meaning friends or elders, or even from reading criticisms—for your taste is essentially irrational. Any such changes are likely to be progressive: step by step from the simple toward the complex, gradually from the familiar toward the exotic, by degrees, from the obvious toward the enigmatic. If you are willing to experience some art works that now seem a bit complex or strange or obscure, you may discover that your tolerance of them will gradually give way to some measure of understanding and then to appreciation and perhaps actual enjoyment. But in the process of acquiring certain new loves, you will discover yourself losing some of your old ones. So, as you become habituated to art works farther up the ladder, the pattern of your likes and dislikes gradually changes.

'Up the ladder' suggests climbing toward some objective. Certainly, if it is true that you can gradually change your art taste—and if it is true that other persons may, by devious and subtle means, change your taste for you!—then it becomes important to consider the goals toward which such changes may be directed. Such conscious changes in your taste directed toward a goal we shall call taste cultivation. As already stated, one of the purposes of this book is to encourage the personal self-cultivation of your taste in the arts. It would be folly to deny that the author of this book would like to share in the venture.

Certainly the most obvious and important task is to set up a goal toward which conscious changes of taste will be directed. The concept of 'good taste' at once suggests itself as the ideal. This good taste, or Taste with a capital T, is sometimes looked upon as absolute, rational, and never-changing! (Individual taste, you will recall, we described as relative, irrational, and ever-changing!) Paul Elmer More once wrote, "The law of taste is the least changing fact of human nature, less changeable than religious creeds, far less changeable than scientific theories. The advent of Christianity has left it untouched, and the waning of faith does not trouble it. The hypotheses of science . . . come and pass and come again, while the central tradition of taste is still the same." Certainly few persons can even glimpse this absolute. Cézanne wrote, "Taste is the best judge. It is rare. Art only addresses itself to an excessively small number of individuals." But perhaps such good taste absolute and eternal, as possessed by rare critics and artists, is not really so absolute or eternal after all.

Let us rather use the phrase 'good taste' to name an abstraction of the tastes of the so-called best people in any social group. This abstraction will consist of those likes and dislikes that are common to the natural or self-appointed or traditionally accepted leaders of the group in question. As was said in regard to beauty, good taste (despite Paul Elmer More to the contrary) differs markedly in different cultures and historic periods. Leafing through old and new art catalogs, thumbing through literary anthologies of a past and the present generation, glancing over musical programs of the turn of the century and the current season will readily demonstrate the shifts in good taste even in one culture and one period. But this good taste in the arts, as established by the individual tastes of the dominant persons in a culture, does have a tremendous influence, and is certainly the goal accepted by many persons for their self-cultivation.

But good taste, as here defined, is too limited a goal for self-cultivation in the arts. It is by no means absolute, but relative to racial, social, and environmental factors. It is by no means rational, but as devious and irresponsible as fashion. It is by no means eternal, but endlessly shifting in the sands of time. Good taste is characteristically narrow and provincial. If you have merely good taste, you simply will not like enough different sorts of things to make your life fully abundant. Furthermore, your good taste will isolate you from those other human beings—of other communities, cultures, and climes—whose arts are sometimes quite different from our own, but for which you may wish to cultivate a taste.

Such a concept of good taste is inadequate as an ideal, so let us explore several other possibilities: 'Undiscriminating taste' suggests itself; but in liking everything and disliking nothing—and that is what the phrase here means—a person really does not exercise taste at all! "It is only the auctioneer," wrote Oscar Wilde, "who can equally and impartially admire all schools of art."

The phrase 'classical taste' names another possible goal for self-cultivation, the systematic preference for those works of art that have remained in the good taste of educated people from year to year and period to period in our cultural past. "The consensus of apparently cultivated persons throughout many generations," writes A. R. Chandler, "will approximately represent humanity at its best and therefore be approximately objective." But a purely classical taste would seem to be a false goal, for, in idealizing the achievements of our great past, it ignores contemporary culture.

Perhaps 'eclectic taste' would be preferable as a chosen end for self-cultivation in the arts. This would suggest that one habituate himself to the great achievements of the past as well as to the significant achievement of the present so as to develop a real liking for them.

But there is a third sort of liking that might well be added to our eclectic taste, and we shall call it 'universal or catholic taste.' A person of a truly universal or catholic taste will have a genuine liking for the best in the arts of all cultures, East as well as West, South as well as North, primitive as well as sophisticated. A person of catholic taste is truly a cultivated citizen of the world. He will not love his classics the less, nor will he withhold his enthusiasm for the contemporary, but he will reach out beyond his own time and culture, and through attention and tolerant interest come to an understanding and then an appreciation and enjoyment of those works of art that at first may seem so remote and foreign to him. And the ideals implicit in the separate phrases 'contemporary [good] taste' and 'classical taste' and 'catholic taste' may be viewed as the three dimensions of magnanimity.

Such *magnanimous taste* may serve as a comprehensive goal for self-cultivation in the arts. The word itself goes back into the classical past and suggests high-mindedness and greatness of spirit, generosity and nobility, tolerance and understanding. To set oneself the ideal of learning to like all good things of all cultures and countries, classical and contemporary, is to develop a tremendous design for abundant living. It is a design that gives expression to the dignity of man and the brotherhood of men, to the Judaeo-Christian tradition and the spirit of Democracy. To become truly magnanimous in your taste for the arts is to learn to know and to love humanity.

3. *Learning to like new things*

It has already been suggested that learning to know is a step toward learning to like. To the indignant comment, 'I know what I like!' the rejoinder may well be: 'You like what you know.' And perhaps the first thing to do in the personal cultivation of your taste is to develop the willingness to have new things about you in your environment. Familiarity will breed not contempt but tolerance, and tolerance may open the way to understanding.

Here are four suggestions that may be of help to you in extending the range of your present taste:

First, when coming upon a work of art of a new and (for you) strange sort, set aside your prejudices and preconceptions. It is true that your own art theory, however vague and fragmentary, and your present art experiences are closely interrelated, and that you tend to listen for or look for or read for those elements that are part of your preconception of what a work of art should be. But it is possible to suspend judgment and come to a new and strange work of art with an open mind.

Second, be willing to experience such works of art fully. You should try to reach out toward the work of art, allowing time for adequate sensory perception of it—listening, looking, reading attentively. You should allow yourself to respond freely and without inhibition, giving yourself up to the experience for what it may be worth. You should, furthermore, alert your keenest intelligence, asking and answering such questions as may seem relevant to an understanding of it.

Third, it is not really important whether, on first acquaintance with a new and strange work of art, you really like it or not. You may prefer and continue to prefer those things that are tried and true. But come back to that strange and new work of art for a second and a third experience. At least, then, the novelty will wear off, and the strangeness will give way to familiarity. By degrees it may come to be liked, and so actually enlarge the pattern of your taste.

Fourth, an almost unnecessary warning: recognize that progress will be made slowly, step by step. Unless you wish to abandon your goal, the cultivation of a discriminating taste—whether you choose the ideal of magnanimous taste or some other—, you will not expect to revolutionize your taste in a single *coup* but will plot a gradual evolution that in the course of time will extend the range of those works of art that you really do like.

To accept such suggestions in principle may be a bit different from

photo by Soichi Sunami

Pablo Picasso, GIRL BEFORE A MIRROR, collection of the
Museum of Modern Art, Gift of Mrs. Simon Guggenheim

carrying them out. You may wonder where exactly to take hold, what sorts of new and strange works to approach open-mindedly and willingly and repeatedly. That will depend, certainly, upon where you at present are in the World of Art. For you, the Romantic composers of the late nineteenth century may still be new and strange, or the contemporary American composers who have experimented in new scales or old modes, or the great music of the Medieval Church. For you, the little Dutch painters of the seventeenth century or the French impressionists may be new and strange, or the contemporary Continental -isms, or the delicate art of the Orient. For you, the Russian novel of the nineteenth century or the French realists may be new and strange, or the modern metaphysical poets, or the tragic drama of ancient Greece. If you are to take seriously the challenge to set for yourself a goal and proceed in the cultivation of your own taste in the arts, you yourself must undertake the strategy and the campaign.

The accompanying picture may serve as a token—and as a subject for discussion.

PART TWO: CREATIVE ACTIVITY AND THE WORK OF ART

Chapter 4. Primary Creative Activity

Sometimes moods which the poet expresses in words come to me in tones: they ring, storm and roar until they finally stand before me in notes.

Beethoven, from *Musical Documents*

If obstacles discourage mediocre talent, they are, on the contrary, the necessary food of genius.

Géricault, from Clément, *Etude* ...

When artists falter, reasoning takes the reins; but when there is no hitch their imagination governs them and achieves the work.

Plotinus, *Enneads*

WE BEGAN this book with a Prelude 'On the World of Art and of People,' surveying the numerous art phenomena in our environments. Part One comprised three chapters under the general heading 'Introduction to Art, Beauty, and Meaning.' Chapter 1 established a 'Definition of Art' in terms of man-made things generally evoking beauty and meaning responses; Chapter 2 provided a framework for individual 'Orientation to Art and Aesthetics'; and Chapter 3 undertook to explore the key problems of 'Beauty and Meaning in Art.' We have just now turned from a brief Interlude 'On the Personal Cultivation of Taste.'

Of the three phases of Art distinguished in the opening chapter, Part Two of this book, upon which you are now embarking, will consider the first two, 'Creative Activity and the Work of Art.' The third phase, 'The Responsive Art Experience,' will be explored in Part Three.

It may have occurred to you while listening to a performance or recording of Chopin's *Prelude* or Debussy's *Clair de Lune* that two different sorts of creative art activity must be distinguished: the creative activity of the composer and the interpretative activity of the performance. Chopin created the composition and wrote it down; the performer, say Cortot, studied the written music and gave a performance of it. Chopin's activity was what we shall call primary creation; Cortot's activity was what we shall call interpretative creation or re-creation. The present chapter will confine itself to primary creative activity, leaving discussion of interpretative performance for the third chapter in this group.

'Why go into the matter of art production,' you may ask, 'in a book intended for the art consumer?'

An answer might be that some knowledge of the way artists work will increase your enjoyment, understanding, and appreciation of the various things they create. If works of art are one means for communicating certain sorts of human experience, then some insight into the artist's activity may be both interesting and helpful. Indeed your general notions about creative activity are, as we have seen, a part of your art theory, which you are in the process of filling out and clarifying.

1. *Characteristics of the creative artist*

There is an air of mystery about the processes of creation. The more we know about historical geology and evolutionary biology, about genetics and embryology, the more truly wonderful the creatures and creations of this world will seem to us. Some of us may see the world and its creatures as the handiwork of God, and think of Him as the Universal Architect and Master Craftsman. Others of us may see the world and its multifarious forms of life as created by Natural Law. Our wonder at the miracle of creation may well be the same in either case.

In his own small way Man too has been creative. Humanity, too, has created for itself a world, and worlds within this world, and one of these we have called the World of Art. And this world, too, is wonderful to behold. Every man is in some measure an artist, occasionally making things that are beautiful and meaningful to those about him, or at times doing things so well that others delight in his performance.

But every man is by no means really a great artist. The psychology of talent and genius is not too well understood. What is it that the great creative artist has that ordinary man does not have? Here are a few suggestions—you will note that these four pairs of characteristics apply quite as much to the creative statesman or scientist and inventor as to the artist.

A *first pair* of characteristics: the artist or inventor is gifted with a more sensitive nervous system and has therefore keener perceptions than the average.

That is, the artist's sense of sight or of hearing may be capable of finer discriminations. The musician may have what is called 'perfect pitch' and the capacity to discriminate the E in the major C scale from the E in the major D scale. (On the piano a compromise is effected; the scale is said to be 'tempered,' and the two E's are the same, but not so on such instruments as the violin. This accounts for the fact that to some ears the piano sounds ever-so-slightly out of tune with an orchestra.) So, too, the architect will be conscious of the slight entasis, or bulging, of classical columns which other persons may only see as cylindrical or slightly tapered. And the painter will note minute differences in colors that the layman will call identical. The artist may, then, have an unusual refinement of some one of his senses.

The artist is also more observant and curious than the rest of us. He not only *can* discriminate, but he *does*. The painter may repeatedly observe his subject or his model under various conditions of lighting at various times of day and with changes in weather. And he may be curious, too, about the absorption and reflection of light, the effect of haze and distance, and so on. The novelist may endlessly watch people, study their postures, their expressions, their conversation, and speculate upon the motives for their actions. And so, too, artists of other sorts may actually use their superior capacity to discriminate, by a more than usual observation of the passing show, about which they are more curious than is common humanity.

A *second pair* of characteristics: the artist or inventor has a more active imagination than most men and the capacity to hold on to and work with images.

The artist is gifted with an especially active imagination. We all dream dreams, of course, and get ideas; we all occasionally have unusual insights as tidbits of past experience piece themselves together in our minds in new and at times amazing combinations. The kaleidoscope of the imagination is in some strange way related to the subconscious. We don't know just how it works, nor do we have much control of it. Its activity may be related to the inhibition or frustration of our basic drives, to deeply hidden fears or anxieties or complexes, to escape mechanisms and compensatory urges. Was Sir Christopher Wren's love of classical forms and orderliness an unconscious revolt against the noisy clutter and confusion of Restoration London? Was Michelangelo somehow impelled by his own ugliness to imagine the idealized beauty of his works of sculpture? Was Shakespeare driven somehow by his own frustrations to conceive characters of such depth and passion? We do not know how or why, but it would seem that artists have more active imaginations than usual. They piece together, in strange and new combinations, the richer observations made possible to them because of their keener sensory systems.

All persons are potential artists: we dream dreams, we are conscious of rare insights, we conceive new thoughts or tunes or forms. But the artist does something about it. He has the rare capacity for holding on to these otherwise fleeting images. He may be able to bring them into focus, fixing them, manipulating them, going to work upon them. Sometimes he can revive these images at another time for further contemplation. Often he takes a pencil and proceeds to make verbal or musical or choreographic or graphic or architectural notes so as to record the images for future use. We all dream dreams, but the artist awakes from his dream and goes to work upon it. This is what is meant by 'being creative': this capacity to make something of the unusual imaginings that are based upon the richer observations made possible to the artist because of his keener sensations.

A *third pair* of characteristics: the artist or inventor has special knowledge of his field and the technical skills necessary to do creative work in it.

The artist is not necessarily a scholar in the history and criticism of his particular art, but he is usually alert to the creative work of his fellow artists and often has an intimate knowledge of many of the masterpieces of his art. Sometimes this knowledge is acquired through formal study in colleges, art schools, conservatories. Just as often it is the result of self-education. The Renaissance painters often sketched each other's work as part of their training. The poets have often written in conscious imitation of favorites among their predecessors. Musicians have often created compositions in the style of earlier works. Whether he is taught or learns without formal instruction, the creative artist must also develop a formidable body of technical knowledge. In the past, painters have studied the composition of pigments, oils, and fabrics, human anatomy and the laws of perspective. Composers have studied harmony and counterpoint, musical form and orchestration. Writers have studied literary form and structure, versification and style, philosophy and psychology, as well as the social and historical backgrounds for particular undertakings. Such special knowledge for one or more of the art fields certainly distinguishes the creative artist from the rest of us.

But the artist is also characterized by his specific technical skill. The painter not only knows about the grinding and mixing of paints, he has developed skills in drawing and painting. Like his more sensitive eye, the artist's more sensitive hand is one of his gifts, but much of his technique is a matter of training and practice. Each of the arts makes its own special demands: the modeling and chiseling skills of the sculptor, the space planning and drafting skills of the architect, the inventive and developmental skills of the composer, the plotting and characterizing and narrative and stylistic skills of the novelist, and so on. This is not merely knowledge; it is know-how based upon knowledge. Without specific technical skill the artist could not be an artist at all. But there is still something more that will be necessary if he is to do creative work.

The *fourth pair* of characteristics: the artist or inventor has a greater abundance of energy and greater control of it than most people.

It takes energy beyond the ordinary demands for daily living to carry through many of the creative projects that artists undertake. The artist may have stronger basic drives than others, and therefore greater creative compulsions. The architect may work long hours over a drafting board; the sculptor may work with mallet and chisel high on a scaffold in strained position; the painter may work for days upon a few square inches of a large canvas; the dancer will work to the point of exhaustion upon a single complex pattern of movement; the mere labor of writing a 1000 page novel! the hours of orchestration that may be involved in one minute of music! the weeks of practicing six or eight hours a day to master one movement of a violin concerto! The old joke about inspiration being nine-tenths perspiration is truer than the new joke about 'the vaporizings of half-baked lazy people.' For it takes superabundant energy, whether the accompaniment of health or illness, to work out our dreams and to imprison them (to use George Jean Nathan's phrase) in tangible form. Perhaps the creative artist has more of what it takes to do this.

The artist not only has this additional energy but he may have more control of it than most people. For he must not only have the energy to do the vast amount of work entailed in the creation of many works of art, he must be able to direct his energies to that end. It is to be wondered at that there are not more *un*finished symphonies, epic fragments, uncompleted novels, and architectural projects. It takes a sort of will power and persistence and stick-to-it-iveness beyond that of most people to carry through such painstaking undertakings. The writer often works against a deadline to complete a certain work by a certain time. So, too, with other artists. It is true that they may actually do their most *creative* thinking in uncontrolled bursts of energetic work, the *furor poeticus* or poetic frenzy of which much is said; but art works of any scope—not a song perhaps but a symphony, not a short lyric perhaps but a long narrative, not a water color but a fresco—demand sustained effort and willful carry-through.

Let us summarize, then, these four pairs of characteristics: *first,* a creative artist is a person of unusual sensory refinement who is actually more observant than most of us; *second,* he is gifted with an active imagination and the ability to hold and work with his images and insights; *third,* he has a special knowledge of his art field and a developed skill in its specific techniques; and *fourth,* he has an abundance of physical and nervous energy and the ability to control its expenditure.

In brief, the artist is characteristically observant, imaginative, skilled, and dynamic. And so, remember, is the creative scientist and the creative statesman and the creative scholar. And so, for that matter and in some measure, may we all be.

2. *Michelangelo as a creative artist*

To illustrate these characteristics of the creative artist, we may cite the personality of Michelangelo Buonarroti—Michelangelo, as we call him. He lived in Italy at the height of the Renaissance. He was a youth of seventeen when Columbus discovered America; he died at the age of eighty-nine in the year of Shakespeare's birth. In his time, young men turned their hands to a variety of activities, so he was not unique in his many-sided development. He not only wrote more than usually good poetry, but he was something of a scientist and inventor. He not only designed the uniforms worn by the Swiss Guards of the Vatican, but he was the architect who redesigned the great dome of St. Peter's Cathedral. He not only carved the heroic statues for the de Medici tombs, but he was also at one time the military engineer concerned with the fortifications of the city of Florence and later of Rome. Although he thought of himself as a sculptor first of all, his most famous work is the vast fresco painting that covers the vaulted ceiling of the Sistine Chapel.

It was Bramante, his long-time rival, who is thought to have connived enviously to have Pope Julius order Michelangelo to paint the vault of the Sistine chapel, expecting that Michelangelo, essentially a sculptor, would fail and be discredited. Raphael then was to take over and carry the day. Michelangelo didn't want to undertake the project, for he realized his limited experience in color; besides, he was at work upon sculpture for the Pope's tomb. But the Pope ordered him to proceed. The chapel, which is 132 feet long by 45 feet wide, was to have been decorated with frescos of the twelve apostles, but Michelangelo persuaded Pope Julius to give him a free hand.

So he began his plans for the expressive and decorative treatment of the entire vaulted ceiling of the chapel, an area of some ten thousand square feet. He drew his subjects from *Genesis,* depicting a series of nine biblical scenes along the center of the ceiling, including the Creation of Adam and the Temptation and Expulsion. Around the lower edge of the ceiling he planned a series of twelve prophets and sibyls, with David and Goliath and other Old Testament scenes in the four corners. In spaces surrounding the biblical scenes he composed expressive nude figures. In all there are some 300 figures of great variety.

Troubles beset him from the start. The scaffolding erected by Bramante would have left unsightly holes in the ceiling, so it had to be completely redesigned. As Michelangelo's early biographer Ascanio Condivi reports, his frescos began to grow mouldy and again he tried to quit. The Pope came frequently to observe the work, climbed the scaffolding with advice and impatience. At one time he pulled away protective cloth so as to peek at fresh work, and broke away a great section of plaster. When all was at last going well and half the work done, Raphael tried to have Michelangelo put aside so that he himself might finish the work—and claim the credit for it. But Michelangelo forestalled this attempt and within four years (1508-1512) completed the frescos—or almost completed them, for the Pope prematurely ordered the scaffolding removed so as to show off the magnificent work, and Michelangelo refused to put it back so as to add the final touches of gold and ultramarine that he had earlier intended.

The mere labor was tremendous. George Vasari relates that "he worked with great inconvenience to himself, having to labor with his face turned upwards, and impaired his eyesight so much in the progress of his work that he could neither read letters nor examine drawings for several months afterwards except in the same attitude of looking upwards." Michelangelo himself wrote:

I've grown a goiter by dwelling in this den—
As cats from stagnant streams in Lombardy,
Or in what other land they hap to be—
Which drives the belly close beneath the chin;
My beard turns up to heaven; my nape falls in,
Fixed on my spine: my breast-bone visibly
Grows like a harp: a rich embroidery
Bedews my face from brush-drops thick and thin.
My loins into my paunch like levers grind:
My buttock like a crupper bears my weight;
My feet unguided wander to and fro;
In front my skin grows loose and long; behind,
By bending it becomes more taut and strait;
Crosswise I strain me like a Syrian bow:
Whence false and quaint, I know,
Must be the fruit of squinting brain and eye;
For ill can aim the gun that bends awry.
Come then, Giovanni, try
To succor my dead pictures and my fame,
Since foul I fare and painting is my shame.

A very different record of Michelangelo's creative activity remains in the small sketches that he made prior to drafting the full size cartoons from which outlines were traced directly on the wet plaster. Here reproduced are the sketches, now in the Metropolitan Museum of Art, that he made for the *Libyan Sibyl*, showing his skill as a draftsman and his interest in human anatomy. Sketches for other figures are preserved in the Cleveland Museum of Art and at Oxford University.

As you study the *Libyan Sibyl* as here represented, bear in mind that the original is but part of a vast system of frescos, that this one figure is some eighteen feet high, and that it is in color. . . .

Now with the *Libyan Sibyl* in mind and the painstaking activity that produced it, let us consider Michelangelo as a creative artist. You will recall the four pairs of characteristics.

First, he seems to have been unusually discriminating and observant. As a youthful apprentice set to copying a master's painting, he went down to the market to study real fish and astonished others with the miracle of his realism. You perhaps noted the result of his close observations of the big toe under various degrees of strain and thrust.

Second, Michelangelo was unusually imaginative. In this one fig-

photo by Braun

Michelangelo, LIBYAN SIBYL, Sistine Chapel, Vatican

Courtesy Metropolitan Museum of Art

Michelangelo, SKETCHES for the LIBYAN SIBYL, Metropolitan Museum of Art, New York

ure of the *Libyan Sibyl*, with its strange but not unnatural posture, you may have seen evidence of his imaginative power and the way he went to work upon the vision of this expressive beauty. You may perhaps gain some feeling for this by projecting yourself imaginatively into the posture and suggested activity of the figure.

Third, Michelangelo was a man of unusual knowledge and technical skill. As a sculptor he studied human anatomy by sketching models and classic statues and by dissection in his own laboratory. Benvenuto Cellini said of him "all that he knows of painting he derived from the carefully studied methods of sculpture." Michelangelo himself said, "That work of painting will be most noble and excellent which copies the noblest object and does so with delicacy and skill. And who is so barbarous as not to understand that the foot of a man is nobler than his shoe, and his skin nobler than that of the sheep with which he is clothed . . .?" His knowledge of human forms he already had when he went to work upon this fresco; his technical skills in wall painting he had to develop.

Fourth, Michelangelo also was a man of great energy and control. It is a matter of record that he had the physical energy necessary to carry on this work almost singlehanded and the will to bring it to triumphant completion.

3. Sources of the artist's materials

Where do artists get the ideas that they give expression to in their works of art? How do they think up all those things? What is the source of their materials?

It is sometimes said that the poet writes out of his head. That ambiguous explanation suggests some measure of truth. We shall consider part of the answer in the next section. Now we shall be concerned with how the artist's material gets into his head.

We have already noted the artist's keen sensory system and discriminating observations. It is from the world of his experience that the artist derives his primary materials. The painter, for instance, is constantly observing the appearance of things, thinking about their forms and relations, noting the effects of light and shade. This steady stream of visual perceptions and thoughts about them is stored for future use. Rummaging about in the storehouse of the unconscious, the imagination pieces together new and sometimes amazing creations. So Michelangelo drew upon his funded knowledge of church doctrine and Old Testament, of human anatomy and expressive posture.

Let us turn to another work of art as an illustration of the way an artist derives his materials from a wide range of experiences.

GRAVE IN THE FOOTHILLS
by *Celeste Turner Wright*

Time is no longer measured by the pipe
Smoked nor the gravel washed; here on the bluff
Thistle and oat have seeded round the rough
Headstone for eighty summers, prototype
Of everlastingness. You are forgot
And your stage properties avail you not,
The ring, the letter, and the Bible page
They buried with you. Chisellings record
You were turned thirty. Even at that age
The fitful weaver oftentimes grows bored
And mars her handiwork; before the gray
Entered her woof you somehow came to stay
Here on the hill. Was there an accident,
Dredging for gold? A robber in your tent?
Or did the typhus burn your life away
After a year or so of banishment
Far from the appletrees and brooks of Maine?

Quiet and drained of youness, here you lie;
And every winter spatters down its rain,
Soaking your private earth. Today the sky
Blazes with heat. The burnished aeroplane
Might scoop below you—for the bluff is high—
Down to the sand bar in the choking stream.

Do you remember in your endless dream
The buttercups; the Jerseys in the pond,
Swishing the waterlilies; and beyond,
The snug, brown-weathered farmhouse half concealed
Against the woodshed and the swallow barn?
There was a boulder in your father's field;
The plowshare veered around it. Winding yarn,
Your mother bade you take the lard-pail lunch
And new McGuffey's reader off to school;
Perhaps you dared the scholars' ridicule,
Honoring teacher with a Mayday bunch
Of violets, cushioned in moss and cool.

Such was the homeland, such the kindly nurse;
But you were centre of a universe,
A gliding harmony of joint and thew;

The self who rose and breakfasted with you,
He was the human norm and he was fate;
Others were all excluded from that gate;
You held out your protesting arms in youth,
But friends drew hardly nearer to the truth
Than I who come a century too late,
I who can see no glimmer of a fact,
The shape of thumbnail or the nick of tooth.

Vainly all mortal kindred have attacked
Separateness they never may compound;
Many have stood like me beside a mound
Lamenting with the ever-clumsy tongue
The barriers on which our souls are flung,
Pressing like salmon to the spawning ground.

Now it is blowing cooler from the south.
Here on the hilltop did you once behold
The sunset like a trumpet's golden mouth?
Glory is liquid round us, and the old
Terror subsides. Audacious overtones
Call from the wind: it does not yet appear
What we shall be within the common sphere
When death has purged the ego from our bones.

(1947)

You may do well to reread this poem a time or two before proceeding to the following consideration of the sources of the artist's materials. . . .

In answer to inquiry about the genesis of this recent poem, the poet was able to supply an amazingly complete account of the creative activity involved in its composition: "One summer I camped overnight in Tahoe National Forest. My friends and I visited Michigan Bluff, now almost a ghost town. Under a rather good stone in the weedy cemetery lay Seth Clark, a Maine man who died in Michigan Bluff in 1864. I was from Maine myself, and Seth Clark happened to be my age when he died. How should we have liked each other?" That night, lonely and restless, the poet wrote "a long stream-of-consciousness thing about Michigan Bluff" and a few days later she wrote "a sonnet on some Chinese graves on the hillside." Two or three years later, in a lonely cabin near her husband's air base, she "began working out the poem, mostly in blank verse." She was annoyed that in two days so little had resulted. The next spring, she "suddenly completed 'Grave' at top speed, practically all in one evening. . . . There was little revision after that.

"The source of each image is clear to me," the poet reports. "Dutchmen in *Hans Brinker*, which I read as a child, measured time by the pipe. Thistle and oat were chosen from a University of California publication on weeds—because they date a long way back. 'Eighty summers' was figured out to permit my hero to use McGuffey, whose readers I learned about in a novel that once ran in *The Youth's Companion*. 'Stage properties' occurred to me while I was a dramatics coach at Davis. Our daily life is full of stage properties. . . . 'Fitful weaver' is probably from Shakespeare's 'fitful fever' [*Macbeth*, III, ii, 23]! Of course the Three Fates were in my high-school Virgil or in Milton's 'blind Fury,' [from *Lycidas*]. Speaking of Milton, the rhyme scheme resembles that of 'Lycidas,' a poem I've always adored, though my idea was simply to rhyme any two or three lines that were conveniently handled in that way. . . Rereading 'Lycidas,' I'm sure that Milton colored a great deal of what I wrote.

"Typhus struck me as an important disease because I'd been reading *Rats, Lice, and History*. A Cal Tech. man at Michigan Bluff pointed out the danger of accidents because of the stupid way the shafts had been sunk.

"The pictures of Maine farming," she goes on, "are all from my grandfather's farm at North Brewer. Elsewhere in Maine (at Kineo) I attended a one-room schoolhouse, knitted sweaters, hung maybaskets, took my lunch in a lardpail. . . .

"The soaked earth is from a basement room in Giannini Hall, Berkeley, whence I, editing, could see the rain spattering into the lawn above my head. . . . The aeroplane was originally a glider, which I pictured in noticing the height of the bluff; at the same period, I often watched aeroplanes during my sunbaths at the Davis swimming pool. The sandbar is imaginary, added to the American River to suggest dryness.

"The 'center of a universe,' the 'human norm,' the ideas on separateness, come from Thomas Mann (the Joseph series), Werfel (*The Forty Days of Musa Dagh*), and Thomas Wolfe (*Look Homeward, Angel*). . . . My two thumbnails are strangely different; I have a nicked tooth in front . . . I've seen salmon in the newsreels . . . In childhood I stood on a hillside in Maine, looking at a golden sunset and remembering the angels, with their trumpets, stamped in gilt on the cover of my *Pilgrim's Progress*. 'It doth not yet appear what we shall be' is from the Bible [1 John 3:2]. . . .

"Several lines of the poem are from a notebook I've long kept—bits I've composed at random, to be included somewhere, sometime. The last line of all is an example."

Such, then, is the poet's own account of the composition of this poem. It is an unusual record of the concrete sources, particular bits of experience that were transmuted by the imagination in the creative activity of writing a poem. To the inevitable question, 'Was the poet fully conscious of the source of each image and phrase as she wrote?' the answer is certainly 'No.' The writing was one thing; the critical analysis came later. With this report of the way the poet drew upon her fund of past experiences, you may wish to reread the poem for further insight into the creative process. . . .

4. *The creative process*

The process of creative activity is by no means exactly the same in all cases. Different arts seem to call for different creative processes; artists are quite individual in their modes of work; the same artist will vary his procedure. Yet, even as with the creative process in the biological world, four general steps may be observed. However, all of these stages in the creative activity are not always easily seen, and sometimes two of them seem merged into one.

The *first step* is the artist's receiving some sort of *initial stimulus*. Often this is a stimulus from the outer world. Such a statement may seem to contradict the suggestion earlier made that the artist's inner drives serve as his creative compulsion. The outer stimulus, however, may do no more than touch the trigger or otherwise occasion the creative response. The composer may be commissioned to write an overture; the artist may be engaged to paint a portrait; the writer may be under contract to write two more novels; the architect is usually employed to design a building. You will recall that Michelangelo was ordered by Pope Julius to decorate the Sistine Chapel.

Or the artist may simply be receptive to some offer or suggestion: competitions are announced, awards offered, exhibitions opened for entry; or 'We could use the extra money, Henry, if you were to sell a story.' Or some especially poignant life experience suggests the poem: some tragic or comic incident or real-life tangle next door inspires the scene for a play; the observation of unusual forms or patterns of light will start the painter's sketching. For Celeste T. Wright the visit to a ghost-town cemetery was the outer stimulus for writing *Grave in the Foothills*.

But sometimes the artist supplies his own stimulus. We said earlier that the artist may have stronger basic drives than others and therefore greater creative compulsions. It would be hard to say what one or combination of these basic drives motivates the artist at any time. The desire to win the favor of his beloved, the need for money to buy food or clothes, the inner demand for social recognition, the accumulation of bodily tensions or the mere exuberance of energy or the sex drive may serve as the stimulus to get the artist started in the process of creating a work of art.

The *second step,* a response to the stimulus, is the *conception of the creative idea.* Sometimes this will flash at once into the artist's mind. He may inexplicably 'see' the painting, full-blown, in his imagination. He may 'hear' the lines of his poem in his mind's-ear ready to write down. More often, however, there will be a delayed response to the outward stimulus. The idea for *Grave in the Foothills* didn't come to the poet for two or three years after the experience in the cemetery.

The artist may simply find himself in a creative mood as a result of his experience. This creative attitude, or readiness to respond to a creative idea when it comes, may last for some time. The painter may simply be open to ideas, or he may await other outward stimuli to urge him on. The writer may engage in exploratory activity, hunting a subject. The architect will doubtless go to work, assembling and analyzing various data. But whether at once or after some considerable time, the response does come; the artist somehow gets hold of a germinal idea. It may be only a stray notion, vague and fleeting. Or it may be a vivid imaginative creation, ready to be set down. Artists' inspirations are, indeed, indescribable mysteries, and we do not know just how or when, after rejecting the twelve apostles as a subject, Michelangelo was first possessed by the creative idea for the chapel ceiling.

The *third step* in the process is the *development* of the germinal idea. After the artist first conceives the work of art in his imagination, he may go to work at once and develop his conception during the process of the actual making of the finished work—the fourth step that will be described next. But this is not usual in the creative process. The artist is more likely to engage in a great deal of developmental activity. The architect, once the scheme for the building comes to him, will sketch various possible plot plans, floor plans, and elevations, and engage in structural research. The sculptor, now possessed of his creative idea, proceeds to graphic or plastic sketching, often from a model. The painter, as we have observed of Michelangelo, also studies and sketches. The choreographer may carry on research in folk music and primitive culture, sketch out possible dance patterns, and engage in experimental creative activity. After he has conceived his dramatic idea, the playwright, the novelist, or poet may spend months in background research, plotting his action and developing his characters. We have noted the developmental work reported by Celeste T. Wright in the process of writing *Grave in the Foothills*—her mulling over the idea, her labored composition of an early version. So too with the composer, whose thematic and other musical ideas will require structural development and often research or experimental work with instruments.

It is in this stage of his work that the artist will make more or less conscious use of his art theory. His generalized notions about what a work of art may do or should do may take the form of 'art principles.' He may have discovered these principles from his own observation of art things, or he may have been taught them in school or by his individual teacher. Sometimes the precepts of a great artist-teacher become the dogma for a succeeding generation of artists. So the definitions and laws of classic beauty set forth by Alberti in 1452 dominated architects for several centuries in the development of their conceptions. And Louis Sullivan's 'Form follows function' has become one of the architectural 'laws' of our times. Although the arbitrary rules of the various academies, conservatories, and schools may control the creative activity of generations of artists, there are always revolutionary forces at work. Some individual artists break with tradition, defy the arbitrary rules—and then proceed to formulate their own rules.

It is during his developmental work, then, that the artist makes more or less conscious use of his art theory, whatever it may be. He may believe that form is all-important or that it is the meaning that counts. He may believe that art should be essentially abstract or that photographic naturalism is the highest goal. He may disapprove of dissonance, or he may believe that the older harmonies are intolerably tame. He may feel that art should be enigmatic, not meaningless but puzzling, or he may hold that clarity and communication of meaning are essential.

However different the art theories may be that guide the artist's development of his creative idea, he is likely to have some deep underlying feelings about human responses to art things. Without giving them articulate expression, he may have some general notions about the work of art which he is in process of creating. He will probably want it to engage and hold the *attention* of other persons—observers or auditors. To do this, he may feel that it must seem to him (and so also, he hopes, to them) to have some sort of *unity;* that is, it must seem to have separateness from other things, and the parts of which it is made up must seem to have a certain relationship. But the work must also seem to him (and he hopes to others) to have some sort of *variety* amongst the parts of which it is made up. The

artist may feel that the work of art must not upset the observer's
sense of *balance,* but that it must at the same time bring his attention
into focus at some *center of interest.* He may also feel that the various
parts of it must seem to be in *harmony* one with the other, but that
there must be sufficient *contrast* to sharpen his attention. He may
feel that the parts may well be so related as to control the *movement*
of the observer's attention, or that their relation should induce a feeling of *rhythm.* He may feel that the parts must clearly be in some
over-all *order,* but that there should be sufficient *complexity* to demand the observer's closer scrutiny. He may feel that the work should
have a general *theme,* but that it should be enigmatic enough to challenge the observer's interest. These *static and dynamic principles*
whether phrased in this way or not phrased at all, may be present in
the artist's mind during the development of his creative idea.

It is apparent from her account that Celeste T. Wright was conscious of certain matters of poetic theory and tradition while writing
Grave in the Foothills. She recognized that she was writing an elegy
and that the manner and music of Milton's *Lycidas* would be appropriate—the iambic pentameter verses run-on and rimed freely, the
fresh outdoor images and atmosphere, the meditative mood. Her report does not indicate the extent to which she consciously organized
her thoughts; but the clarity of its opening image 'here on the bluff,'
the sequence of her reflections, and the closing 'sunset like a trumpet's
golden mouth' are doubtless the result of her ordered thinking in the
process of development.

Michelangelo's art theory is to be studied in part through his letters. In his opinion "painting should be considered excellent in proportion as it approaches the effect of relief [sculpture]." He believed
strongly in symmetry and balance as principles, and said that "architectural members ought to follow the same rule as members of the
human body. He that has not mastered, or does not master, the
human figure, and especially its anatomy, can never comprehend it."
He is reported to have said, "What one must most toil and labor
with hard work and study to attain in painting is that, after much
labor spent on it, it should seem to have been done almost rapidly and
with no labor at all." We can see in the *Libyan Sibyl* evidences of
Michelangelo's sculptural principle for painting, of his sense of bodily
balance, and his belief that the final result must seem deceptively
easy.

So much, then, regarding the developmental stage in the creative
process.

The *fourth step* in the creative process is the *execution* of the work of art, the actual making of the work of art as the germinal idea is finally developed. Often, the developmental work keeps right on after the final execution of the work begins. The architect begins the final execution of the plans for the structure he has designed, but he is still changing things as he works, further developing his creative ideas. The sculptor begins to execute in marble the statue that he has given detailed development in modeling clay. The painter after many preliminary sketches and studies undertakes the final execution of his painting, sometimes carrying it through in a single sitting, sometimes laboring upon it for years. The hour comes when the dancer performs before an audience what has been so painstakingly developed through hours of study and rehearsal. The novelist or playwright types off his final draft and finishes his creative work. The composer inks in his completed score and copies the parts. For him and for the playwright the essential execution of their creative works, however, remains incomplete, as with the dancer, until the necessary interpretative artists rehearse and perform them before an audience. But of this interpretative performance something will be said in a later chapter.

You will recall that finally *Grave in the Foothills* was suddenly written through 'at top speed, practically all in one evening,' and that Michelangelo finally transferred the full-scale cartoon to a section of fresh plaster, working rapidly before the wall dried.

5. Cellini's creation of 'Perseus'

It is difficult to study the artist at work, for he may not himself realize what outward event started him off upon his work; he may not recall just when or in what form the germinal idea struck him; he may have been engaged upon other projects while much of the developmental work was under way; he may have left no record of the activity involved in the final execution of the work of art. For certain works of art, like the *Grave in the Foothills,* the data are available for studying the creative process. Another of these is Benvenuto Cellini's statue of *Perseus and Medusa.*

Benvenuto Cellini (1500-1571) was born at the height of the Italian Renaissance, the son of a musician and maker of musical instruments in Florence. The boy Benvenuto became an accomplished flute player and was later appointed one of the Pope's court musicians. But during his teens he developed an interest in sculpture, studied the work of Michelangelo, and became a goldsmith and seal cutter. He designed medals, set jewels, and created works of small sculpture. It was his skill as a goldsmith that attracted Michelangelo's attention and won his friendship. In 1545 Cosimo de Medici, the Duke of Florence, asked Cellini to make him a statue of Perseus, something that had long been in the Duke's mind.

Perseus, you may recall, was the son of Danae by Zeus himself. Because it was prophesied that the child would grow up to kill his grandfather Acrisius, Danae and Perseus were set adrift in a chest. They arrived finally at the island of Seriphos where Polydectes fell in love with Danae. She rejected his affection, but Polydectes persisted, and Perseus grew to young manhood. To get Perseus out of the way, Polydectes sent him on a dangerous adventure to obtain the head of the snake-haired gorgon Medusa, one sight of whose face would turn a man to stone! But the gods helped Perseus: Pluto lent him a magic helmet to render him invisible; Hermes (Mercury), wings for his feet; Athena, a mirror so that he need not look directly at the gorgon. With this help he safely slew Medusa and beheaded her without looking at her face. In later adventures the head was useful, turning a monster to stone, petrifying a rival for the hand of Andromeda, transforming Atlas into a mountain. Later, however, Perseus killed his grandfather by accidental discus throw, but refused to benefit by his death. Perses, his son, became ruler of the Persians, whence their name! So much for the Perseus of Greek myth in whom the Duke was interested.

So Cellini set to work and within a few weeks completed a model, as he describes it, "made of yellow wax, about a cubit [18 inches] in height." The model, here reproduced, still survives in Florence. The Duke was so pleased that he asked Cellini "to carry out this little model on a large scale."

The record of this creative activity, as well as his various adventures, is to be found in the latter third of Cellini's famous *Autobiography,* where you may read about his besetting problems and the slow progress in his work. The patronage of the Duke wavered; a jealous rival intrigued against him; he needed and couldn't get enough skilled help. Then there were technical problems and other creative demands upon his time.

Working at first in a basement with one of his little apprentices, Cencio, "a very handsome lad," as a model, he began his large statue. He describes elsewhere (in a letter to Benedetto Varchi) some of his art theories, for instance that "a statue has eight views and they must be equally good." And he describes his method of studying "the effects of foreshortening" by taking "a well-formed young man" as a model and, using a lamp, projecting his shadow upon the whitewashed wall of his studio, sketching the outline in a variety of "the most beautiful and natural postures," adding "a few lines that were

photo by Alinari

Cellini, PERSEUS AND MEDUSA. Loggia dei Lanzi, Florence

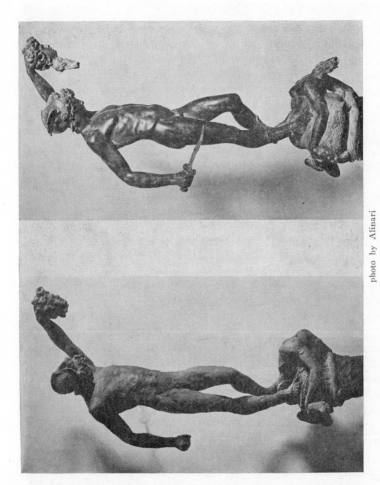

Cellini, WAX AND BRONZE MODELS for the PERSEUS, National Museum, Florence

not visible in the shadow, for some details are always concealed in the thickness of the arm at the elbow, near the shoulders, both under and over, and on the head, and in various points of the torso, legs, and hands."

As he records in his *Autobiography*, he abandoned his first plan to make the statue in gesso (or plaster) and then cast it in bronze. Instead, he made a framework of iron, then laid on clay, modeled to within a half inch of the ultimate size of the more than life-size figure. After baking the clay, he "spread wax on the top, modeling this with the utmost care."

First he completed and cast the headless figure of Medusa, above which the triumphant Perseus stands holding her head. Finally the figure of Perseus was complete and ready, six cubits (about nine feet) high.

Cellini describes in detail how he made a 'tunic' of clay about the wax-on-clay figure. Then he built up a brick furnace about it, and baked the mould and melted away the wax between it and the inner clay core. Then he sank the mould and core into a deep pit. He built another furnace to melt the metal, the "pigs of copper and pieces of bronze," that was to flow through tile conduits into the mould.

Cellini recounts the actual casting with a sense of high drama. Pine resin and "the well-contrived draught of the furnace" made a terrific heat, necessary to melt the metal. Then the shop roof caught on fire—wind and rain blew in and began to cool the furnace—Cellini himself was overcome with fever and fatigue—his assistants had to go after more wood—then the fire on the roof required their attention again—the metal began to melt, the lid of the furnace blew off with a great noise, the bronze began to flow, but too slowly—in that desperate moment he called for all the household pewter, dishes and porringers and plates, to speed the flow of molten metal. "In an instant my mould filled up; and I knelt down and thanked God with all my heart; then turned to a plate of salad lying on a bench there, and with splendid appetite ate and drank, and all my gang of men along with me."

After two days he removed the mould, and his work, except for some minor repairs and surface detail, was finished. The statue with elaborate pedestal containing a bas relief of Perseus and Andromeda was completed in 1554 some nine years after its beginning.

There is no need to comment in detail upon the four steps in the creative process as here exemplified. The Duke, of course, supplied the outer stimulus. There is no record of the second step, the conception of the creative idea; he simply 'set to the task with great good will.' His developmental work upon the small model and his sketching and modeling the clay heroic figure are clearly a third step, and the dramatic casting of the *Perseus* a fourth.

It may be of interest, however, to re-examine the statue considering the significance of the posture and of the accessory details in relation to the mythological sources of Cellini's materials. Why is Medusa's head held high and facing out? What is the nature of its locks? What is peculiar about Perseus' helmet? Why does he look down? How does the statue differ from the model in this regard? Why is Perseus represented as so powerful in physique? What is the meaning of the posture of his left foot? What is bound to his heels? What issues from the Medusa's neck?! . . .

It may be of further interest to you to consider Benvenuto Cellini and his activity in the light of the characteristics of the creative artist.

6. *'The Mastersingers'* as a final example

Richard Wagner's comic grand opera *Die Meistersinger von Nurnberg*, or *The Mastersingers* as we shall call it, will serve as a final illustration for this chapter on 'Primary Creative Activity,' because (as with *Perseus*) we are fortunate in knowing a great deal about the history of its composition. But before discussing the activity that created it, let us experience this work of art. Without an actual performance of the full opera, not from records but in the theater, *The Mastersingers* can only be represented in a fragmentary way. But in this case, perhaps, half measures are better than none.

First, the well-known *Overture* or Prelude which anticipates the musical themes to be developed throughout the work. This can be effectively studied by means of a recording. Several such are readily available. The following notation may be of help, fixing in mind the important themes upon which it is built.

Thematic Notes for the

OVERTURE to THE MASTERSINGERS

by *Richard Wagner*

The story of Wagner's libretto is briefly this:

Young Walter (Walther von Stolzing), a Franconian knight, falls in love at first sight with Eva, daughter of old Pogner, who is a member of the Nuremburg guild of mastersingers. But Pogner has decided to give his daughter in marriage as a prize to whatever mastersinger shall win the forthcoming contest. Walter, discovering this condition, presents himself as a candidate to become a mastersinger. His song follows his inspiration rather than the complicated guild rules of composition; and Beckmesser, the marker, covers his board with marks against the song. Despite the appeals of Hans Sachs, the cobbler-poet, on his behalf, Walter is voted down.

In the second act, Eva learns of the failure of Walter to gain admission to the guild. She and Walter then plan to elope, but are prevented by the arrival of Beckmesser who has come to serenade Eva, whom he would woo and win as the prize. Hans Sachs, who guesses that Eva is in love with Walter, disconcerts the elderly and jealous Beckmesser by serving as *his* marker during the serenade and raps out his criticisms on the cobbler's last. The street brawl that ensues is ended by the approach of the night watchman. Eva goes home with her father; the cobbler pulls Walter into his shop to prevent more trouble.

Next morning Walter comes downstairs having had a wonderful dream. Hans Sachs encourages him to make a master-song of it. Walter, at first contemptuous of the guild rules, allows the cobbler to help him, and to write it down. But Beckmesser, finding the music, accuses Hans Sachs of intending to enter the contest. The cobbler insists not and gives the music to Beckmesser. At the contest

Beckmesser does his miserable best to sing the song, but is laughed to scorn for his effort. He goes off in a rage, saying that anyway *he* didn't write the song but that Hans Sachs did! The cobbler says, No, he didn't write it either, but it's a good song if well sung. Walter comes forward to sing *The Prize Song*! The mastersingers are won over by it; they proclaim him a master and winner of the contest— and of Eva.

The Prize Song, which Walter thus sings at the climax of this music drama, is also readily available as a recording, one by Lauritz Melchior. The musical notation for the melody line is here given with an English translation of Wagner's German lyric. You may wish to follow it while listening to the recording.

THE PRIZE SONG

from 'The Mastersingers'

by *Richard Wagner*

Morn-ing was gleaming with ro - - - - seate light, the air was filled with scent dis-tilled, where beauty beam - - - ing, past all dreaming, a garden did in - - - -vite. Wherein, beneath a wondrous tree, with fruit superb - ly la - - den, in blissful love-dream I could see the rare and ten - - der maid - en, whose charms, be-yond all price, entranced my heart— E - - va, in Pa - ra - - dise! Eve-ning was dark - ling and night closed a - - round. By rugged way my feet did

A good bit is known about Wagner's composition of *The Master-singers*, which was first thought out and a first sketch written in 1845, when he was 32 years old. But he did not actually begin to write the libretto or book itself until the end of 1861; he completed it before the end of January, 1862, in thirty days of intensive work. The musical score was not completed until 1867; and the first performance was not given until 1868, almost a quarter of a century after the idea for the opera first struck him.

The story of *The Mastersingers*, which we summarized at some length, bears an important relation to Wagner's own life. Some would say that the character of Walter is indeed Wagner himself. However, as Henderson says, "This is not justified by anything in the work or in the other writings of its creator. Nevertheless we have ground, and the support of Wagner, for the assumption that he really designed Walter to represent the spirit of progress in music, while the masters embodied that of pure pedantry. These two powers have always been at war in the world of art and always will be." But, if Walter is by no means Wagner personally, the bitterness that Wagner felt at the unfriendly reception of his operas was very great. Tovey says, "Wagner ingeniously made poetry and drama out of an explicit manifesto to musical critics." And the critics recognized it as such. On one occasion before the music of *The Mastersingers* was complete, he read the libretto aloud to a group of persons including 'the dangerous critic,' Dr. Hanslick, who took it as a lampoon aimed directly at himself and left in a huff before the reading was finished. Musicians, too, sharply criticized Wagner's work, while recognizing that here and there it contained some good things. Schumann went so far as to write, "It is the empty and unpleasing music of an amateur!" But *The Mastersingers* is not merely the defiant outburst of a revolutionary. Wagner was, indeed, active in the political revolution of 1849; but his music-dramas also broke with operatic tradition. However, like Walter, Wagner did learn from the mastersingers who had preceded him, from Weber and from Beethoven; and his musical inspirations were truly shaped by his vast and exacting musical knowledge.

Let us conclude this consideration and the chapter as well by a more detailed study of the four steps in the creative process of Wagner's composition of *The Mastersingers*.

First, the outward stimulus for Wagner's work came (he wrote in a pamphlet published in 1851) "from the advice of well-meaning friends who wished me to write an opera in a 'lighter style,' because this, they said, would procure my admission to the German theatres, and thus insure that success for the continual want of which my outward circumstances had been seriously threatened."

Second, the germinal idea came to him during the summer of 1845, while he was on a much-needed vacation at Marienbad in Bohemia, from some reading about the 16th century mastersingers in Gervinus's *History of German Literature.* In his autobiography, Wagner wrote: "On my lonely walks, without knowing anything particular about Hans Sachs and his poetic contemporaries, I thought out a humorous scene in which the cobbler—as a popular artisan-poet—with the hammer on his last, gives the Marker a practical lesson by making him sing, thereby taking revenge on him for his conventional misdeeds." And a vivid image came to his mind of a Nuremburg street scene ending in a brawl. "Then suddenly the whole of my Meistersinger comedy took shape so vividly before me that, inasmuch as it was a particularly cheerful subject, and not in the least likely to over-excite my nerves, I felt I must write it out in spite of the doctor's orders. I therefore proceeded to do this."

Third, it was while he was on another holiday with friends in Venice (1861) that he received the stimulus to take up his earlier story idea and develop it. In the Academy of Arts, he stood looking at Titian's painting of the Assumption of the Virgin. He later wrote that it "exercised a most sublime influence on me, so that, as soon as I realized its conception, my old powers revived within me, as though by a sudden flash of inspiration." And he adds, "I determined at once on the composition of the work." After four dreary days in Venice, he started back to Vienna by train, following the round-about overland route. During this trip, he later wrote, "The music of the *Meistersinger* first dawned on my mind, in which I still retained the libretto as I had originally conceived it. With the utmost distinctness I at once composed the principal part of the Overture in C major."

This was in 1861. He set to work at once on the development of his creative ideas. Asking his friend Peter Cornelius to help him find books, he· began an intensive study of the 16th century mastersingers, of Hans Sachs the cobbler-poet, and of the old *Nuremburg Chronicle.* He also wrote his publishers, B. Schott and Sons of Mainz, on October 30, 1861; he proposed that they undertake to publish *The Mastersingers,* which he said he would engage to deliver "complete and ready for performance" next winter. But the monetary advance he asked for (about $4000) seemed too much for the publishers to hazard, and the financial security that he felt he needed was not to be his. Schott did pay him $600 for a piano arrangement of his *Walkure,* and then $600 more as an advance on *The Master-*

singers. So Wagner went to work on a detailed scenic sketch of his comic opera.

Fourth, in December he went to Paris, and in one month completed the execution of the libretto, a hundred-and-twenty-page drama in poetic form! Meanwhile he was on the alert for melodies. One came to him "on the way to the Taverne Anglaise, whilst strolling through the galleries of the Palais Royal." He borrowed paper and pencil from a friend, and jotted it down. In the spring, while looking at a magnificent sunset, "the prelude [overture] for my *Meistersinger* again suddenly made its presence closely and distinctly felt in my soul. Once before had I seen it rise before me out of a lake of sorrow, like some distant mirage. I proceeded to write down the prelude exactly as it appears today in the score; that is, containing the clear outline of the leading themes of the whole drama." And he proceeded then to continue his composition of the music.

However, by August, 1862, he had completed less than one act of the score. At that time, he was bitten on the thumb by a dog, and was unable to hold a pen for two months. Financial troubles ensued; Schott backed out; Wagner had to devote his time to work that would earn immediate money. He continued to be plagued by domestic troubles. The score for his comic opera was repeatedly put aside, and taken up again with the determination to complete it.

Indeed, the music for *The Mastersingers* was not completed, as we have observed, until October 10, 1867; and the first performance (which marked its final execution as a work of art, the realization of Wagner's twenty-three-year dream) was given in Munich on July 21, 1868.

Chapter 5. The Work of Art

Remember that a picture—before being a battle horse, a nude woman, or some anecdote—is essentially a plane surface covered with colors assembled in a certain order.

Maurice Denis, *Theories*

What we transport from Egypt to London is merely a set of signs, from which a suitable interpreter . . . can produce a certain state of mind.

I. A. Richards, *Principles of Literary Criticism*

A melody of Mozart, or Beethoven, stands solidly on its own feet, as does a verse by Goethe, a quotation from Lessing, a statue of Thorwaldsen, a painting by Overbeck.

Edward Hanslick, *Vom Musikalisch-Schoenen*

WE HAVE so far given some thought to artists who, like the painter and writer and composer, engage in primary creative activity. We shall postpone until the next chapter consideration of those other artists, like the actor and musical performer, whose creative activity is interpretative. Artists of both sorts create works of art, which are the subject of the present chapter.

1. An art work as a public object

Keeping in mind the triadic relation of artist, art work, and artee, we shall say simply that a work of art is the material product of the artist's activity, the objective result of his creative efforts, the thing that the artist makes. On the other hand, the work of art may be looked upon as the thing that the artee sees or hears, the objective stimulus for his responses, the complex cause of his perception and enjoyment and understanding. The work of art is therefore the link between the mind of the artist and the mind of the artee. It exists *outside the mind* of both of them.

To speak of a work of art as existing outside of the mind involves us in a key problem of philosophy. But we cannot avoid asking, as regards a work of art, what 'it' is that we are talking about? what the referent of our thought is when we speak of the statue of *Perseus?* what the nature of the referent is? Perhaps, with John Locke, whose *Essay Concerning Human Understanding* established the direction for so much subsequent thought, we shall for our practical purpose state our belief that a world of external things does exist. These external things, let us say, have certain *primary qualities,* to use Locke's phrase, such as solidity, extension, figure (that is, form) and motion, which are capable of precise measurement. But these external things also have certain secondary qualities such as greenness, smoothness, and other sensory effects produced in a person by the primary qualities. So we shall, for our present purpose, accept the reality of physical substances without denying other sorts of reality, and say that the physical substance of the work of art does exist outside the mind as something possessed of certain primary qualities that can be apprehended by weighing, measuring, and counting—all very complex activities, by the way, *in* the mind of man!

There are, however, two other things that we *might,* but do *not,* mean by 'work of art.' *One* of these exists in the mind of the artist; it is his full and complete conception, what he tried to give expression to in creating the material work of art—the rich and meaningful experience that finally synthesized in his imagination as the work of art or that he finally saw as embodied in the physical work of art. The *other* thing that we *might,* but do *not,* mean by 'work of art' exists in the mind of the artee; it is his full and complete perception, what he sees or hears by giving close attention to the material work of art, the synthesis of the work of art in his own mind. It must be clear that in these two senses the phrase 'work of art' spreads over into the first and third phases of the aesthetic triad. The work of art in the mind of the artist is part of what we have called creative art activity; and the work of art in the mind of the artee is part of what we have called the responsive art experience. As each of these two somewhat different mental works of art exists only *in* the mind of one person, neither of them can be seen or heard by another person. As works of art, they are what are called private objects. It is *only* the material work of art, the work of art outside the mind of both artist and artee, that will here be called *the public object.* And it is only the public object that we shall continue to call, without qualification, 'the' work of art.

Considered as regards the nature of their physical materials, works of art are of various sorts. You will recall that some, such as buildings and statues and paintings, exist in space, consist of inanimate materials, and are perceived primarily by the visual sense. So, too, are works of literature and musical scores, but with a difference. However, art works such as dances, stageplays, and musical performances exist in time as well as in space, consist of animate human beings and sounds, and are perceived both by the visual and auditory senses. But speech and music-as-sound are different yet: they exist essentially in time, consist of intangible and invisible sound waves, and are perceived by hearing alone. These differences in spatiotemporal existence, physical material, and consequent mode of sensory perception are the basis for the following four sections discussing works of art as public objects.

You will have no difficulty in thinking of the statue that we called *Perseus and Medusa* as existing outside of your own mind and outside the mind of Benvenuto Cellini. He, of course, first conceived the work of art in his mind, made small models, developed the statue in clay and wax, and then made the bronze casting. Cellini is dead and the work of art in his mind, a private object, is dead with him. But the material work of art exists today as a public object. You may go to Italy to see it, or you may verify its objective existence by studying the evidence presented by innumerable photographs and reports. But as you piece together your experience of various photos and facts about this public object, and as your perception of this work of art is gradually synthesized, the 'Perseus and Medusa' *in your mind* is again a private object, for no one else can see 'it' exactly as you see it in your own mind. And for every individual, the work of art as a private object in the mind will be ever-so-slightly different. We might say that the work of art outside the mind, the public object, is the link between the private worlds of all those persons who behold and contemplate it.

But something besides the material statue exists outside the mind and is as public as the work of art: the fleeting and ever-changing pattern of light rays reflected from the bronze surface. Light is as subject to physical measurement and discrimination as the tangible substance of the bronze statue, as everyone realizes who makes use of the common photographer's light meter. So, at the end of this chapter we shall consider this essential public medium that, in the case of the spatial and spatiotemporal arts, links the artee and the art work.

2. *Solid art works*

What can be said about the *Perseus* as a work of art, as a public object existing outside the mind of man?

First of all, we can say that it exists in space. It has physiochemical substance; it has measurable form; it has 'color', if by that we at present merely mean that it has the property of absorbing light rays of certain measurable wave lengths and reflecting others. If you were in the presence of the statue *Perseus,* you could touch it, if no guard prevented you; and you could see it, if there were adequate light. You could take the sense-stuff of the statue into the scientist's laboratory for analysis.

The substance would be discovered to be a bronze alloy of copper, lead, and tin in a certain proportion that could be determined precisely by the quantitative analysis of samples—if they were available! Certain physical properties, also, could be studied, such as the tensile strength, malleability, specific gravity, melting point, superficial smoothness and durability.

The substance of the *Perseus* has a certain form. Its gross bulk can be measured easily as being so many feet and inches high, wide, and thick, and made up of parts that also have measurable dimensions. A complete and detailed analysis of the measurable aspects of its form would, however, become unbelievably complex. To measure and to plot all of the complex curvatures of its form would be well-nigh impossible, a terrifyingly complicated problem in descriptive geometry! But even if precise description is impracticable, the substance of this work of art will readily be granted as existing outside the mind of both artist and observer in a certain definite physical form.

You may wish to say that the substance and form are the only fully objective properties of the work of art, and you may add that the substance cannot exist without form or the form without substance. But we have added a third property, 'color.' By this we mean that, because of the physiochemical nature of its substance, it absorbs light rays of certain wave lengths and reflects others. The nature of its form, too, determines the reflective character of the work of art. The color sensation is not a primary quality of the public object; it is a secondary quality and does not exist outside the mind, but it will be convenient to use the word 'color' within quotation marks as an abbreviation for the primary quality of reflecting light rays of measurably different wave lengths. Although the *Perseus,* then, is relatively of a single 'color,' the originally monochromatic bronze has weathered; and the oxidation, or natural patina as it is called, has significantly and variously altered the 'color' of its more exposed surfaces in contrast to the protected concavities.

Such, then, are the substance, form, and 'color' (in our special sense) of the *Perseus* as a work of art. What else can be said about it as a public object?

You may at once say, "It was made by Benvenuto Cellini; it was commissioned by Cosimo de Medici; it was modeled and cast in the years 1545-1554; it is now in the Loggia dei Lanzi in Florence, Italy." These facts, indeed, are verifiable; they are true reports of events and data existing outside the mind. So, we might add, is the title of this work of art—or, in this case, the several titles by which it is or has been called: 'Perseus,' 'Perseus and Medusa,' and 'Perseus with the Head of Medusa.' But such facts and reports, public as they are and objectively verifiable, are not truly a part of the work of art itself as a public object; they are a part of the history of the work, and that is a very different thing.

But let us introduce a fresh illustration. Here is a small reproduction of a picture by the recent American painter Grant Wood, who was born in Anamosa, Iowa, in 1892, the son of a Quaker farmer, and died in 1942.

As a young man, he did odd jobs at farm and forge. He studied crafts and succeeded as a craftsman with his own shop. Then he was able to go to Paris to study art. He wore a Basque beret and a crop of pink whiskers and painted canvases undistinguishable from the mill run of impressionist works produced by his fellow students. On a visit to Munich he saw some portraits by Hans Holbein and various works by Albrecht Durer, and he was struck by the thought that here were real and recognizable folk like his own relatives back home. So he came back to the United States without the beard and beret to study the people and the landscape of his native Iowa. With courage and independence he proceeded to develop his own very distinctive regional style, choosing as his subjects Iowa landscapes and American themes. In later life he was artist-in-residence at the State University of Iowa, where he had earlier spent a year in a life class whose absent-minded professor neglected to see that he paid his tuition.

His method seems to have been to choose a subject, mull it over in his mind for as much as a year before even sketching. Then he proceeded to make preliminary sketches and detailed working drawings on brown wrapping paper. He studied minutely the persons and the objects that he pictured, engaged in careful research relative to details. The painting itself was a painstaking process—he averaged only two pictures a year—and he finally applied as many as eight layers of pigment to his canvas. The picture here presented, typical landscape of Cedar River Valley, was painted in 1931, and is now in the collection of Marshal Field III, with whose permission it is reproduced.

Grant Wood, FALL PLOWING, collection of Marshall Field III

You may do well to observe it closely and thoughtfully, at first with the idea of experiencing it as fully as you can and enjoying it, and then with the idea of considering it as a work of art outside the mind. . . .

Now, what can we say about this painting as a public object? I mean, of course, the picture itself, of which this print is but a representation.

First, it is made of paint and canvas, substances that can be analyzed in the laboratory. The canvas, which is open to more direct observation by looking at the back of the picture, consists of organic fibers twisted and woven, so many coarse strands to the inch. The pigments which completely cover the front surface of the canvas, are compounded of zinc and chromium and various mineral elements held together with the dried residue of certain oils and chemical driers. The substance of the wooden stretcher and surrounding frame also can be analyzed. How different are the various substances of the painting from the relatively uniform substance of the statue!

Second, the material substance of this picture is of certain form and occupies measurable space, $40\frac{1}{4}$ inches wide by 30 inches high, and is perhaps one-eighth inch thick including the pigment. The plotting of each particular pigmented area—with regard to its size, shape, and 'color'—would be a difficult task. But, there is no denying, I believe, that the physiochemical pigments do exist in a certain objective relation to each other—the substance and form of the work of art as a public object. However, notice how different the form of the picture is from the form of the statue just described!

Third, the basis for discriminating the forms of the pigmented surface of the picture is, as we have just seen, the 'color'—the fact that different measurable areas of the surface reflect light rays of various measurable wave lengths. The so-called 'white' light striking the picture contains all of the visible wave lengths. What you see as a certain 'green' has the property of absorbing from the 'white' light all the wave lengths except those of 525 mu (millimicrons, as we shall abbreviate it)—that is, except the 'green' rays, which are reflected from the surface into the observer's eye. Each of the areas of other 'colors'—the various hues and values and intensities of 'color'—will absorb certain of the wave lengths and reflect others from the 'white' light that strikes it. How different in complexity is the 'color' of the painting from the relatively monochromatic statue!

Disappointed by the thought that this picture is no more than analyzable substance in measurable form, you may at once say, "The subject matter is certainly part of the picture." So I ask in return: "Just what is the subject of this picture?" You may at once reply,

"A plow and hills." But would you consider the man mistaken who answered: farm scene, or Iowa landscape, or plowed fields, or the cereal cycle? . . . "Well," you may persist, "if the general theme is a matter of interpretation, everyone recognizes the individual items in the picture—the plow, the freshly turned earth, the sheaves of grain, the separate fields and hills, the closer and more distant trees, the far-off house and barn!". . . But had you noticed the fence posts and barbed wire—and the windmill—and the absence of man and beast?

Have you forgotten that the picture is a complex sign? A sign, you will recall, is not the referent; it only 'stands for' the referent. This picture makes use of resemblative signs; they stood in a similarity relation to their referents in Grant Wood's world of experience, and they now stand in a similarity relation to their referents in your own world of experience. But the meaning is not *in* the sign, as we earlier observed; the meaning is evoked *by* the sign. The subject matter is not *in* the painting; it was in the mind of the painter. And the truly amazing thing about the picture is its ability, owing to the artist's skill in designing and painting it, to evoke comparable subject matter in the minds of various beholders.—By the way, are those sheaves of grain in the middle distance? or are they haycocks? or straw bundles? or corn stalks? Your experience may be too limited for such discrimination; but you may rest assured that Grant Wood knew what he meant.

"Well, the balance is certainly in the picture," you may add, "and the rhythm." . . . Indeed you may point out how, with the plow holding down the lower center of the picture, the forms or objects depicted.to left and right balance each other. You may further assert that since Grant Wood as a professional artist put balance into the picture, it is there without a doubt, and you for one can see it.

But the balance is not something an artist *can* put into a picture. All he can do is to fashion his painting in such a way as to satisfy his own feeling of balance, if that is one of the formal feeling states that is a part of his creative experience. This he may do carefully and consciously perhaps by providing forms of what he considers equal weight to the left and right of a central axis, or he may intuitively give expression to his feeling of balance by the placement of forms of what he unconsciously feels to be equal interest. But one cannot say that the balance is a part of the picture as a work of art. It is true, however, that a skillfully designed picture is more than likely to evoke such a balance response in the beholder, or he may simply feel that it is somehow 'right,' without specific reference to balance or imbalance.

Even the color, as we have already said (except in that special sense of the measurable wave lengths of the reflected light) is not a part of the work of art as a public object—as you realize, with some amusement, when talking to persons with various sorts and degrees of color blindness.

No, the subject matter, the formal balance, the color, and, we may add, the function or usefulness are, like the beauty of the picture, aspects of the art experience. They are not, in our sense, properties of the public object. But you will recall that we defined an art work as 'a man-made thing generally evoking beauty and meaning responses.' If the man-madeness is part of the creative activity and if the beauty and meaning are parts of the art experience, what is there left to distinguish and characterize the work of art itself? That's a good question. The answer is simply that what is left is the *quality* of having been made by man and the *quality* of generally evoking beauty and meaning responses. These are the qualities that characterize a work of art. Neither of them is a physical property of the public object; but both of them can be publicly verified—that is, you may secure objective reports of the fact that the picture was made by man, and you may make an objective study of an adequate sampling of persons' reports of their subjective responses to it.

So *Fall Plowing*—for that is the title of this picture by Grant Wood—consists of analyzable substance in measurable form, but this substance in this form is such as generally to evoke beauty and meaning responses in beholders.

This description of a painting may be very discouraging to you. Agreeing that, of course, paintings are made of inanimate matter, you may still maintain that a work of art certainly has something more to it than just material substance and form! You may feel that *Fall Plowing* so characterized as a public object is little short of contemptible—like the assertion that man is made of 98 cents' worth of chemicals and twenty gallons of water! Besides, this materialism, you may say, takes all the joy and inspiration and beauty and deeper meaning out of art!

Perhaps it is enough to realize that joy and inspiration, beauty and deeper meaning may be a part of the artist's experience to which he gives expression in a work of art; and that joy and inspiration, beauty and deeper meaning, not identical but similar to the artist's, may indeed be evoked by the work of art as a part of the beholder's art experience. How amazing, in truth, is the thing, the merely physical work of art, which is capable of communicating in this way some of the richest values of life! Without itself having beauty, it may yet express the artist's feeling of beauty; without itself having beauty, it may yet evoke a beauty response in the observer.

So instead of looking for inspiration *in* a picture, you may well study closely the variegated surface of the painting with a lively interest in its variously pigmented areas, the shapes and hues and values as you are made aware of them by the selective reflection of light. For this complex art work outside the mind is the stimulus to which all the richness of a full art experience will be the response. That a material thing of physical substance and a certain form may occasion such varied, delightful, or profound psychological activity within an observer is truly one of the major wonders of the world.

3. *Symbol art works*

When we turn from Painting to Literature in considering the work of art as it exists outside the mind of man, we face both a simpler and a more difficult problem. It may be of special interest to consider in this connection the following well-known poem about a picture. Robert Browning, a nineteenth century English poet who lived for many years in Italy, wrote a good many poems about the arts and humanity. He had an unusual understanding of both. This well-known poem, *My Last Duchess,* is a dramatic monologue. The Duke of Ferrara is presumed to be speaking. His listener is an emissary from some Count with a marriageable daughter. The two of them are standing before the portrait of Ferrara's 'last' duchess.

MY LAST DUCHESS
Ferrara
by *Robert Browning*

That's my last Duchess painted on the wall,
Looking as if she were alive. I call
That piece a wonder, now: Fra Pandolf's hands
Worked busily a day, and there she stands.
Will't please you sit and look at her? I said
"Fra Pandolf" by design, for never read
Strangers like you that pictured countenance,
The depth and passion of its earnest glance,
But to myself they turned (since none puts by
The curtain I have drawn for you, but I)
And seemed as they would ask me, if they durst,
How such a glance came there; so, not the first
Are you to turn and ask thus. Sir, 't was not
Her husband's presence only, called that spot

Of joy into the Duchess' cheek: perhaps
Fra Pandolf chanced to say "Her mantle laps
"Over my lady's wrist too much," or "Paint
"Must never hope to reproduce the faint
"Half-flush that dies along her throat"; such stuff
Was courtesy, she thought, and cause enough
For calling up that spot of joy. She had
A heart—how shall I say?—too soon made glad,
Too easily impressed; she liked whate'er
She looked on, and her looks went everywhere.
Sir, 't was all one! My favour at her breast,
The dropping of the daylight in the West,
The bough of cherries some officious fool
Broke in the orchard for her, the white mule
She rode with round the terrace—all and each
Would draw from her alike the approving speech,
Or blush, at least. She thanked men,—good! but thanked
Somehow—I know not how—as if she ranked
My gift of a nine-hundred-years-old name
With anybody's gift. Who'd stoop to blame
This sort of trifling? Even had you skill
In speech—(which I have not)—to make your will
Quite clear to such an one, and say, "Just this
"Or that in you disgusts me; here you miss,
"Or there exceed the mark"—and if she let
Herself be lessoned so, nor plainly set
Her wits to yours, forsooth, and made excuse,
—E'en then would be some stooping; and I choose
Never to stoop. Oh sir, she smiled, no doubt,
Whene'er I passed her; but who passed without
Much the same smile? This grew; I gave commands;
Then all smiles stopped together. There she stands
As if alive. Will't please you rise? We'll meet
The company below, then. I repeat,
The Count your master's known munificence
Is ample warrant that no just pretence
Of mine for dowry will be disallowed;
Though his fair daughter's self, as I avowed
At starting, is my object. Nay, we'll go
Together down, sir! Notice Neptune, though,
Taming a sea-horse, thought a rarity,
Which Claus of Innsbruck cast in bronze for me!

(1842)

Before discussing this poem as a work of art, we shall do well to consider the portrait of the Duchess as suggested by Browning's lines. Through the Duke's words you are given a glimpse of the artist Fra Pandolf in the process of creating the portrait. Notice that this is not an objective report but is highly colored by the Duke's suspicions and jealousies. 'The depth and passion of its earnest glance' is not, of course, part of the portrait as a public object, though others besides the present visitor have made similar interpretations in looking at it. The 'glance,' the 'spot of joy' in the Duchess's cheek, the faint/Half-flush that dies along her throat,' the 'blush,' the 'smile'—it is interesting to speculate as to what existed in the forms and 'colors' upon the pigmented canvas of this (hypothetical) picture that evoked these interpretations . . . So much, then, for our present thoughts about this imagined portrait of the Duchess, the activity that created it, and the responses that it evoked.

As for the poem itself, all that exists outside the mind of the reader is the paper and ink marks upon it. The substance is analyzable cellulose with a particular fibrous character and a certain combination of carbon, linseed oil, and drier residues. The superficial form is the measurably smooth surface of the paper of a certain size and the calculable configurations of ink of microscopic thickness which penetrates into the fibers of the paper. This public object is of a determinable reflectivity, the paper reflecting and the ink absorbing most of the wave-lengths of the light striking the page.

This poem, then, is much like a painting. The chemical difference in substance and even in over-all size is not particularly significant. One difference, however, is in the surface complexity of the two. The surface of the painting is relatively complex; it is made up of innumerable small areas of widely various shapes and 'colors.' The surface of the poem is relatively simple: the paper background reflects light quite uniformly and the lines of printing, all of one 'color,' are superficially similar. A second difference is in the nature of the two considered as signs. If you recall our earlier discussion, the painting has the quality of consisting of resemblative signs; they have a similarity relation to the things that they stand for. The poem, on the other hand, has the quality of consisting of symbolic signs; they have a conventional relation to the things that they stand for.

But there is another point. The poem on this page 'is' the poem; the picture on the page is only 'a print of' the picture. Of course you could say that the poem *My Last Duchess* really is Browning's original manuscript of the poem, or the printing of it in the original edition of the *Dramatic Lyrics* (1842) where it appeared as the first of a pair of poems under the general heading, 'Italy and France,' and with the title 'I. Italy.' (The second poem in the pair is 'Count Gismond.') But Browning made some changes in the poem in later editions of his work, and gave it the present title 'My Last Duchess: Ferrara' in 1849. And he made slight changes even after that time.

We might say that the final manuscript of the poem, or the edition of it as printed from his finally corrected proof, 'is' the poem. And scholars are often concerned with textual criticism and the establishing of the text of an author's work. But once this is established, as Browning experts have determined the final version of *My Last Duchess,* is not one printing of the words as much 'the' poem as another? That is, as long as it is like the final version *verbatim et literatim,* word for word and letter for letter and, we might add, point for point in punctuation. Yes, we might say that this poem exists, not uniquely like a picture, but in thousands of identical books, impressions in the original edition of the poem as finally revised by the author, and in the countless copies of other editions since that time that have followed the original word for word and point for point.

My Last Duchess on these pages may be said to be the real thing in a way that even a color print of Grant Wood's *Fall Plowing* is not. Therefore the substance and form of *My Last Duchess,* as a work of art existing outside the mind, will vary somewhat, though not greatly and significantly, depending upon what copy of what edition is taken into the laboratory for physiochemical analysis and measurement.

What has here been said about the poem as a public object may likewise be said of all music on the page. Such a work of art is no more than a particular configuration of measurable black marks upon otherwise blank paper!

But, again, if this seems to you to be a disillusioning definition of a poem or musical score as a work of art outside the mind of man, you may again be reminded of the magical power, the potential of these particular black marks to reflect such a pattern of light into the human eye as will set in motion a train of thoughts and images and feelings that fuse as a richly integrated human experience which you call *My Last Duchess!*

4. *Activity art works*

Let us now consider those works of art that we earlier called spatio-temporal, that have animate human beings and sounds as their physical materials, and that are perceived through both the visual and auditory senses—art works like the dance, the stageplay, and we may add the musical performance.

The substance of a dance is essentially the body and costume of the dancer. This could be subjected to bio-physio-chemical analysis and measurement, complex as such a study would be. And the form and 'color' of the exposed surfaces of this substance too might be determined and plotted—if you could get the dancer to stand still! For the property of this dance as a public object, distinguishing it from the statue and the picture, is its movement. This motion, however, can also be measured, plotted, and recorded. But there is still another property of the dance as a work of art, and that is 'sound,'— the musical accompaniment, the footfalls, etc. More will be said of 'sound' in the next section. But it must be said here that 'sound,' which like 'color' as a primary quality will be set off by quotation marks, is here used to name the complex pattern of sound waves in the air, the components of which are measurable in terms of so many vibrations per second.

Whereas a painting may be represented quite adequately by a fine color print, the dance as a work of art will require a moving picture film in both color and sound to represent it; and even then the reproduction will be less than adequate, for the essentially animate human being, the dancer in person, will not be there.

Several observations should be made about a dance as a work of art. First, it is here called an activity art work. Its substance consists of animate beings in motion; it is spatiotemporal; it is audiovisual. Second, the creative activity of the performer is inseparable from the thing created. The final step in the creative process, the execution of the work of art, actually is the work of art. Third, after the creative activity of the dancer stops, the dance ceases to exist as a public object. What is called 'the' dance may be repeated on another occasion; but each performance is in reality the creation of a new work of art, no matter how nearly identical the pattern and timing of the component bodily movements, for on each different occasion the artist engages in creative activity, the execution or final step in the creative process. Fourth, since the dance does not survive as a public object and cinema records of it are but recent, the history of the dance is most difficult to study. So, one of the oldest and most widely practiced arts is by far the least known and understood today.

The same observations may be made of the art of the theater. A stageplay is also an activity art work—animate human beings in motion and (in this case) speaking, spatiotemporal, therefore audiovisual. The stageplay, as a public object, is also inseparable from the final stage in the creative activity that produces it. So, too, when the curtain comes down at the end, the performance is over; nothing remains outside the minds of the spectators and actors. It is true, of course, that the playscript remains and can be published, and may be considered a work of art in its own right—one of the dramas of Literature. Yes, and the scenery and costumes may last a generation, and certain of the actors survive a thousand or more performances. But that stageplay—that performance, that night—is gone forever! Another day, a matinee, will again require creative activity for the actors to give another performance, ever so slightly different from that of the preceding night; and it too will pass without a trace. So, since the stageplay does not survive as a public object—and cinema records of actual plays on the stage are recent, few, and unsuccessful—the history of theatrical art is also difficult to study.

Parallel observations may be made for the art of musical performance but with this difference: whereas for the dance the visual component is most important and the auditory component much less important, for musical performance, the auditory component is paramount and the visual is, some might say, relatively unimportant. (For the stageplay sight and sound are nearly equal.) Although more will be said of this matter in the next chapter, here it is necessary to indicate that the musical performance as a work of art exists inseparably from the creative activity of the performing artist; that when the last note has died away, nothing remains of the public object; that the phonograph does record the auditory component of such performances, but it takes sound film to record the musical performance more adequately. For, whether one 'should' look at the pianist or not, many or perhaps most listeners do; they watch for his appearance upon the platform, his adjustment to his instrument, his pause for audience attention, his attack, his hands, his pedaling, his evidence of technical mastery, his head gestures, perhaps his climaxing burst of energy, and his response to their applause. These are a part, albeit a less important part, of the musical performance as a public object. The more important part will occupy us in the next section.

So much, then, for the activity art works: dance, stageplay, and musical performance. As public objects they are immeasurably more complex than the statue and painting. To substance and form and 'color'—the primary qualities of the purely space arts—are added the primary qualities of motion and 'sound.' As motion and 'sound' can only be suggested or symbolized on the printed page, you can readily appreciate the problem of representing in a book the animate, spatiotemporal, audiovisual arts!

5. *Intangible works of art*

We have already mentioned the music-on-the-page as a public object, and have now commented on the musical performance as a work of art. It remains to consider the music-in-the-air, as one may be inclined to call the complex pattern of the sound waves that issue from the piano during a performance, or from your record player or radio. Perhaps we need do little more than present an illustration and then make a few comments on it.

Let us take as an illustration *Jesu, Joy of Man's Desiring*, the best known portion of Cantata No. 147 by Johann Sebastian Bach (1685-1750). A thematic outline is presented on two of the following pages. The piano arrangement by Myra Hess is readily available, as is a recording of her performance. This chorale, however, was originally scored for chorus and small orchestra, and has been recorded by the Bach Chorus, Cantata Club Orchestra, and Leon Goossens.

Certainly Bach is one of the great composers of all time. He came from a family that was prominent in the history of music in Germany for 200 years. In eight generations, 50 of the 136 persons were musicians, practically all of them composers as well as performers. Taught the violin by his father who died when the boy was ten, Bach was raised by his brother, an organist who taught him the clavier—ancestor of the modern piano. In convent school he sang for his tuition, and became a church organist. Later as court organist and university instructor, his skill and reputation increased. At one time he invented an instrument midway between 'cello and viola, and devised a clavier with catgut strings. He advanced the technique of piano playing, adding the regular use of thumb and little finger to the early limited fingering. And he wrote a great wealth of musical compositions, of wide range of types and forms, for voice, solo instruments, and various ensembles. Some music lovers would say that his work marks the highest development of counterpoint or polyphonic music, which is characterized by the concurrence of two or more melodies, or, as in the fugue, the simultaneous playing of two or more phrases from the same theme by two or more voices, as in 'Three Blind Mice.'

Now get someone to play the piano arrangement of Bach's *Jesu, Joy of Man's Desiring*, or listen to a recording—preferably of the original choral and instrumental composition rather than of the piano arrangement, for the differences in tone quality will help you to distinguish the several concurrent themes. Even if you have small skill in reading musical notation you may find the thematic outline of help in your listening to and experiencing this music. By giving attention to first one and then another of the melody lines as you play the recording, you will increase your ability to be conscious of the several themes going on at the same time. . . .

Thematic Outline of
JESU, JOY OF MAN'S DESIRING
Chorale from Cantata No. 147
by *Johann Sebastian Bach*

How many different themes were you able to keep track of at one time? As the outline is here arranged to be a guide for your attention, the thematic materials are designated by letters on their first and second appearance. You probably can do well enough in 'hearing' two of them together as at bar 14. Can you follow the C theme at bar 17 and again at 21? And probably the bass figure is easy to identify at 24. But how do you manage at bar 29? Can you feel the bass rumbling along and the A theme on top? But can you keep these going in the back of your mind and concentrate on the B theme, in the middle, now in octaves? Then how do you fare at bar 52 when the C theme also appears? Can you put the deep bass, the simple B voice, and the restless oboe theme all three in the background without losing them, and then follow briefly the elusive alto theme? If you have increased your ability to hear them all as separate themes yet all together, you have thereby enriched your experience of this work of art.

Having listened to this Bach chorale, you may ask the question, What is 'it,' the work of art outside the mind, the public object? This question was suggested in the preceding section wherein 'sound' was named as one property of the activity art works. And 'sound,' thus within quotation marks, was defined as naming a complex pattern of sound waves in the air, the components of which are measurable in terms of so many vibrations per second. We have said 'in the air;' we must add that sound waves are also conducted by water, ground, wood, metal, and bone, but this is not to our present purpose. The time-honored question, Does the tree make a noise when it falls in a deserted forest? is pertinent here. We may be sure that it does make a 'sound' as we have defined 'sound' here in terms of sound waves in the air; but it does not make a *sound* as we shall define our use of the word without quotation marks to mean auditory sensations within the mind of man or beast.

What, then, can we say about the 'sound' of *Jesu, Joy of Man's Desiring* as a public object? It does not have material substance and occupy space, like bronze or pigment or the dancer's body. It is intangible and invisible, yet it is capable of measurement in the physics laboratory. It is not a property of solid extensional matter. 'Sound' exists as vibrations of the air; it is a primary quality of the air, motion in the air as substance. These vibrations of the air were first produced by instruments—human voices, oboe, violins, etc.—as the essential part of a musical performance; and they are now reproduced by record player. You may prefer to say that the air is merely the medium for the complex of 'sound' initiated by musical instruments; however, the music as a public object does not exist as a property of motion in the separate instruments important as that is in the musical performance, but as the confluence of the vibrations set up in the air by the several instruments.

So we may well think of the complex of sound waves in the air as being the music itself, the work of art existing outside the mind of both performer and auditor, the public object. This 'sound' does not itself have substance or form or 'color' or motion in the sense we have used these words. It has existence in the air, a substance; it consists of motion (vibration) of the air, a substance. This music-in-the-air, as we have therefore called it, is both intangible and invisible, yet it can be taken into the laboratory for precise study and measurement; it can be recorded accurately and can then be reproduced mechanically.

The reality of 'sound' as a public object can easily be demonstrated by the use of a pair of identical tuning forks. Strike one of them and you set it in vibration. You can then hear a buzzing, which becomes a clear if odd tone if you hold the end of the tuning fork against the table. You can also feel a certain tingling sensation as you hold the tuning fork, and you can actually see the motion of the vibrating fork as a sort of blur. So, sight and feeling and hearing provide corroborative sensations relative to the vibration of the fork.

Now let someone else strike this tuning fork while you hold the second tuning fork at some distance, and you will observe—by faint hearing, feeling, and seeing—that your tuning fork is set in vibration. You cannot see the sound waves in the air, caused by the first fork and affecting the second; you cannot feel them; but you can hear them, for the sound waves in the air that affect the second tuning fork also set up a comparable vibration of your eardrum. And if there is a piano in the room, those of its strings that are in tune with the forks will be, in the same way, set a-buzzing.

An A tuning fork of present standard pitch is one that vibrates 440 times per second when struck. It also is set in vibration when in the presence of sound waves of 440 v.p.s. (vibrations per second). Each piano string, because of its length and tautness, produces and responds to only one frequency. But the eardrum is so constructed as to be set in vibration by any frequency of sound waves from (roughly) 10 to 10,000 v.p.s. And, what is yet more remarkable, it can at one and the same time be set in vibration by sound waves of different v.p.s. That is, you can hear sounds of different pitches simultaneously.

It is not possible here to discuss the physical complexity of 'sound' and the delicate devices for measuring it. But two or three points may be of general interest: When the C string on the piano is struck by its key, it is set in vibration not only in its whole length at 264 v.p.s., which is called the fundamental, but also in each of several fractions of its whole length, setting up lesser sound waves of other v.p.s. of progressively higher frequencies, called upper partials, overtones, or harmonics. Each fundamental is thus accompanied by its own series of partials. Owing to the material of which they are made and to their shape, different musical instruments amplify certain ones of these partials. So the sound waves of 440 v.p.s. produced by the oboe are accompanied by one set of partials; whereas the sound waves of 440 v.p.s produced by a human voice are accompanied by a somewhat different set of partials. Each is heard as a single sound, the musical tone A; but each is heard as a distinct quality of sound because of its particular complex of partials. The mathematical relation of these partials has been established, and the overtone structure of a particular tone can be studied.

The ratio of the v.p.s. of the tones in the various musical scales is also a matter for public discrimination. In the major diatonic scale (our ordinary C scale for instance), the v.p.s. of middle C has a 1:2 ratio to the v.p.s. of the C one octave above it. That is, the 'sound' of middle C consists of 264 v.p.s.; the 'sound' of octave C, 528 v.p.s. As played on the violin, for instance, the other ratios of the notes of the C scale are as follows:

The true C major diatonic scale

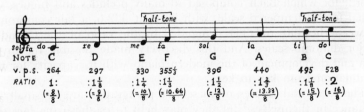

solfa	do	re	me	fa	sol	la	ti	do
NOTE	C	D	E	F	G	A	B	C
v.p.s.	264	297	330	355⅓	396	440	495	528
RATIO	1:	:1⅛	:1¼	:1⅓	:1½	:1⅔	:1⅞	:2
	(=$\frac{8}{8}$)	:(=$\frac{9}{8}$)	(=$\frac{10}{8}$)	(=$\frac{10.66}{8}$)	(=$\frac{12}{8}$)	(=$\frac{13.33}{8}$)	(=$\frac{15}{8}$)	(=$\frac{16}{8}$)

With a scratch pad to help, you can easily figure out that one-eighth of 264 is 33. D, which has a ratio to C of one-and-one-eighth to one, has therefore 264 plus 33 v.p.s.; that is 297, as you will note in the table above. E, which has a ratio to C of one-and-two-eighths to one, has therefore 264 plus 33 plus another 33 v.p.s.; that is, 330. Note that E stands in a simple fixed ratio to C, not to D, the next note below it; for this is the C scale, and all of the notes are proportionally related to the fundamental note of the scale, which is called the tonic.

Now say that we build a similar major diatonic scale on the D tone of 297 v.p.s. Remember that the ratios will be the same, but that one-eighth of 297 is 37.12 v.p.s.; therefore E will have 297 plus 37.12 v.p.s.; that is, 334.12.

As indicated in the last chapter, the difference between 330 and 334 is not only a mathematical and measurable discrimination, but it is also perceptible to persons of keen hearing. So the equitempered scale, referred to in the preceding chapter, was devised:

The tempered scale of the piano

Compare the v.p.s. for the similar D, E, G, A, B, notes on the three scales given above.

The compromises of the tempered scale are such as to make the one tuning of the piano strings sound almost-if-not-quite in tune for *all* the major and minor diatonic scales. The well-tempered clavichord, for which Bach composed so many preludes and fugues, was tuned to this tempered scale, with its E at 332.6, a fair compromise between the 330 and 334 demanded by the ratio of the C and D major diatonic scales. And this discovery made possible the invention and development of the modern piano with its capacity for rich modulation from key to key.

The facts and figures of these last paragraphs are of small importance in themselves. But they may help to establish the fact that the music-in-the-air, the music as 'sound,' does exist in the outer world of measurable time and space. Even brief attention to the intricacy of the fundamental-overtone structure of a single tone, or to the vibrational ratios involved in a simple scale, or to the well-tempered tuning of the piano may provide at least a glimpse into the complexity of, say, *Jesu, Joy of Man's Desiring*, the public object, as a work of art. And what has here been said about music as 'sound' can be said, with certain characterizing differences, of human speech as 'sound' which we encountered in our brief comment on the performance of a stageplay as an activity art work.

6. 'Color' and Light

Early in this chapter we noted that in considering a statue or a painting there are two sorts of things existing outside the mind both of the artist and of the observer: first, the work of art itself, which we said has substance and form and 'color'; and second, the pattern of light rays reflected from its surface. Both the work of art and the pattern of light rays are *public* and may be studied objectively by analysis and measurement.

'Color' within quotation marks has been defined in a preceding section as the primary quality of reflecting light rays of measurably different wave lengths. In this sense, the picture as a public object may be said to possess 'color,' and it continues to possess 'color' in this sense whether or not it is reflecting any light at all at the moment. In the middle of the night and the dark of the moon, the so-called 'green' pigment of the painting continues to possess the primary quality of, or should we say for, reflecting the light wave lengths of 525 mu (millimicrons, as here abbreviated). Turn on the same and only the same light at any time of day or night, and the reflection from the surface will be the same.

"Radiant energy within a certain range of wave lengths or frequencies is capable of arousing a chain of events in the visual sense which enables one to see. For convenience this may be termed light." So Luckiesch defines it. "Furthermore, light per se possesses but one inherent or fundamental characteristic—spectral quality. However as visual stimulus, it may be varied in both intensity and in duration. . . ."

It is not to our purpose to undertake a technical consideration of the complex question of light and its nature. But a word must be said about it as the requisite medium for all visual perception of objects outside the mind. By requisite medium we mean no more than that light is the essential go-between or middleman. Unless light is directed at the picture, no light can be reflected from it. Unless the beam of light falling on the picture contains wave lengths of 525 mu, no 'green' wave lengths can possibly be reflected from even its 'greenest' pigment.

The importance of light has long been recognized by those artists whose creative work is in the spatial and spatiotemporal arts. In the Middle Ages the Gothic architects were especially concerned with the problem of lighting the interiors of their cathedrals. They developed the flying-buttress and clerestory construction so as to allow the penetration of an adequate *quantity* of sunlight, the only strong light source they had for use. They developed, with the aid of special artists and artisans, the amazing stained-glass windows, which controlled and patterned the *color*-rays that filtered in. And they also controlled (within the limits of seasonal change) the *direction* of the sunlight, not by moving the sun of course, but by the compass placement of the structure and by the placement of various windows, the lantern (skylight), and reflecting surfaces. It is by no means an accident that the interior of a cathedral is so beautifully and variously illuminated.

The sculptor, also, is concerned about the lighting of his statue. Daniel Chester French, whose enormous statue of the Emancipator is housed in the Lincoln Memorial, gave years of attention to developing what he considered the best artificial lighting to supplement the sunlight which the building itself was designed to admit for the illumination of his work. Painters are concerned to have adequate light in their studios; designers and directors of art galleries study the problems of natural and artificial lighting. But perhaps the most conscious use of light as a physical medium is to be found in the modern theater, where the quantity, color, and direction of light can be subtly controlled and changed at will, to be woven into a meaningful and beautiful pattern.

It takes but a few simple experiments to show how important lighting is.

Study a white plaster cast, preferably of a portrait bust, in a room darkened so as to control reflected light. Use a strong flashlight, holding it at various angles. Note the strong highlights and deep shadows. Then manipulate a piece of cardboard so as to reflect some light toward the statue from various angles. Now use two cardboards of different colors. You will discover that light from two directions, of different intensities and of different color-rays, is very important for the revelation of form and surface textures.

Try another experiment with a picture, using a baby spotlight or a strong flashlight in a dark room. (It would be best if you had two paintings, one smooth-surfaced and one rough-surfaced.) First, move the light about and vary the angle of the picture. You will discover that a glare occurs when the direct source of light, the plane of the picture's surface, and the observer's eye are in a mirror-relation to each other. (If you are experimenting with two paintings, you will discover that the glare is much worse from the one that is smooth-surfaced.) But all light follows the same law: the angle of reflection is equal to the angle of incidence. Light rays are reflected, not by the general plane of the picture, but by the plane of each separate minute area of the surface. Now put up the blinds and note that light is directed at the picture from many sources; it comes through a window and is bounced off the floor up against the wall, angles up to the ceiling and is reflected back down at a comparable angle. It becomes diffused.

If a fairly uniform and moderate amount of light strikes a smooth-surfaced painting from all of the innumerable angles that are in the mirror-relation to the eye, then the picture will seem to be well lit, all areas of the surface will be equally visible. This accounts for the advantage of tubular lights with curved reflectors in the lighting of paintings. But, on a rough-surfaced painting, each individual lump of paint presents its own surfaces, and lighting of various intensities from various angles will reflect a pattern of minute high lights and shadows as from a sculptured surface. This may be seen as you move the rough-surfaced painting over into a beam of sunlight or the spot-light.

But try a third experiment, again in a darkened room. This time use a few frames of colored gelatine or cellophane with the spot-light. First, direct a red light toward the painting. By calling it 'red,' remember, we mean that almost all of the wave lengths except those of approximately 685 mu have been filtered out by the jelly. Now, the areas of 'red' pigment on the canvas are chemically such as to reflect the 685 mu rays but no others. The 'white' areas will reflect all wave lengths equally; the 'gray' areas will absorb and reflect some of all wave lengths; the 'black' areas will absorb all of them. The 'green' areas will absorb the 685 mu (red) rays; for the 'green' areas are chemically such as to reflect the 525 mu (green) rays. And areas of other 'colors' will also reflect only their own wave lengths. Notice that the areas that were vivid 'green' in the sunlight are murky and dark under the 'red' light; they are not 'red' and certainly not 'green.' What was 'red' in the sunlight is still 'red,' but everything that was 'white' or 'gray' is also 'red.' So we could go on. But now use a 'green' jelly, or a 'blue' or a 'yellow' jelly, and study the results.

Perhaps these simple experiments have demonstrated how important light is as the physical medium in the spatial and spatiotemporal arts. It is not the work of art, as we have defined it, but it also exists outside the mind, and can be analyzed and measured in the physics laboratory. It is the essential middleman for the visual and audiovisual arts, the means by which the observer becomes aware of those art works from which it may be reflected.

Chapter 6. Interpretative Creative Activity

It is our actors, singers, and musicians upon whose own instincts
all hope for the attainment of artistic objects must rest, even when
these objects themselves may be incomprehensible to them.
> Richard Wagner, *Purpose of Opera*

You must make enough progress to comprehend a piece of music on paper.
> Robert Schumann, *Precepts of Art and Life*

... the vanity of translation: it were as wise to cast a violet into
a crucible that you might discover the formal principle of its color
and odor, as seek to transfuse from one language into another the
creation of a poet.
> Percy B. Shelley, *A Defense of Poetry*

In the present group of three chapters under the heading 'Part
Two: Creative Activity and the Work of Art,' we began by considering 'Primary Creative Activity' such as the painter's production
of a picture, the poet's writing of a poem, or the composer's creation of a musical work. We then proceeded to discuss 'The Work of
Art' created by these activities of artists: the picture, the poem, the
music. But in considering music, as we noted, there are three things
of quite different sorts to be taken into account as works of art: the
music-on-the-page, the musical performance that interprets the musical notation and creates the audible music, and the music-in-the-air
so created. The present chapter will say something more about this
'Interpretative Creative Activity,' which, in the case of music, turns
one sort of art work into another, black marks into enjoyable sounds.
It will not, however, confine itself to the art of musical performance,
for there are other sorts of interpretative creative activity as well.

The interpretative artist is the essential intermediary in many of
the arts; he communicates to auditors or spectators his understanding of the primary artist's creation. You may be surprised when your
attention is called to the wide range and diversity of interpretative

creative activity. Like musical performers and an orchestral conductor, actors and their stage director interpret a playscript, creating a stageplay which communicates to the audience their understanding of the playwright's lines and stage directions. Similarly, the master builder interprets the plans of the architect and creates the building with the help of various special artists and craftsmen and workmen. Unlike Benvenuto Cellini, most sculptors send their completed clay models to special foundries where skilled artisans make and often finish the bronze casting. Until the recent advent of photoengraving, the work of painters was reproduced in books by the artful handiwork of steel engravers. Translators and illustrators also are interpretative creative artists of somewhat different sorts. And we must not forget that Shakespeare was a dramatizer of popular history, short stories, and romances. Though he was of surpassing creative originality in doing this, his activity was not different in kind, but only in degree, from the current dramatization of a recent best-seller.

There is, then, an amazing variation within the range of what is here called interpretative creative activity.

1. *Several sorts of interpretative activity*

Let us begin with an example.

Composed when Franz Schubert (1797-1828) was eighteen, *Der Erlkönig* ('The Erlking') is labeled opus 1, though by no means the earliest among his many works. Since his death he has come to be celebrated as the greatest writer of German 'lieder,' as such songs are called; and he left 538 different songs, enough to fill 10 volumes. Some of these, like *Who Is Sylvia* and *Hark, Hark, the Lark* were composed as musical settings for lyrics from Shakespeare's plays. The well-known *Ave Maria* is based upon a lyric from Scott's *Lady of the Lake*. A number, such as the popular *Am Meer* ('By the Sea'), have song-lyrics by Heinrich Heine. The verse for a larger number, such as *Heidenröslein* ('Hedge-roses') and *Gretchen am Spinnrade* ('Margaret at the Spinning Wheel'), come from the works of Goethe, and it is to this last group that *The Erlking* belongs.

One afternoon two friends called on Schubert. They found him in high excitement walking up and down in his room, book in hand, reading aloud Goethe's ballad about the elf-king who in Danish legend worked his special mischief and ruin upon children.

DER ERLKOENIG

by *Johann Wolfgang von Goethe*

Wer reitet so spät durch Nacht und Wind?
Es ist der Vater mit seinem Kind;
er hat den Knaben wohl in dem Arm,
er fasst ihn sicher, er hält ihn warm.

„Mein Sohn, was birgst du so bang dein Gesicht?"
„Siehst, Vater, du den Erlkönig nicht?
den Erlenkönig mit Kron und Schweif?"
„Mein Sohn, es ist ein Nebelstreif."

„Du liebes Kind, komm, geh' mit mir!
gar schöne Spiele spiel' ich mit dir;
manch' bunte Blumen sind an dem Strand,
meine Mutter hat manch gülden Gewand."

„Mein Vater, mein Vater, und hörest du nicht,
was Erlenkönig mir leise verspricht?"
„Sei ruhig, bleibe ruhig, mein Kind;
in dürren Blättern säuselt der Wind."

„Willst, feiner Knabe, du mit mir gehn?
meine Töchter sollen dich warten schön;
meine Töchter führen den nächtlichen Reihn
und wiegen und tanzen und singen dich ein,
sie wiegen und tanzen und singen dich ein."

„Mein Vater, mein Vater, und siehst du nicht dort
Erlkönigs Töchter am düstern Ort?"
„Mein Sohn, mein Sohn, ich seh' es genau,
es scheinen die alten Weiden so grau."

„Ich liebe dich, mich reizt deine schöne Gestalt,
und bist du nicht willig, so brauch' ich Gewalt."
„Mein Vater, mein Vater, jetzt fasst er mich an!
Erlkönig hat mir ein Leid's gethan!"

Dem Vater grauset's, er reitet geschwind,
er hält in Armen das ächzende Kind,
erreicht den Hof mit Müh' und Noth;
in seinen Armen das Kind war todt.

Schubert's friends watched him as he read on. Then suddenly, they later reported, he sat down; and as fast as he could make the notes, he dashed off the whole song composition, almost in its present form.

Because Schubert had no piano, he and his friends hurried off to the neighboring school where fourteen-year-old Randhartinger sang it for excited teachers and pupils, with Schubert dashing off the accompaniment. This accompaniment is built upon a continuous galloping of octaves and chords in triplets—almost impossible for the pianist to keep up!—with a characteristic upsurging figure in the bass. A few bars will suffice to suggest it.

With the musical notation for the voice is here printed an English translation of Goethe's words by Arthur Westbrook. Many different recordings of this well-known art song are available. Franz Liszt, the brilliant pianist and composer, who after Schubert's death referred to him as 'the most poetic musician that ever lived,' arranged *Der Erlkönig* as a piano solo, which also has been recorded. The musical score for solo voice and piano accompaniment is readily available. Whether you are listening to a recording or to an immediate performance, you may find it helpful to follow the notes and English words, given on the following pages. . . .

As you think of the history of *The Erlking*—from Goethe's writing of the ballad to the making of recent recordings—you will doubtless note that a number of different artists have been involved in various sorts of interpretative creative activity.

First of all, there is the work of Schubert. You may be inclined to say that his composition of a musical setting for this ballad was just as much primary creation as Wagner's composition of the *Prize Song*; there certainly does not seem to be much difference between the two. Yet Schubert was, in effect, interpreting Goethe's poem; and he apparently tried to give expression to the vivid experience that he had had in reading this ballad of the supernatural. It is worth noting that when Goethe first heard the song, he didn't like it at all. Apparently he felt that Schubert had not interpreted his poem satisfactorily; but some years later he heard it again, sung by 'the great Schroeder-Devrient,' and he was enthusiastic, kissed the singer on the cheek and thanked her 'a thousand times for a great

THE ERLKING
Lyric by *Goethe*, translated by *Westbrook*
Music by *Franz Schubert*

Who rid-eth so late through night and wind? It is the fa-ther with his child. He has the boy so safe in his arm; He holds him tightly, he holds him warm.

"My son, in ter-ror why hid-est thy face?" "Oh, fa-ther, see, the Erl-king is nigh! The Erl--king dreaded with crown and robe." "My son, 'tis but a streak of mist."

'My dear--est child, come go with me! Such mer--ry plays I'll play-- with thee, For man-y gay flow-ers are bloom-ing there, and my moth-er has man-y gold-en robes for thee.' "My fa-ther, my fa--ther, and hear-est thou not What the Erl-king whispers so soft in my ear?" "Be qui-et, oh, be qui-et my child; 'Tis but the

dead leaves stirred by the wind." 'Come, lovely boy, wilt thou go with me? My daughters fair shall

wait on thee. There my daughters lead in the revels each night; They'll sing and they'll dance and they'll

rock thee to sleep, They'll sing and they'll dance and they'll rock thee to sleep.' "My fa-ther, my

fa-ther, and see-est thou not   the Erl-king's daugh-ter in yon dim   spot?"

"My son,   my son,   I   see and I know 'Twas on-ly the old-en

willow so   gray."   'I   love thee so, thy beau-ty has rav-ished my

sense; and, will-ing or   not, I   will car-ry thee hence.' "My fa-ther, my

fa-ther, now grasps he my arm, The Erl-king has seized me, has done me

harm!"   The fa- -ther shud-ders, he rides like the wind, He

clasps to his bos-om the pale, sob-bing child.   He reach-es

home with fear and dread;   Clasped in his arms-- the child was dead.

(From the book *Fifty Master Songs by Twenty Composers* as published and copyrighted, 1902, renewal 1930, by Oliver Ditson Company. Words re-printed by permission.)

artistic achievement' and proclaimed the song as she sang it 'a true picture'—that is, a faithful interpretation of his ballad.

Another sort of interpretative creative activity is the musical performance of the singer and accompanist. If you have listened to two or more solo vocal performances of *The Erlking*, you may have noticed considerable difference in their interpretations. It is true that both vocalists sang the same words (or one may have used an English translation) and that both sang the same relative pattern of musical sounds (or one used a transposition into a key more suited to his vocal range). But the general tempo, the rushing and lingering; the changes in volume; the differentiation of the voice of the narrator, father, son, and elf; the handling of the other dramatic elements and the recitative at the end—these are individual matters, part of the vocalist's creative activity as an interpreter, his creative contribution to the musical performance. And so, too, as regards the accompaniment. It is unfortunate that we cannot hear a performance by Schubert's friend Vogl with the composer himself at the piano. A contemporary wrote that "Schubert had little technique, and Vogl but little voice," yet it is said that their hearers were moved to tears when they performed. Schubert himself said, "The way in which Vogl sings and I accompany, *so that for the moment we seem to be one*, is something quite new and unexpected to these people." And another added: "Voice and piano became as nothing; the music seemed to want no material help, but the melodies appealed to the ear as a vision does the eye." All of the singers who give fine performances of *The Erlking* are interpretative creative artists, for they study the Goethe ballad and Schubert music and then practice to communicate their full understanding of it to others in a performance.

Yet another sort of interpretative creative activity has been noted in our consideration of *The Erlking*. Arthur Westbrook translated Goethe's German ballad into English, or perhaps we should say that he translated the words of Schubert's song. That might be a slightly different thing. A literary translation to be read and a vocal translation to be sung may be somewhat different, for the singer can make some sounds more articulately and effectively than others. You may question whether the translator is a creative artist at all. According to our definition, he is, if he makes something generally evoking beauty and meaning responses—which is more than can be said for many translations, it is true. The successful translator is an interpretative creative artist, because he first comes to a full and rich understanding of the work of art in its original language, and then he seeks to communicate this complex art experience in another language. Always he tries to be faithful to the meaning and the spirit of the original as he interprets them; and often he tries to preserve something of its verse form, though Westbrook felt it more important to keep the sense clear than to follow the ballad riming. Somewhat comparable to the translation of Goethe's verses, printed with the music, is Franz Liszt's arrangement of Schubert's *Erlking* as a piano solo. This too may be called interpretative creative activity. Such musical arrangements by creative artists are not mere transpositions (as from one key to another, a purely mathematical and mechanical matter) or transcriptions; for they are in the nature of translations of the artist's full understanding of the original into the 'language' of another instrument or ensemble. So Liszt made of a song a tone poem for piano alone, and you may be interested in observing, by listening to a recording, what he did in the process of arrangement.

Such, then, are the three quite different sorts of interpretative creative activity that we have considered in relation to the Schubert song *The Erlking*; but we cannot leave Goethe's ballad without noting that some thirty-eight composers have created musical settings for it, and that the one by Loewe has been regarded highly by many critics.

2. *The interpretative artist*

Since interpretative artists engage in such a variety of activities and since there are at times several of them serving as essential middlemen between the original producer and the ultimate consumer, it may be well to say something rather general about the interpretative artist and his creative activity.

What was said in Chapter 4 about the characteristics of the creative artist was there applicable especially to the primary creative artist. There it was said that the creative artist is a person of unusual sensory refinement who is actually more observant than most of us; that he is gifted with an active imagination and the ability to hold and work with images and insights; that he has a special knowledge of his art field and a developed skill in its specific techniques; and that he has an abundance of physical and nervous energy and the ability to control its expenditure. The interpretative artist also is thus characteristically observant, imaginative, skilled, and dynamic. But it must be said that he is sensitive and observant of somewhat different things, imaginative in a different way, possessed of different skills, and different in his expenditure of dynamic energy.

Similarly the four steps in the creative process—initial stimulus, conception of creative idea, development of the germinal idea, and final execution of the work of art—were discussed with particular reference to the primary creative artist. Perhaps it went unnoticed that a rough parallel may be seen in the four pair of characteristics and the four steps in the process:

sensitive and observant   — initial stimulus
imaginative and tenacious — conception of idea
informed and skilled   — development of idea
dynamic and controlled   — execution of art work

Because he is sensitive, he responds to the initial stimulus; because he is imaginative, he conceives the idea; because he is skilled, he can develop the idea; because he is dynamic, he can carry his work to completion. And the creative process of the interpretative artist may also be viewed as comprising these four steps.

Whatever the happy accident may be that first introduces him to the primary art work that he later re-creates, the initial stimulus in the creative process is that original work of art. For Schubert, it was Goethe's ballad *Der Erlkönig*, which, because of his sensitiveness to the words as symbols and his observant discrimination of their meanings for him, he was able to read.

As a second step in the process, the interpretative artist, because of his imaginative gift, is suddenly struck with a creative idea, an idea of what the original 'really means' or 'the feel of it' of 'how it should go' or 'what to do with it.' We shall never know just how far in his reading Schubert had gone before he suddenly 'felt' the on-rushing triplets and the up-surging wind and 'heard' the several voices of the characters. And this was his imaginative experience, the meaning of Goethe's poem for him in terms of music, not as speech, but as song.

The third step, the development of the idea, is also to be seen in interpretative creative activity. With Schubert, an accomplished song writer at eighteen, there was already a great musical knowledge and compositional skill that went to work for him in the swift development of his first conception. Perhaps it took a second or third reading of the poem—we do not know when in the process the friends called on him—until that first conception for a musical setting was fully developed in Schubert's mind.

The fourth step in the interpretative creative process is the execution of the work of art. In the case of Schubert's work, with friends waiting, he dashed off the manuscript, writing the notes as fast as his pen would go, controlling his expenditure of energy until the work was done. And apparently there was comparatively little revision and correction at a later time.

Now let us look at, say, Alexander Kipnis as an interpretative artist and his creative activity in performing Schubert's *The Erlking*. As a singer he was sensitive to the musical notation and words as symbols. He was observant of the key signature, time, and tempo; of the pitch and time value of each note; of each sharp and flat; of each slur and rest. Doubtless his musical score had only the German text. As Kipnis was a Ukrainian by birth, he probably gave very close attention to the words themselves, making sure that he understood their meaning. At some point in the complicated process of reading the music and words, the singer's imagination must have been fired with an idea of just how *he* would interpret it, how *he* would differentiate the narration from the dialog of father and son, how *he* would create the illusion of the supernatural elf king that the child alone can see and hear, how *he* would recite the climactic words.

These first two steps in the singer's activity are essentially interpretative; the next two steps are outwardly creative.

Now came the developmental work, in which Kipnis brought to bear his vocal technique. He practised, both alone and with his accompanist Dougherty, to achieve in his singing the outward expression of his interpretation of the song. This may indeed have involved him in arduous work and self-criticism; it may have included enriching study and perhaps coaching with his gifted 'old teacher' E. Grenzebach, and there may have been try-outs before groups of critical friends. It was, however, in the first or subsequent performance or in the flawless recording, perhaps after many false cuttings, that the final execution of the singer's work of art took place. It was at this time that his energies must have been most abundant and most controlled. Many singers and other performing artists condition themselves with great care, with rest and proper food and even meditation of one sort or another, before appearing before an audience; then they 'give themselves' without stint, often with the display of terrific energy under amazing control, in their interpretative creative activity. You may be even more conscious of this in observing a living musical performance of *The Erlking* than in listening to a recording.

We may say two things, then, about the interpretative creative artist—whether he be translator or arranger, illustrator or composer of a musical setting, builder or performer. First, he is a discriminating and imaginative reader of the primary work that he interprets. Second, he is a technically skilled and disciplined creator or performer of his interpretation of this primary work.

3. *Translation and similar creative activity*

There have been three general sorts of interpretative creative activity suggested in the preceding sections—translation or arrangement; illustration or composition of musical setting; building or performance. There is no one word commonly used to name each of the three, so we shall call them translation, etc.; illustration, etc.; and performance, etc., and take them up one by one in these next three sections.

By *translation, etc.* we shall mean interpretative creative activity that tries to put the meaning and beauty and form of the original work of art into a *related medium*. That is, the German ballad of Goethe was put into English. German and English are both symbol systems, or languages as we call them; they are what is here meant by related media. Westbrook's effort was to put into English as much of the meaning and beauty of Goethe's ballad (as he interpreted it) as he could, and at the same time save as much of the ballad form as possible.

In much the same way Liszt arranged Schubert's song for piano solo. You can see that, by eliminating the voice as an instrument, Liszt did away with the words as a sequence of meaningful symbols. But for those who know their folk-lore, or for those who have read Goethe's ballad or heard Schubert's song, the title of Liszt's arrangement, *Der Erlkönig*, is enough of a symbol to stand for the whole sequence of events otherwise symbolized by the words of the ballad, and this is suggested by the music as a sequence of natural and resemblative signs. The person who does not have this knowledge will have a markedly different experience in listening to a performance of Liszt's interpretative composition. Voice with piano accompaniment is one medium of musical expression; piano alone is another. So Liszt, who had unusual command of the expressive potentialities of the piano—he was perhaps the most brilliant performer of his day—translated the meaning and beauty and form of the Goethe-Schubert song (as he interpreted it) into the piano medium, of which he was such a master.

The Roman sculptors who copied the late Greek statue of the discus thrower did much the same sort of thing. A reconstruction of the original *Discobolus* by Myron, which was probably in bronze, is to be seen in the Terme Museum in Rome. The copy now in the Vatican is of marble. The bronze original was cast; the marble copy was carved. The bronze has great tensile strength, which allows the weight of the whole figure to be carried on the right foot, balanced

Terme Museum, Rome   photo by Alinari   Vatican Museum   photo by Alinari   Harvard Univ.   photo by J. K. Ufford

(a) Plaster reconstruction of bronze   (b) Marble copy of bronze, restored   (c) Bronze copy of marble

Three copies of DISCUS THROWER by Myron

by the left toe; but the marble has much less strength than the bronze, so the interpretative sculptor had to leave a stump-like mass to support the weight of the figure. He also altered the position of the head. Perhaps he considered the forward look a better interpretation of what he thought Myron really meant, than the looking-back position as represented in the reconstruction of the original bronze. So the Roman sculptor who carved the marble *Discobolus* really translated or arranged the late Greek original. The third of the accompanying illustrations is of a bronze copy of the marble version of the bronze original! It was made by Jonderia Chiurazzi of Naples, and stands by the Hemenway Gymnasium on the Harvard University campus. You will notice that the stump-like mass, that was necessary to support the stone, survives without necessity in the present bronze copy. . . .

Other examples of this sort of interpretative creative activity may be cited briefly: The steel engraver, mentioned at the beginning of this chapter, translated the painter's large and colorful picture into his black and white medium in which the values and forms of the original are expressed by means of closely arranged lines finally printed from a plate. The painting and the engraving may be looked upon as related media. So, too, may the theater, radio, and cinema; and it is not uncommon for a stageplay to be adapted to one of those different yet related media for production as a radio-drama or moving picture. Such adaptations are similar to literary translations, musical arrangements, and sculptural copying.

As a present illustration of interpretative creative activity, let us consider the Aesopic fable called *The Man and the Lion*. It is quite impossible to put one's finger definitely on the original of this or any particular Aesopic fable; but let us assume that this one was written by the man called Aesop. For there doubtless was such a man, though some have questioned his very existence. Of uncertain origin, place and date of birth, Aesop lived during the 6th century B.C. A slave of one Iadmon by name, who lived on the Greek island of Samos, he was apparently freed. Perhaps a Negro (an Ethiop, Aethiop, whence Aesop's name), perhaps a hunchback, he was certainly quick-witted and disguised his criticism of contemporary tyranny in the form of fables. He met a violent death at the hands of the inhabitants of Delphi, who were perhaps enraged by his veiled insults; but the Delphians repented, when struck by a later pestilence, and offered to pay for their wrong-doing. Grandson Iadmon stepped forward to claim the wergild.

Aesop probably did not write down the fables. They were collected, about the year 300 B.C., by Demetrius of Phaleron, founder of the Library at Alexandria. They were translated into Latin by Phaedrus, a Greek freedman of Augustus, in the first century A.D. Later Greek and Latin versions also survive. But the fables or apologues that accumulated about the name of Aesop are by no means all Greek in origin; some of them are Hindu, and many of them later in origin. Everyone who retold the fables as he heard them seems to have felt free to interpret them as he wished, adjusting the moral to the occasion. So, of course, many different versions have survived, of which the following represents one version.

Ἄνθρωπος καὶ λέων ⟨συνοδεύοντες⟩.

Ὤδευέ ποτε λέων σὺν ἀνθρώπῳ. Ἕκαστος δὲ αὐτῶν τοῖς λόγοις ἐκαυχῶντο. Καὶ δὴ ἐν τῇ ὁδῷ ἦν ἀνδρὸς στήλη πετρίνη λέοντα πνίγοντος. Ὁ δὲ ἀνὴρ ὑποδείξας τῷ λέοντι ἔφη· « Ὁρᾷς σὺ πῶς ἐσμεν ὑμῶν κρείττονες. » Κἀκεῖνος εἶπεν ὑπομειδιάσας· « Εἰ λέοντες ᾔδεισαν γλύφειν, πολλοὺς ἂν ἄνδρας εἶδες ὑποκάτω λέοντος. » Ὅτι πολλοὶ καυχῶνται διὰ λόγων ἀνδρεῖοι εἶναι καὶ θρασεῖς οὓς ἡ πεῖρα γυμνασθέντας ἐξελέγχει.

For those who have less than a little knowledge of Greek, this literal translation may be of interest.

MAN AND LION
by *Aesop* (?), translated by *William Tudhope*

On one occasion a lion made a journey with a man. Each of them boasted in their conversation. On the roadside there was a statue of a man strangling a lion. Pointing it out the man said to the lion, "Do you see how we are stronger than you?" The lion said with a smile, "If lions knew how to carve, you would see many men in the grip of a lion."

The moral is that many people boast in words that they are brave and fearless, but that experience strips them and shows them up.

A medieval Latin version of this fable will, for our purposes, be attributed to Phaedrus, whose name became almost a synonym for Aesop.

HOMO ET LEO
by *Phaedrus* (?)

Homo certabat cum Leone, fortior
Quis esset, litisque hujus testimonium
Dum quaerunt, ad sepulcrum tandem venerunt,
Elisis in quo ab homine pictum faucibus
Leonem ostendit, argumentum virium.
Leo respondit: Humana hoc pictum manu.
Videres hominem dejectum, si pingere
Leones scirent. Sed ego testimonium
Dabo virtutis certius. Ad spectaculum
Induxit Hominem, monstrans ubi bona fide
Enectos a leonibus homines, ait:
Non est colorum testimoniis opus;
Hic exhibetur vera virtus actibus.
Colore frustra mendaces uti docet
Fabella, certa cum datur probatio.

Two English versions of *The Man and the Lion* fable are here presented. The first is by Sir Roger L'Estrange, one of the most famous English translators of Aesop. The second version is by Sir Richard Steele who wove it into one of the *Spectator papers*.

A LION AND A MAN
by *Sir Roger L'Estrange*

There was a controversy started betwixt a lion and a man, which was the braver and the stronger creature of the two. "Why, look ye," says the man, after a long dispute, "we'll appeal to that statue there," and so he showed him the figure of a man cut in stone with a lion under his feet. "Well," says the lion, "if we had been brought up to Painting and carving, as you are, where you have one lion under the feet of a man, you should have twenty men under the paws of a lion."

The Moral

'Tis against the rules of common justice for men to be judges in their own case.

(1692-9)

THE LION AND THE MAN
from *The Spectator* No. 11, by *Sir Richard Steele*

[The character Arietta is speaking:]

The man, walking with that noble animal, showed him, in the ostentation of human superiority, a sign of a man killing a lion. Upon which the lion said very justly, "We lions are none of us painters, else we could show a hundred men killed by lions, for one lion killed by man."

(March 13, 1711)

L'Estrange includes in his version a full paragraph of 'Reflection,' common in some versions of the Aesopic fables, in which it is said that " 'Tis against common equity for the same people to be both parties and judges, and that's the case betwixt the man and the lion. Now the lion is much in the right, that characters, pictures, and images are all as the painter, the carver, or the statuary pleases; and that there's a great difference betwixt a flight of fancy and the history of nature. 'Tis much easier for a man to make an ass of a lion upon a pedestal than in a forest. . . ."

The moral is a regular part of the Aesopic fable, but the various translators and adapters have enjoyed some freedom here. Steele's Arietta uses the fable as a leonine defense against female detractors. For L'Estrange, writing during the time when Englishmen were much concerned for their human rights, the significance of the fable is essentially legal. For the Rev. G. F. Townsend (1871), the moral was that "One story is good, till another is told." For Joseph Jacobs (1854): "We can easily represent things as we wish them to be." The moral for one of the Greek versions: "Boasters brag even when they have no grounds for what they say"; and of another: "He who treats his equals with justice will not fail in vanquishing them."

The famous French version of the Aesopic fables is by Jean de La Fontaine, one of the most celebrated poets of the golden age of Louis XIV, a friend of Molière and Racine, of Boileau and de la Rochefoucauld. La Fontaine drew freely upon both Greek and Latin sources for his materials. Here is

LE LION ABATTU PAR L'HOMME
by *La Fontaine*

On exposait une peinture
Où l'artisan avait tracé

Un lion d'immense stature
Par un seul homme terrassé.
Les regardants en tiraient gloire.   `
Un lion en passant rabattit leur caquet.
Je vois bien, dit-il, qu'en effet
On vous donne ici la victoire;
Mais l'ouvrier vous a décus;
Il avait liberté de feindre.
Avec plus de raison nous aurions le dessus
Si mes confrères savaient peindre.

(1668)

We can never be sure just which version of an Aesopic fable was the original or what several versions may have colored the interpretation of a particular translator. But certainly La Fontaine did more than simply put the Aesopic fable into French, and he did more than substitute the Phaedrus picture for the original statue. He quite changed the dramatic setting and incident, and really developed in a tightly knit poetic form a somewhat different fable on the same theme. Most persons would call it a miniature work of art. But let us turn to interpretative creation of another sort.

4. *Illustration and similar creative activity*

In translation, etc., the interpretative artist studies the original and then tries to recreate it in a related medium. In what we shall call *illustration, etc.*, the interpretative artist studies the original and then tries to give expression to its essential meaning in some *quite different medium*. 'Related medium' and 'quite different medium' are at best relative terms, so there may be no agreement about where to make the division; but, for the most part, translation and illustration will be seen to be quite different. Along with illustration, you may recall, we shall consider the composition of a musical setting, and we have already commented on Schubert's *The Erlking* as an example. So we shall give but brief attention to illustration and other similar creative activity in which the artist expresses his interpretation of a primary work of art in a medium quite different from the original.

As an example of illustration, the Doré headpiece for La Fontaine's fable is here reprinted. It was drawn by Gustave Doré and engraved by Delduc.

Doré depicted the people as fleeing in all directions from the lion, who seems more zoological than fabulous. An illustration attributed to J. J. Grandville and engraved by Verdell (?) shows a beaux arts

lion in the African desert, with palette and brush, rustic easel and great canvas, painting a lion triumphantly mauling not one but several men.

It's worth noting that neither Doré nor Grandville tried to represent literally the scene suggested by La Fontaine's fable. Doré chose to show what he thought logically should follow, and Grandville chose to show what even the lion implied could never be! Perhaps neither one of them studied the original quite closely enough. But the illustrator is always faced with the problem of deciding just what moment or moments in a story he will try to depict in his graphic medium, what moment will best represent the meaning of the original, and what moment will provide the basis for an effectively composed picture.

Somewhat different from graphic illustration, yet interpretative creative activity of the same general sort, is dramatic adaptation. The theatre represents a quite different medium from prose fiction. A novel is a book to be read alone by the fire. A stageplay is the acting out of a story upon a stage before an audience. A novel may involve twenty hours of reading; a stageplay is a two-hour spectacle. To turn a successful novel into an equally successful stageplay is not like translating that novel into a different language. It involves a complex adaptation, dramatization and production. Changes inevitably are made in the plot construction, in the characters, in the dialogue; and the over-all meaning will undergo a change in the process.

Similar to dramatization is the interpretative creative activity of the dancer who takes a literary or musical work as the basis for choreography.

In such dance-adaptations, in dramatizations, in the composition of musical settings, and in illustrations you may observe a general

sort of interpretative creative activity different from translation, etc.,
different also from the musical and dramatic performances to which
we now turn.

5. *Performance and similar creative activity*

In TRANSLATION, ETC., the meaning of the original or primary
work is given expression in a *related medium*. In ILLUSTRATION, ETC.,
the meaning of the original or primary work, or of some part of it,
is given expression in a *quite different medium*. In PERFORMANCE,
ETC., (not only in musical and dramatic performance but in similar
activities to be mentioned shortly), the meaning of the original or
primary work is given expression in the intended or *implicit medium*.

That is, the composer's musical score is intended to be performed;
the playwright's script is intended to be acted out upon a stage in a
theater. Musical performance is thus implicit in the music on the
page; the notes and various marks are symbols which mean, first of
all, various complex activities of performance. The words in the
playscript are symbols standing, first of all, for speech sounds to be
made and actions to be performed by actors. La Fontaine did not

intend that his Fables be translated, and he did not write them in order to have them pictured by an illustrator. But Schubert did write out the music of *The Erlking* so that Vogl and other singers could perform it; and Shakespeare did write out *A Midsummer-Night's Dream* so that his fellow actors might present it as a stageplay.

Again you may be surprised that there is so much interpretative creative activity of this third general sort. The work of the master builder, mentioned in an early paragraph of this chapter, involves the careful study of every minute aspect of the architect's blueprints and written specifications. He interprets each resemblative and symbolic sign, and gradually the building takes shape in his imagination. Then comes the organizational and developmental work, his own planning of procedures, securing of materials, ordering and scheduling; and this preliminary creative activity is followed by the processes of the actual building. So the general contractor, as we call the master builder in our day, really gives a sort of performance of the primary work of the architect.

The dancers who interpret the directions of their choreographer and practice to perform their parts in a group dance are also interpretative artists of this same general sort. So also is the orator who studies the delivery of his own manuscript—and the public official who practices reading aloud the words prepared for him by his ghost writer. Like the master builder, the singer, or the actor, their activity is again twofold: first, to study and so come to an understanding of the original or primary work of art; and second, to give that understanding expression in the implicit medium. That is, first to interpret and then to create.

The characteristic performance—not the building, but the musical recital, the stageplay, the dance, and the oration—implies an audience. Now an audience consists of people who come together, usually sit down, and are prepared to give attention to the performance. An audience behaves, not as so many individual persons, but as a group. The individuals respond, not only to the work of art created by the performers, but also to the forces within the social group. By responding to the performers—with rapt attention, laughter, tears, breathless hush or wild applause—the audience actually stimulates the performers or, if the response is cold and restless and disapproving, frustrates them. In a sense, the audience therefore becomes a part of the performance.

The following merry scene from Shakespeare's *A Midsummer-Night's Dream* may well serve to illustrate this brief discussion of performance and so conclude the present chapter on interpretative creative activity. In this fantastic comedy Shakespeare developed three sets of characters: First, the Athenian court—Theseus, Duke of Athens, and his betrothed, Hippolyta, Queen of the Amazons; and two pair of young lovers—Lysander and Hermia, Demetrius and Helena. Second, the fairies—Oberon and Titania, king and queen of the fairies, Puck, and other fairies. Third, the Athenian artisans—Bottom, the weaver; Quince, the carpenter; Snug, the joiner; Flute, the bellows-mender; Snout, the tinker; and Starveling, the tailor. In the complexities of the plot the fortunes of these three groups of persons cross and recross.

In the generation after Shakespeare's time the scenes involving the last group of characters were made into a droll, or short play, and it was "acted at Bartholomew Fair and other markets in the country by strollers." It was published in several editions as *The Merry Conceited Humours of Bottom the Weaver*. And in our own time a somewhat similar arrangement of comic scenes from *A Midsummer-Night's Dream* is often performed separately as a one-act play.

In an amusing early scene (Act I, scene ii of Shakespeare's play), we are introduced to Nick Bottom, Peter Quince, Francis Flute and the rest of the 'rude mechanicals.' They have gathered at Quince's house to cast the interlude that they are to present before the duke and duchess on their wedding night. Quince serves as stage director, and assigns the roles, but with much advice from Bottom, who can see himself playing all the good parts in turn. But Quince's decision stands, and Bottom will play Pyramus and Flute will play Thisbe his beloved; Snug will be the Lion, and so on. Each is given his lines to learn, and Quince himself will 'draw a bill of properties such as our play wants.'

At their rehearsal the next night (III,i), held a mile from town in the privacy of the woods, a problem arises: how shall they represent the moonlight, essential to the romantic scene, and the wall that keeps the young lovers apart? The decision is that each of these shall be portrayed by an actor. The rehearsal proceeds, but is thoroughly disrupted when Bottom makes his second cue entrance from a thicket transformed by the fairy magic of Puck—and now possessed of an ass's head on his own two shoulders! It is not to our present purpose to summarize the incidents of Queen Titania's awakening and her magically induced love for Bottom in his monstrous form (III,i; IV,i) and of his own later waking as from a dream, there in the woods and once more with his natural head. Then he rejoins his fellow actors, once more at Quince's house (IV,ii), and preparations are concluded for the play.

The performance itself, 'The most lamentable comedy, and most

cruel death of Pyramus and Thisbe,' is here presented somewhat
abridged and condensed (V,i). It is indeed 'a tedious brief scene'
and 'very tragical mirth.'

PYRAMUS AND THISBE

from A MIDSUMMER-NIGHT'S DREAM, V.I

by *William Shakespeare*

[The scene is the palace; it is the duke's wedding night. Theseus and
his Hippolyta, Lysander and Hermia, Demetrius and Helena, Lords and
attendants are seated about in readiness now for the show. The light-
hearted banter is interrupted by the re-entrance of Philostrate, master
of the revels:]

PHILOSTRATE. So please your Grace, the Prologue is address'd.
THESEUS. Let him approach.   [*Flourish of trumpets.*]

   [*Enter* QUINCE *as the Prologue.*]

PROLOGUE. If we offend, it is with our good will.
   That you should think, we come not to offend,
   But with good will. To show our simple skill,
   That is the true beginning of our end.
   Consider, then, we come but in despite.
   We do not come, as minding to content you,
   Our true intent is. All for your delight,
   We are not here. That you should here repent you,
   The actors are at hand; and, by their show,
   You shall know all, that you are like to know.

THESEUS. This fellow doth not stand upon points.

LYSANDER. He hath rid his prologue like a rough colt; he knows
   not the stop. A good moral, my lord: it is not enough to speak,
   but to speak true....

THESEUS. ... Who is next?

   [*Enter* BOTTOM *as Pyramus,* FLUTE *as Thisbe,* SNOUT *as Wall,*
      STARVELING *as Moonshine,* SNUG *as Lion.*]

PROLOGUE. Gentles, perchance you wonder at this show;
   But wonder on, till truth make all things plain.
   This man is Pyramus, if you would know;
   This beauteous lady Thisbe is certain.
   This man, with lime and rough-cast, doth present
   Wall, that vile Wall which did these lovers sunder;
   And through Wall's chink, poor souls, they are content

To whisper. At the which let no man wonder.
This man, with lanthorn, dog, and bush of thorn,
  Presenteth Moonshine; for, if you will know,
By moonshine did these lovers think no scorn
  To meet at Ninus' tomb, there, there to woo.
This grisly beast, which Lion hight by name,
The trusty Thisbe, coming first by night,
Did scare away, or rather did affright;
And, as she fled, her mantle she did fall,
  Which Lion vile with bloody mouth did stain.
Anon comes Pyramus, sweet youth and tall,
  And finds his trusty Thisbe's mantle slain:
Whereat, with blade, with bloody blameful blade,
  He bravely broach'd his boiling bloody breast;
And Thisbe, tarrying in mulberry shade,
  His dagger drew, and died. For all the rest,
Let Lion, Moonshine, Wall, and lovers twain
At large discourse, while here they do remain.

[*Exeunt* PROLOGUE, PYRAMUS, THISBE, LION, *and* MOONSHINE.]

THESEUS. I wonder if the lion be to speak.

DEMETRIUS. No wonder, my lord: one lion may, when many asses do.

WALL. In this same interlude it doth befall
That I, one Snout by name, present a wall;
And such a wall, as I would have you think,
That had in it a crannied hole or chink,
Through which the lovers, Pyramus and Thisbe,
Did whisper often very secretly.
This loam, this rough-cast, and this stone, doth show
That I am that same wall; the truth is so:
And this the cranny is, right and sinister,
Through which the fearful lovers are to whisper.

THESEUS. Would you desire lime and hair to speak better?

DEMETRIUS. It is the wittiest partition that ever I heard discourse, my lord.

THESEUS. Pyramus draws near the wall: silence!

[*Re-enter* PYRAMUS]

PYRAMUS. O grim-look'd night! O night with hue so black!
O night, which ever art when day is not!
O night, O night! alack, alack, alack,
I fear my Thisbe's promise is forgot!

And thou, O wall, O sweet, O lovely wall,
Show me thy chink, to blink through with mine eyne!
[WALL *holds up his fingers.*]
Thanks, courteous wall: Jove shield thee well for this!
But what see I? No Thisbe do I see.
O wicked wall, through whom I see no bliss!
Cursed be thy stones for thus deceiving me!

THESEUS. The wall, methinks, being sensible, should curse again.

PYRAMUS. No, in truth, sir, he should not. 'Deceiving me' is Thisbe's
cue: she is to enter now, and I am to spy her through the wall.
You shall see, it will fall pat as I told you. Yonder she comes.

[*Re-enter* THISBE.]

THISBE. O wall, full often hast thou heard my moans,
For parting my fair Pyramus and me!
My cherry lips have often kiss'd thy stones,
Thy stones with lime and hair knit up in thee.

PYRAMUS. I see a voice: now will I to the chink,
To spy an I can hear my Thisbe's face.
Thisbe!

THISBE. My love thou art, my love I think.

PYRAMUS. Think what thou wilt, I am thy lover's grace;
And, like Limander, am I trusty still.

THISBE. And I like Helen, till the Fates me kill.

PYRAMUS. Not Shafalus to Procrus was so true.

THISBE. As Shafalus to Procrus, I to you.

PYRAMUS. O, kiss me through the hole of this vile wall!

THISBE. I kiss the wall's hole, not your lips at all.

PYRAMUS. Wilt thou at Ninny's tomb meet me straightway?

THISBE. 'Tide life, 'tide death, I come without delay.

[*Exeunt* PYRAMUS *and* THISBE.]

WALL. Thus have I, wall, my part discharged so;
And, being done, thus wall away doth go. [*Exit.*]

THESEUS. Now is the mural down between the two neighbours.

DEMETRIUS. No remedy, my lord, when walls are so wilful to hear
without warning.

HIPPOLYTA. This is the silliest stuff that ever I heard.

THESEUS. The best in this kind are but shadows; and the worst are no worse, if imagination amend them.

HIPPOLYTA. It must be your imagination then, and not theirs.

THESEUS. If we imagine no worse of them than they of themselves, they may pass for excellent men.
Here come two noble beasts in, a man and a lion.

[*Re-enter* LION *and* MOONSHINE.]

LION. You, ladies, you, whose gentle hearts do fear
  The smallest monstrous mouse that creeps on floor,
May now perchance both quake and tremble here,
  When lion rough in wildest rage doth roar.
Then know that I , one Snug the joiner, am
A lion-fell, nor else no lion's dam;
For, if I should as lion come in strife
Into this place, 'twere pity on my life.

THESEUS. A very gentle beast, and of a good conscience.

DEMETRIUS. The very best at a beast, my lord, that e'er I saw.

LYSANDER. This lion is a very fox for his valour.

THESEUS. True; and a goose for his discretion.

DEMETRIUS. Not so, my lord; for his valour cannot carry his discretion; and the fox carries the goose.

THESEUS. His discretion, I am sure, cannot carry his valour; for the goose carries not the fox. It is well: leave it to his discretion, and let us listen to the moon.

MOON. This lanthorn doth the horned moon present;—

DEMETRIUS. He should have worn the horns on his head.

THESEUS. He is no crescent, and his horns are invisible within the circumference.

MOON. This lanthorn doth the horned moon present;
  Myself the man i' the moon do seem to be.

THESEUS. This is the greatest error of all the rest: the man should be put into the lantern. How is it else the man i' the moon?

DEMETRIUS. He dares not come there for the candle. . . .

LYSANDER. Proceed, Moon.

MOON. All that I have to say, is, to tell you that the lanthorn is the moon; I, the man i' the moon; this thorn-bush, my thorn-bush; and this dog, my dog.

DEMETRIUS. Why, all these should be in the lantern; for all these are in the moon. But, silence! here comes Thisbe.

[*Re-enter* THISBE.]

THISBE. This is old Ninny's tomb. Where is my love?

LION. [*Roaring*] Oh——

[THISBE *runs off.*]

DEMETRIUS. Well roared, Lion.

THESEUS. Well run, Thisbe.

HIPPOLYTA. Well shone, Moon. Truly, the moon shines with a good grace.

[*The* LION *shakes Thisbe's mantle, and exit.*]

THESEUS. Well moused, Lion.

DEMETRIUS. And then came Pyramus.

LYSANDER. And so the lion vanished.

[*Re-enter* PYRAMUS.]

PYRAMUS. Sweet Moon, I thank thee for thy sunny beams;
   I thank thee, Moon, for shining now so bright;
For, by thy gracious, golden, glittering gleams,
   I trust to take of truest Thisbe sight.
      But stay, O spite!
      But mark, poor knight,
   What dreadful dole is here!
      Eyes, do you see?
      How can it be?
   O dainty duck! O dear!
      Thy mantle good,
      What, stain'd with blood!
   Approach, ye Furies fell!
      O Fates, come, come,
      Cut thread and thrum;
Quail, crush, conclude, and quell!

THESEUS. This passion, and the death of a dear friend, would go near to make a man look sad.

HIPPOLYTA. Beshrew my heart, but I pity the man.

PYRAMUS. O wherefore, Nature, didst thou lions frame?

  Since lion vile hath here deflowr'd my dear:
Which is—no, no—which was the fairest dame
That lived, that loved, that liked, that look'd with cheer.
   Come, tears, confound;
   Out, sword, and wound
  The pap of Pyramus;
   Ay, that left pap,
   Where heart doth hop: [*Stabs himself.*]
  Thus die I, thus, thus, thus.
   Now am I dead,
   Now am I fled;
  My soul is in the sky:
   Tongue, lose thy light;
   Moon, take thy flight: [*Exit* MOONSHINE.]
  Now die, die, die, die, die.   [*Dies.*] ...

HIPPOLYTA. How chance Moonshine is gone before Thisbe comes
back and finds her lover?

THESEUS. She will find him by starlight. Here she comes; and
her passion ends the play.

  [*Re-enter* THISBE.] ...

THISBE.   Asleep, my love?
   What, dead, my love?
  O Pyramus, arise!
   Speak, speak. Quite dumb?
   Dead, dead? A tomb
  Must cover thy sweet eyes.
   These lily lips,
   This cherry nose,
  These yellow cowslip cheeks,
   Are gone, are gone:
   Lovers, make moan:
  His eyes were green as leeks.
   O Sisters Three,
   Come, come to me,
  With hands as pale as milk:
   Lay them in gore,
   Since you have shore
  With shears his thread of silk.
   Tongue, not a word:
   Come, trusty sword;
  Come, blade, my breast imbrue: [*Stabs herself.*]
   And, farewell, friends;
   Thus Thisbe ends:
  Adieu, adieu, adieu.   [*Dies.*]

THESEUS. Moonshine and Lion are left to bury the dead.

DEMETRIUS. Ay, and Wall too.

BOTTOM. [*Starting up*] No, I assure you; the wall is down that parted their fathers. Will it please you to see the epilogue, or to hear a Bergomask dance between two of our company?

THESEUS. No epilogue, I pray you; for your play needs no excuse. Never excuse; for when the players are all dead, there need none to be blamed. Marry, if he that writ it had played Pyramus and hanged in Thisbe's garter, it would have been a fine tragedy: and so it is, truly, and very notably discharged. But, come, your Bergomask: let your epilogue alone. . . .

(c. 1594)

Perhaps no comment is necessary in regard to this performance. These artisans are something less than artists, it is true. Quince is not skilled in interpreting the punctuation of his set prologue, and Bottom has small knowledge of classical mythology; but such understandings as they have, they express with ingenuous ingenuity. And certainly the audience is unrestrained in its participation in the performance. Possibly the reader may himself be encouraged to interpretative creative activity and, with others, will read aloud or prepare a performance of this *Pyramus and Thisbe* or of a fuller version of *Bottom the Weaver* out of *A Midsummer-Night's Dream*, with its own elf-king and fabulous lion.

On the Human Need for Art

We all stand in need of art, whether as creators or as appreciative witnesses. Art marks the only ends of life which give full rest and repose, which can excite vivid moments without ulterior conflicts or consequences.

R. M. Ogden, *The Psychology of Art*

THIS INTERLUDE II serves as a fence that separates two fields in the layout of this book. Having come through Part Two, the discussion of 'Creative Activity and the Work of Art' and before beginning Part Three, the exploration in some detail of 'The Responsive Art Experience,' let us sit a while on the top rail and ask a big Why or two. The obvious question may assert and reassert itself: Why should good ordinary people, with no special interest in any one of the arts and with an eager desire to ride some other hobby or gallop off in some other direction—why should we give so much attention to the arts? Answers have already been suggested. It was pointed out in the Prelude that we do live, willy nilly, in the World of Art, and it behooves us to Know Ourselves and to explore our immediate as well as our more remote environments.

But the more important question is this: Why do people engage in creative art activities of one kind or another, and why do they devote conscious time and money and energy to responsive art experiences? This also is a good and fair question, though sometimes it is asked in a why-waste-your-time tone of voice, and we shall take time out to answer it in this Interlude II, 'On the Human Need for Art,' whose very title implies that people create and experience art works because for some reason they must, to satisfy certain deep human needs.

1. *Variety of art activities and experiences*

We may well recur to the thought, suggested in the Prelude, that there are worlds of different activities and experiences that comprise the World of Art. For the time being let us not be concerned with the accomplished artist and the professional critic. "Each of us," it has been maintained by Croce, "has in him a little of the poet, of the sculptor, of the musician, of the painter, of the prose writer. . . ." Each of us, possessed of at least a rudimentary art theory, is also something of a critic. And most of us engage, many of us engage daily, in creative or responsive art activities or experiences of one kind or another.

It was earlier said that when you whistle as you work, doodle on the phone pad, choose a particular tie, take a snapshot, or write a personal letter, you are engaging in creative art activity. Many persons indeed have various art hobbies, as our earlier survey of your own art activities may have revealed. You like to dance and sing with a group; perhaps you're clever at imitations and like to help put on a show; you may like to make things in your basement or garage shop, refinish furniture, or redecorate a room. You may be one who turns his dreams of the good and abundant life into house plans, or who actually remodels the attic. You may while away an hour at the piano, replaying music learned long ago or improvising sequences of chords or melodic patterns. Or you may be one of that somewhat smaller number that does sketch and paint, that does carve or model, that does write verse or short stories, that does study and practice voice or a musical instrument.

Though these various goings-on may all be qualified as creative art activity—they are certainly of the *sort* that might eventuate in works of art, whether or not the actual things created are 'generally' considered works of art or not—yet they are quite different one from another in the nature of the activity involved. So, too, there are many kinds of goings-on to be found among responsive art experiences. Again we may well loosen up our definition, and include responses to some man-made things that, while popularly evoking beauty and meaning responses, are not 'generally' considered works of art.

You may be one of those persons who regularly read magazine fiction and glance at the art features, who read pocket books on the bus or streetcar, who buy book-club romances, who listen to radio dramas and music broadcasts, who follow popular music. Or perhaps you respond with delight to a garden of flowers and shrubs, to a vase of unusual proportions and design, to a decorative arrangement on the coffee table, to a particular ensemble in dress, to the furnishing of a room, to the lines and finish and appointments of a new car. Or it may be that you enjoy the experience of only some of these works in the popular and the applied, practical, household, and industrial arts, but that you more particularly respond to works in the so-called Fine Arts. You may listen to radio or recorded performance of classical music or attend recitals and concerts, operas and dance performances, stageplays and works of cinema art. You may read the more substantial contemporary novels and significant poetry. You may go out of your way to visit great cathedrals and public buildings, memorial sculpture, and exhibitions of the old masters and modern painters, and enjoy such works of art in reproduction.

Such a wide range of responsive art experiences, as well as the great variety of creative art activities already suggested, must be kept in mind when we ask the question: What *human needs* do these art activities and experiences satisfy? Why do people create and respond to art things? Why do individual persons need art? What does art mean, what value does it have, for you and for me?

But before attempting to answer this important question, let us turn to the accompanying reproduction of *The Lacemaker*, one of the small pictures by Jan Vermeer (1632-1675), who was one of the Little Dutch painters of the seventeenth century. Not much is known of the artist's life, beyond his birth in Delft, his marriage at twenty, his family of eight children, his early death in poverty. Nor are there very many, less than fifty, of his canvases that survive. But if he had no great success in his own time and remained pretty well unknown for more than two centuries, he has come to prominence in our own day as one of the minor masters of European painting. Except for some exterior views of his home town, most of his subjects were interior domestic scenes, usually a single figure or two engaged in some household task or recreation—a servant pouring milk, a girl making lace, a woman with a water jug or reading a letter, the music lesson, a lady with a lute or girl with a flute. But the impression that these small pictures makes upon many beholders is one of unusual realism in the representation of life and of light— reflective surfaces, the texture of materials, transparency and translucency, human forms as modeled by high light and shadow.

Allow yourself ample time for a full and untrammeled response to this work of art before considering thoughtfully the questions: What human needs of Vermeer may the creation of this work of art have satisfied? and what human needs of your own may the contemplation of this work of art satisfy? . . . Perhaps you will wish to commit yourself to a few scratch paper notes before reading further. . . .

Jan Vermeer, THE LACEMAKER, National Gallery of Art
Washington, D. C. (Mellon Collection)

2. *Various human needs for art*

Why does humanity need the arts? The answer cannot be a simple one, unless one simply says that people need the arts because creative and responsive art activities and experiences satisfy a great variety of human needs. A full answer would of necessity take us deep into the springs of human behavior, the pinions and cogs of personality, the motives and cues for action, the checks and balances of mental and spiritual health. The author has written elsewhere: "Poetry—other literature, too, and works in the other arts—poetry may indeed 'minister to a mind diseas'd'; it may indeed bring peace to 'that noble and most sovereign reason' when 'like sweet bells jangled' it is 'out of tune and harsh'; it may indeed be 'the balm from Gilead'."[1]

In considering the arts as satisfying deep human needs and as having definitely therapeutic value, there is no implication that everybody is a bit crazy or that the arts are all well and good for people who are a little out of their minds. "But each and every personality," to quote again from the same passage, "is in constant need of at least minor repair and adjustment; the healing of inner hurts, the resolution of doubts, the regulation of desires, the deflation of egocentricity, the restoration of ideals. Perhaps the deepest of human ills, those of the spirit, find their remedy in the widely various practices of religion. Some such maladjustments are in this day the concern of psychiatry. Many, very many, however, of the lesser maladies of the mind respond to the ministrations of art."

Without any attempt at completeness, five interrelated human needs will be considered briefly with some comments on the way art activities and experiences may serve to satisfy them.

The first of these is the simple human need for *relaxation and recreation*. It has always been true, but is especially true in this day and age, that the activities of daily life—in the market place or schoolroom, home or industry—tend to build up physiological and psychological tensions. In order to maintain bodily and mental health, it is necessary that release from such tensions be found. The bow must be unbent to keep it strong. Physical exercise and group play are common ways to work out, to expend excess energy, and to let off steam. The result is relaxation which is conducive to good sound rest and sleep, the restoration of bodily and mental tonus, and preparation for the next job to be done. Less violent sorts of physical and social activity, such as social dancing, may have the same thera-

---

[1]*Preface to Poetry*, p. 304.

peutic effects, and sunbathing and bridge may be included in the same general category. But among the various forms of essential human recreation, art certainly is conspicuous and important. Edmund Burke wrote of 'the inward sense of melting and languor' that may accompany the contemplation of what we call works of art, and said: "... beauty acts by relaxing the solids [*sic!*] of the whole system. There are all the appearances of such a relaxation, and a relaxation somewhat below the natural tone seems to me to be the cause of all positive pleasure."

Although suggested a century earlier by Kant and Schiller, the Art as Play theory was really developed at the beginning of this century by Lange and Groos; and various creative art activities, making use of drawing, singing and rhythm games, and mimetic and dramatic play, are a part of our present day system of early education. It is almost unnecessary to point out how many adults find recreation and relaxation in group singing or other musical activities, in folk dancing and little theater work, in gardening and household arts. And much has been written of the importance of the arts as a constructive and creative use of that leisure time which modern technology will make more abundant. But the person who is weary from the full day's work can, if he has even moderate skill, sit down at the piano or pick up his musical instrument, and his playing will dispel his fatigue and perhaps discouragement, release his nervous tensions, and redispose his attitudes. However, this same sort of relaxation will come, for other persons, through the more passive activity of responsive experience, the listening to records or radio, reading a novel or short story or poetry. And then—as Schopenhauer said in regard to 'aesthetic pleasure'—"Then all at once the peace which we were always seeking, but which always fled from us on the former path of the desires, comes to us of its own accord, and it is well with us."

A second human need is for *escape*. It has long been recognized that one of the functions of literature, the theater, and the movies is to provide a means of escape for persons who find their immediate surroundings and life drab or unhappy or unendurable. And sometimes it is added that escape is no solution for present problems. But vacationing in the Never-never-land of the mysteries and romantic fiction, whether via pulps or stage or screen, may serve as a means to that relaxation of which we have spoken; and many persons return from such trips refreshed and ready to go on, if not actually to solve their discouraging life problems. Music, too, may provide such an outlet. Many listeners escape by way of music to a realm of fantasy, and some performers 'lose themselves' in the intricate patterns of their re-creative activity. So, too, the actor, for whom self-identification with the character he is creating may actually bring release from the cares and worries of his daily life.

There are other means of escape from reality besides art, of course. Although 'the shortest way out of Manchester' may be a book, it may also be a bottle. And for yet other people it is the World Series and sports page, or the Woman's Page and a flurry of meaningless social activities. It is necessary at times to escape, to get away from it all, to go on a vacation. But there is always the homecoming, the return to work, the reawakening into reality. If the experience has given one a new perspective, renewed strength, and the ability to cope with the problems of the real world, then the adventure has indeed fulfilled a great human need. C. E. Montague has spoken of the artist's outlook as being like that of "an Adam new to the Garden and just looking around." The artee also may be wide-eyed with wonder as he enters into the new world of art. His vacation has been well spent if he returns to his real world with that new look of an Adam or an Eve seeing the Garden of daily life in a new light.

The third human need is for *enrichment*. This is implicit in the need to escape from the drabness of ordinary life. But getting away for a week-end and going on a prospecting trip for gold are two different ventures, though some persons are skillful in combining business with pleasure. We have already discussed 'beauty' as the comprehensive value word often associated with the arts, and our definition of art was in terms of beauty and meaning. There must be some deep human need for beauty and meaning. From the most primitive man onward, in the unfolding pageant of anthropology and history, man has created all manner of things, not only to be useful, but to be beautiful and meaningful. And it is so today, when persons find satisfaction in decorating their homes and fixing up their yards, adorning their persons and treasuring all manner of oddments that they somehow happen to value.

But the mind, too, may be enriched by the arts. The person who reads first of all to escape from boredom, may return with all manner of information about distant lands and ancient times. So, too, the theater and especially cinema art may enrich the beholder with the veritable shape of far places and strange sights, people from beyond the seas and their modes of life. And the art of painting may in some measure do this too, but more particularly it will take one into the artist's mind and show you his vision of some bit of the outer world. Nor should we forget the enrichment that comes from the experiencing of music and the acquisition thereby of myriads of melodic and harmonic patterns.

"And this," writes Plato in his *Symposium*—"this is the true discipline of loving or being loved: that a man begin with the beauties of this world and use them as stepping-stones for an unceasing journey to that other beauty, going from one to two and from two to all, and from beautiful creatures to beautiful lives, and from beautiful lives to beautiful truths, and from beautiful truths attaining finally to nothing less than the true knowledge of Beauty itself, and so know at last what Beauty is." And indeed there is a deep human need both for love and for beauty in life and art.

A fourth great human need is for *companionship*. We have a deep need for friends as well as acquaintances, for loved ones as well as friends. In part, at least, this is based upon the necessity of sharing our experiences. And man, because of his much more complex organism and the capacities for thought and refined emotion, not only enjoys richer and more highly differentiated experiences than do lower forms of life, but he has incomparable means of expression and communication in language and the arts. "For the arts," writes I. A. Richards, "are the supreme form of communicative activity," and we have already quoted John Dewey as saying, "Art is the most effective mode of communication that exists."

In saying this we must keep clear in our minds what it is that we can share with other persons most effectively by way of the arts. It is, of course, human experiences of value and significance, of beauty and meaning. Richards has said further, "In the arts we find the record in the only form in which these things can be recorded of the experiences which have seemed most worth having to the most sensitive and discriminating persons." And when you respond fully and thoughtfully to such a record of the artist's worthwhile experience, you indeed share vicariously in that experience. Certainly, through the epic and novel, the drama and stageplay, the cinema and other media of fiction—and only in a somewhat different way through the other arts—you enlarge and deepen your understanding of humanity. And in so far as you put pen to paper to share, through letter writing, the rich moments or the trials or the daily routine of your life with some friend far away—or when you sit down to play the piano for some friends close at hand—you are engaging in creative activity to fulfill this same general need for human companionship, the sharing of experience. Tolstoy once said, "The task for Christian art is to establish brotherly union among men."

The fifth one of the great human needs is for mental *order and balance*. This has already been referred to in the opening paragraphs of this particular section, and it is implicit in what was said in regard to the other human needs. The bodily tensions which must be released are often the result of mental tensions, confusions that result from the pressure of work, or fatigue; and the arts—and other sorts of activity too—may serve as remedial relaxation, as a vacation from reality, as a means of quiet enrichment and the sharing of experience, all of which may incidentally restore perspective, re-establish balance in one's interests, and bring order once more out of chaos. But there is another and more immediate way that the arts may serve this end, and this is especially true of the temporal and spatiotemporal arts. During the time that you listen to a symphony, for instance, your conscious life is given a certain order and pattern by the design of the successive stimuli that claim your attention. When you read a novel or a poem, see a stageplay or ballet, the same thing is true: whatever the confusions and conflicts and chaos of your previous consciousness, now and for this period of time at least, your life is given a single direction and your mental processes are ordered and organized by the work of art to which you are responding. And the same thing is true, without being bound to a certain time-scheme, while you are contemplating a picture, work of sculpture, or building.

For the person engaged in creative art activity, the same ordering of the mind takes place. When you sit at the piano playing a Chopin *Prelude* or the latest song hit, your present activity controls your consciousness and organizes your mental life. Writing a poem or letter, sketching or carving, drawing plans or refinishing an old chair will do the same thing. We are all acquainted with the therapeutic use of the arts and crafts in the treatment of various mental disorders, but we must not overlook the human need for art in maintaining mental health in normal people by restoring order and balance after the chaotic and upsetting and disturbing activities of our daily life. In his *Timaeus* Plato wrote that melody "is given us to help us in ordering and assimilating to it the discordant motions of our souls. And rhythm again was given us . . . for the same purpose, to help us in dealing with what is unmeasured and chaotic in the minds of most of us."

These five interrelated human needs—for relaxation, for vacation, for enrichment, for companionship, and for order—are ministered to, in one way and another, by the arts. So it can be said, Humanity needs the Arts to meet its human needs.

3. *Other needs and other times*

But these five human needs are by no means the only ones that may be served by creative and responsive art activities and experiences. It will be sufficient, however, merely to mention a few of the others. For instance, there is the human need for recognition, some form of social success; and certainly skill in primary or interpretative creative activity provides some persons with that public acclaim that is requisite for their happiness and health. Then there is the human need for the opportunity to serve some higher or greater authority, and many have been the jugglers who have brought such talents as they have had and offered them in service to God. Another and certainly very human need is for daily bread, and professional and commercial musicians, artists, and writers are impelled, in no small measure, by the demands of the family larder. And it would only be right to add that there are human needs beyond our ken, that people engage in art creatively and responsively for reasons other than here suggested, to fulfill needs but dimly felt and hardly understood.

It is perhaps unnecessary to point out the extent to which persons of great achievement in our own and other times have recognized the need of the arts in their own lives. Let us not cite the artists themselves or the professional critics, or those persons who have achieved success both in the world of affairs and in one of the arts, such as Richard B. Sheridan (statesman—dramatist), Alexander Graham Bell (inventor—painter), Lawrence Langer (patent attorney—theatrical producer), Wallace Stevens (insurance executive—poet), John Erskine (English professor—musician). We have already referred to Jefferson and the place that creative architecture and music occupied in his life. Other presidents may be named also who have felt a need for the arts: Hoover read mysteries, Roosevelt treasured boat models, Truman plays the piano. No one can forget that Winston Churchill took his paints and palette with him when he went to the Casablanca Conference.

Enough has been said, certainly, to remove the arts from the luxury category in relation to humanity. It is true that, when economy clamors to eliminate the frills from education or from the civic budget, the arts often come under attack and the 3 R's of basic literacy are extolled. And the arts for mere entertainment, for killing time, for surface decoration, for superficial culture—the arts conceived as serving no fundamental human needs are, doubtless, an extravagance and gross waste of the taxpayers' good money. But this is, in our opinion, a dim view of the real human need for the arts.

The public library and art association, summer concerts in the park and the community theater program, folk dancing and civic festivals, instruction in the arts and extracurricular art activities—these are, indeed, some of the necessities of a full and healthy life. Give us these too as daily bread!

It must be said, however, that creative or responsive art activity or experience will not always minister to the individual's particular human need. Nor will you always put your hand upon the particular work of art that would be most suited to your psychological condition of that moment. There are times when listening to a symphony simply isn't it, when scraping varnish off that old dresser will do the trick. And a work of art that at one time will speak to your own needs with terrific instancy will, upon another occasion, seem relatively valueless or insignificant. So you should not expect every work of art that you come across, or that is presented to you, to speak to your present condition. But it may have something to say to you at a future time, when the residue of the present experience is dimly recalled to be reinterpreted. One can indeed, by consciously putting oneself into a physical and psychological attitude of readiness to accept whatever may be of future value, store up art experiences as treasures to be drawn upon at times of future stress and strain, doubt and dismay, confusion and chaos, and then revive these earlier responses to fill the then present human need.

Therefore, the music with which this Interlude will close—Samuel Barber's *Adagio for Strings*—may seem quite useless to you today. But, if you attend to the recording, which it is expected you can arrange to hear, and allow yourself a full and thoughtful response to it, it may somehow contribute to such personal needs as those suggested above.

The Theme of
ADAGIO FOR STRINGS
by *Samuel Barber*

(Copyright, 1939, by G. Schirmer, Inc. Printed by permission.)

Samuel Barber is a contemporary American composer, born in 1910 in Pennsylvania. He was encouraged in his musical career by his aunt, the celebrated singer Louise Homer. He studied at the Curtis Institute in Philadelphia, and he early won important prizes for his work in composition. His music includes songs, chamber music, and orchestral works. His *First Symphony,* in one movement, was performed in Rome and at Salzburg before the World War II, during which Barber served in the Army Air Corps. The *Adagio for Strings* comes from his *String Quartet in B minor,* which was rewritten for string orchestra at the suggestion of Toscanini, who conducted and recorded the performance of it.

Perhaps your responsive art experience of this musical work will serve some one of your present or future human needs.

PART THREE:
THE RESPONSIVE ART EXPERIENCE

~~~~~~

Chapter 7. Perception of the Work of Art

There is nothing in the intellect unless it has first been in the senses.

Aristotle, from Vico's *New Science.*

What we perceive is a combination of direct sensuous knowledge and interpretation.

F. R. O'Neill, *The Relation of Art to Life.*

A fool sees not the same tree that a wise man sees.

William Blake, *The Marriage of Heaven and Hell.*

FROM THE OPENING chapter onward the discussion of successive problems of art theory has proceeded hand in hand with a consideration of specific art experiences. Now we come to Part Three, and shall give more particular attention to the nature and structure of the responsive art experience.

You will recall the art triad—the artist, the art work, the artee—mentioned in the first chapter; and you recognize its relation to the art process—creative activity, (the art work), the art experience. That is, the artist creates the *work of art* that the artee experiences. But we discovered that in many instances it is not as simple as that. The primary artist creates a musical composition (a symbol art work) that the interpretative artist recreates in a musical performance (an activity art work) that creates the music-in-the-air (an intangible art work), which the artee experiences. The 'which' refers rather elastically to the third of the three art works in the series, or to the last two or to all of them. That is, the listener may hear a record or he may disregard the living performance before him and attend only to the sound that he hears; or, at the other extreme, he may listen, watch the performer, and follow score at one and the same time. But whether 'the work of art' is multiple, as in this case, or single, as when one looks at a picture, it certainly is pivotal in both the art triad and the art process; that is, it is the central member of both sets of three terms each.

It may still seem to you that we belittled the work of art in our discussion of it as a public object. You may still feel that somehow a great picture or symphony or novel, even as a work of art outside the mind, is something more than a mere physical structure, a configuration of matter and motion. This materialism, you may say again, robs art of all its beauty and meaning, value and inspiration! And again I say, 'No, it need not.' You may well stand amazed before any great work of art—any man-made thing that has evoked great beauty and meaning responses in great numbers of discriminating observers and/or auditors in a great portion of the time since its original creation; and you may wonder at its potential power as a stimulus for valued human experience. The work of art is in no way lessened when we have stripped from it 'the' beauty and meaning, value and inspiration that in itself it never 'possessed.' Nor are beauty and meaning belittled when they are 'removed' from the work of art (where they never existed) and are 'relocated' in the art experience.

1. *Art experience as a total response*

The phrase 'art experience' is here used to mean the sum total of what goes on in a person as his response to a work of art. This includes the neuro-muscular activity of his receptors, a wide range of feeling responses, as well as the sequence of thoughts upon the surface of consciousness. When you listened to a recording of Schubert's song, your art experience included, first of all, the auditory activity of your hearing it. Then, it included some modifications of bodily states of which you may have been but vaguely conscious, such as increased heart beat or altered breathing, foot-tapping or head-nodding, perhaps mind-pictures of storm and the awful event, and some vague feeling of supernatural terror. And your experience also doubtless included a running fire sequence of thoughts of one kind or another, perhaps confined to the meaning of the verses of the lyric and to the succession of musical ideas, perhaps including references to your art theory and certain value judgments.

This and the following two chapters will consider the sensory and perceptual, the naive and emotive, the critical and interpretative as three separate aspects of the art experience. However, it is important to observe at the start that these three sorts of response do not occur in a neat 1-2-3 succession. It is true that you must 'see' a picture before you can feel stirred by it or interpret its meaning. But after the first look, you do not close your eyes while you continue with the other parts of the response; you keep right on looking, and what you look at and look for is partly the result of your various naive and critical reactions. So these three aspects of the art experience are intimately interrelated, and, though it will be convenient to consider them separately, we must constantly remember that they exist as a complex unity.

It will be apparent, as we proceed through the next chapter, that an experience of a work of art is by no means confined to the recipient's perceiving it and thinking about it. It is important to say at the start that listening to music, looking at a picture, reading a drama or novel involves a total personality response of the auditor, observer, or reader. This response is richly inward and may call into play remembrances, images, feelings, taste, basic drives, and all sorts of personal aspirations and frustrations, accumulated knowledge, thoughts, judgments, and so on. But this response may at the same time be noticeably outward and may include incipient bodily actions and attitudes, head-noddings, foot-tappings, adjustments of position, and other muscular activities. *An art experience, then, is the total response of a personality to a work of art.*

As an example of what is meant by 'total response', turn your thoughts back to *Pyramus and Thisbe* and consider it as a work of theater art—acted out upon a stage whose setting represents the Court of Theseus. This will call for some imaginative effort on your part as a reader. For you must try to visualize the Duke and his bride, the other paired lovers and attendants as well as Bottom, Quince, and their fellows—a stage picture in the mind's eye. As you glance back at the dialog on the pages that conclude the last full chapter, consider the printed words as symbols of the sounds uttered and as suggestions of the actor's bodily movements. Make an effort to see and hear this bit of comedy produced in the theater of your imagination, as though you were one of a jolly crowd forming a carefree audience in the theater of your mind. Now consider what your total response would be in attending a performance of this stageplay. . . .

As each reader will interpret the dialog independently and imagine a unique production of the scene, the only way the present writer can proceed with a consideration of this art experience is for you to let him refer to *his own particular* response. This he will do in the immodest first person singular, and you, the reader, will note how *different* the effect of *your own* imagined production has been upon your own personality.

I give but scant attention to the slight and tinkly music as the lights dim and restless chattery people about me gather themselves into an expectant common attitude of attention, watching the lighted curtain as I do in anticipation of what will be revealed. Now I hear distant laughter and the gay tones of inarticulate conversation as the curtain goes up and the scene is disclosed: a sort of open loggia or veranda, columns and curtained double doorways on the sides, but a wide expanse of night sky, above a balustrade, moon lighting up the right side of the loggia, leaving the left in shadow. I take it all in at a broad glance, and my eyes jump to the branched candelabra in the shadowed left side of the stage. Between them are two seated figures: a large man, regal in appearance, seated beside—ah, holding hands—tiara sparkling on her queenly head! An engaged couple in silhouette seated nearby on the railing—faces dimly visible. Another couple seated on pillows over to the left, their close faces catching the light. Love scene—with other persons barely to be seen in the background.

The music and voices have faded as my eyes are caught by the entrance in the moonlight on the right of a man in dark period attire. With slight bow he announces, "So please your Grace, the Prologue is addressed" (whatever 'addressed' means—'is dressed' perhaps? or 'has his speech ready'?). But I was right, 'Your Grace' confirms my notion that the big man is a duke or a king or something, for it is he who answers. Long trumpets back of the Duke flash, and from somewhere comes a rip-snorting fanfare.

Before it has faded away, the tail of my eye is again caught by some movement over to the right—the entrance of a fellow in rough tunic and leather breeches, hair slicked down above a pale and timorous face with square glasses over which he looks—wrists out of sleeves, awkward stance in long stockings and crude shoes. Standing alone in the empty part of the stage in the bright moonlight, he stares across at his stage audience, awkwardly awaiting the end of the toodle-doodle-do. He speaks now—his tone is more confident than his manner—but what he says is strangely confused in sense—I get it: his phrasing doesn't follow the meaning! Oho, he's memorized the words without understanding them! So when the Duke and the others laugh—"The fellow doth not stand upon points"—I get it: he hasn't bothered to observe the punctuation in his script, and I titter, too, knowingly, as do those around about me.

Others enter and line up stiffly behind the prologue speaker—what a bunch of 'characters!' I glance from one to the next as they are

introduced: the big ruddy-faced fellow, Pyramus, with a shock of red
hair and a crude yellow stage beard tied over his ears, sash and
wooden sword; the next figure in a woman's mask, obvious wig, ill-
fitted milk-maid's dress; and so on down the line. ... Again I'm
smiling and amused, as are others near me, and join with the spirit
of the Duke and his friends. ... Now the actors are all gone but one,
'Snout by name,' who doth present a wall, and I see the plaster daubed
on his coarse tunic, the stone as a symbol of the wall's substance, and
the fingers representing the hole. And so on and on...

I see the actors entering and moving about the stage, gesturing,
acting out their business; my eyes sweep over to the amused and
critical stage audience—with side glances at the persons about me. I
hear the music, the trumpeting, the dialogue, the laughter and comments from the stage—whispers, snickering, and occasional guffaws
from those about me. I'm more or less conscious, furthermore, of straining to see faces in the shadows, shifting in my seat to see past the large
man in front of me, moving forward and straining to hear the Duke's
lady, who doesn't speak loudly enough, and to hear Moon, some of
whose words aren't clear. I'm also aware of my own release of tensions
in laughter, my frame shaking, diaphragmatic spasms, facial contortions; tears in my eyes, nudging my companion, slapping my knee.

But these external actions are but manifestations of a rich and complex set of internal goings-on. The innumerable data of sight and sound
form the basis of numerous perceptions, and to these I make a wide
variety of naive responses. Like Bottom—for I recall reading the
whole drama—I would play all the parts in turn, and can imagine
myself there upon the stage, ranting with Pyramus, making like a Wall,
reassuring the ladies before Lionizing, embarrassed for Moon at his
interruption, speaking in 'a monstrous little voice' as Thisbe. I can
now see the courtly audience through the eyes of these 'hard-handed
men that work in Athens here.' With Bottom, I feel my heart swell at
the Duke's commendation, 'a fine tragedy' and 'very notably discharged.'
And my eyes are filled with merry tears—not in ridicule at the crude
efforts of this amateur theatrical, though outlandish it certainly is, but
with a rich and warm feeling of having had a part with them in their
creative play.

Even while observing closely and listening attentively—even while
responding naively in a variety of ways—I have been using my head.
Interpretation of the words uttered by the actors upon my imaginary
stage has been a critical process calling for the more or less conscious
discrimination of relevant senses of the word-sounds as heard, and the
relationship of these word-meanings to make sense of the statements.
And I'm immeasurably helped in this by catching meaning clues from
the actor's speech patterns, phrasing, emphasis, and explanatory gestures.
So when Wall describes the 'crannied hole or chink,' he represents it

by the forefinger and thumb of his left hand; and when he says 'this
the cranny is, right and sinister,' he points at this crannied hole from
first the right and then the *left* side to insure my catching the double
sense of 'sinister.' But I have a continuous discharge of all manner of
relevant thoughts as I witness this performance, not only about the
sense of what the actors say, but about its implications—the relation
of this interlude to the rest of the play as I recall it, to my other experiences in theater-going, to my larger views of life...

Certainly enough has been said to illustrate the assertion that *an
art experience is a total personality response* and that the many different sorts of sensory, affective, and logical events which make up
such a response exist in complex unity. Let us turn, therefore, to a
closer consideration of the first-named of the three separable aspects
of an art experience—sensory perception—which will occupy our
attention throughout the remainder of this chapter.

2. *Sensation, attention, perception*

In our discussion of 'the work of art' early in chapter 5, it was
pointed out that we must distinguish three things that might possibly be meant by the phrase: the work of art as conceived by the
artist, the work of art as a public object, and the work of art as perceived by the artee. The central one of these three, the public object,
which we have called pivotal, exists outside the mind of both the artist and the artee. The first and third of the three, private objects,
exist respectively in the mind of the artist and in the mind of the artee.

The work of art as perceived is a response to the public object. It
is the first of the three aspects of the complex art experience. It is
first because it is first in point of time; that is, the beginnings of
sensory activity and perception precede the other sorts of response. It
is also first because without it there can be no other aspects of the
art experience. It is also first because the naive responses and critical
interpretations are really responses to it, not to the work of art as a
public object. That is to say, when you experience a work of music,
your various naive responses (images, feelings, etc.) and your
various critical interpretations (thoughts about its meaning, etc.)
are evoked by the art work as perceived, not directly by the work of
art outside the mind. It is the music as you hear it that is gloomy,
or exciting, or melodramatic, or fateful, or pulsing for you. It is the
music as you hear it that tells you the supernatural story of elf and
child, or that is in 4/4 time for you and in minor mode, or that
you note as 'durchkomponiert' rather than in strophic form, or that

illustrates for you Schubert's attachment to Goethe's lyrics and his timely romanticism.

Indeed the only response that you make directly to the art work as a public object is to perceive it. It is important, therefore, to consider the process of sensory perception in some detail. In this process a sense organ is exposed to outward stimuli and, as a consequence, the person becomes conscious of 'something.' We earlier mentioned light waves and sound waves as the causes of sensations; now we must deal with the sensations that result from such stimulation.

It used to be said that there were five senses: sight, hearing, smell, taste, and touch. These five still stand, though touch is now looked upon as consisting of four different sensory systems that respond to surface-pressure, warmth, cold, and pain. But there are other senses as well: the sense of equilibrium, the muscle sense, and the various organic senses. Sight and hearing, both of which are distance senses, are by far the most important in considering the sensory perception of a work of art, but many of the other senses are also utilized in one way or another in art experiences.

Each of the sensory systems includes sense organs with receptor nerve-endings that are specialized to receive certain stimuli. Boring says, "A stimulus is any event that activates a sense organ and its receptors." In the sense organs, stimuli are transformed into neural impulses and transmitted along nerve fibers to various ones of the nerve centers. Those that reach the higher centers of the brain, and of which the individual therefore may become conscious, are called sensations.

The sense organs are constantly in the presence of potential stimuli: light waves, sound waves, direct contacts of varying pressure and temperature, and bodily states such as equilibrial and muscular and organic positions or conditions. And even during sleep a certain amount of sensory data is constantly being transmitted from the end organs to the lower nerve centers. Fortunately most of these communications are taken care of by the clerks in the waiting room. Only certain ones reach the self-conscious executives in the upstairs office. We would go crazy if every potential stimulus actually stimulated, and if every stimulus became a sensation. If every separate nerve end at the surface of the body or deep within its organs and muscles were to get a constant flow of messages through to consciousness, it would indeed be sensational! But we are capable of receiving a number of these sensations at the same time. Indeed we are likely to become aware of them as groups. And this general awareness of one group of sensations (or of free images or of thoughts, for that matter) of which we are conscious, and the disregard of other neural impulses (which are potential sensations), we shall call the 'field of consciousness.' The word 'attention' itself will be used to name the keen awareness of one item in the field of consciousness.

A good bit is known about the psychology of attention, this selective response in one's consciousness. Attention is unstable; it jumps from one thing to another as various ones of a group of sensations (or other items in the field of consciousness) become momentarily clearer. When strong impulses of another sort are simultaneously sent up from the nerve ends and competing sensations crowd in, attention upon the original group of sensations is accompanied by a strain that may be called 'effort.' On the other hand, when attention moves easily from one sensation to another in the group without competition or effort, it is sometimes called 'interest.' The fleeting nature of attention and the limited number of items that can be attended to at one time are both very important to an understanding of the art experience. But even though our attention jumps from one to another of the momentary sensations, we are not aware of them separately, but in groups or patterns, 'Gestalten' as some psychologists call them. The awareness of these 'things' (as our attention shifts fleetingly from sensation to sensation in the field of consciousness) is one of the mental phenomena known as *perception*.

We are not usually concerned with simple perceptions, the integration of simple sensations, but with complex perceptions which consist of two parts: immediate sensory data, and items from past experience, memories, images, etc. These two, 'the core and the context' as they have been called, are the basis for a *complex perception*.

It is important to realize that we don't 'see' with our eyes; we 'see' with our brains, and our eyes are but sense organs that transform light waves into neural impulses that are sent up to the brain for interpretation. And what we do 'see' or perceive is not alone dependent upon the sensations that we may give separate attention to, but is also dependent on our imagination, our memories, our past experiences.

3. Visual sensation and perception

The visual process involved as one looks at a picture is not so simple as it might at first seem, for the eyes are very active sense organs that make amazing adjustments to the demands of one's attention.

The eye is roughly an egg-shaped structure with a transparent small end. The inside of the large end consists of a closely packed pattern of nerve endings called the retina. These nerve endings are of two sorts, rods and cones. According to one theory the *rods* are sensitive to all the light waves that fall upon them; they send up impulses that are interpreted as white and the many shades of grey. The *cones*, this theory maintains, are sensitive to the various wave lengths of light: they send up impulses that are interpreted as red or yellow or green or blue. The rods are primarily responsible for our visual sensations of shape; the cones are responsible for sensations of color.

The retina is not uniform in the pattern of nerve endings. At the center, the fovea, there is a depressed area into which are crowded a great many cones. Because the cones are sensitive to color rays, because there are so many nerve endings in this area, the fovea is the area that provides for clear vision of color and form, whereas the greater part of the retina, with relatively few cones and rods, provides only hazy vision.

The pattern of light rays comes into the eye through the cornea (the glassy small end of the egg) and the aqueous humor or watery liquid. Then it goes through the pupil (the apparently black center which is surrounded by the iris, a blue or brown adjustable diaphragm) and the lens (a crystal-clear slightly-adjustable muscle, double-convex in shape, which inverts the pattern of light rays and brings them into focus). The light proceeds through the vitreous humor (the clear gelatinous substance that fills the eyeball); and the inverted pattern of light rays then falls upon the retina (the sensitive inside of the back of the eyeball, an arrangement of rods and cones, the optic nerve ends). Each one of these optic nerve ends transforms the particular ray of light that falls upon it into a neural impulse; and together they are sent out along the optic nerve (made up of about half a million nerve fibres) to the visual center of the brain. It is there, as we have said, that the sensation of 'seeing' takes place—the sensations of dark and light, of line and shape, and of color.

But only the center of the immediate vision will be clear, the rest hazy or blurred out of focus. However, the eye is provided with pairs of outside (extrinsic) muscles that control its position and movement within its socket. You have noticed that your eyes are almost continually in motion. Only rarely does one stare at something; children are scolded when their attention is concentrated upon some inner thought and their eyes remain fixed, apparently focused on some object. 'Don't stare' is like the policeman's warning, 'Keep moving.' Normally the eyes are engaged in a sequence of alternate saccadic (jumpy) movements and fixations—jerk (pause) jerk (pause) jerk (pause), etc. It is during the pauses that the pattern of light rays stimulates particular rods and cones. It is by means of these jerky eye movements that different parts of the larger pattern of light rays are brought to bear on the fovea (that central area of the retina) which alone provides clear vision.

A scientific study of these eye movements has been made and is described in the book, *How People Look at Pictures*. Guy T. Buswell developed special laboratory equipment at the University of Chicago for photographing the eye movements of an individual while he is looking at a picture. It is his assumption that "the center of fixation of the eyes is the center of attention at a given time." That is, *we jerk our eyes to a position which will give us clear vision of that which claims our momentary attention.* The pause will not be long: it may be as little as one-tenth of a second; it averages one-third of a second; it is seldom longer than a full second. Even during this short pause, attention, which we described as very unstable, is on the move. At first it moves restlessly among the group of sensations within the area of clear vision; then some vague sensation from the field of less clear vision demands attention, and jerk go the muscles that pull the eyeball around to a new position that brings this demanding stimulus into focus upon the fovea. Sometimes a change in vague sensation on the periphery (outer edge) of vision demands attention, and the eyes are jerked clear away from the picture for a momentary fixation upon a red hat that has come into the art gallery! Remember that we can give attention to other events in the mind besides sensations from our outer nerve endings; sensations from the muscular and visceral nerve endings may be just as demanding. But memories, images, and concepts also demand attention, and often crowd the immediate sensory data out of the field of attention.

Buswell demonstrates that the pattern of eye movements and the duration of fixations are notably individual, but that there are also notable similarities among the eye-movement patterns of most people. "Two general patterns of perception are apparent," he says. "One of these consists of a general survey in which the eye moves with a series of relatively short pauses over the main portions of the picture. A second type of pattern was observed in which series of fixations, usually longer in duration, are concentrated over small areas of the picture, evidencing detailed examination of those sections." The survey usually comes first; the detailed examination later, though some people only make the general survey and then pass on to another picture. "The longer fixations seem to indicate a mental process of reflection or at least a higher degree of interest than is occasioned by the ordinary survey of the picture."

Other conclusions that Buswell draws from his work are these: The pattern of eye movements does not follow the general pattern of a design, as is so often said. Art students and students generally, children and adults show no great difference in regard to their eye movements. But verbal directions given the subject before looking at a picture do influence the character of his eye movements and perception.

So much, then, for the eye movements during the active process of looking at a picture. It would be helpful if other parts of the process could be studied in the same objective way. But at the present time they cannot. Yet we must go on in, and explore as best as we can the process of mind involved in the perception of a picture.

We might say that *perception is the organizing of sensory data with our past experiences.* This is 'the core and context' of which we spoke a few pages back. The sensory data are supplied by the optic nerve ends, which keep on sending up fresh data as the eye movements bring various patterns of light into focus upon the fovea for clear vision. The picture as perceived, the image of the whole picture, grows as one contemplates it. As more sensory data are brought in by additional eye movements and fixations, the general outline of the 'picture in the mind' is filled in with more and more details. Also, more and more of the observer's past experience is brought to bear to be organized into the complex perception. After a period of thoughtful observation, the picture as seen is like the face of an old friend; it looks quite different from what it did upon first acquaintance. By a process known as *funding* the perception has become richer and more complex. To the bare consciousness of visual sensations there have been added organization, recognition, beauty, and meaning, which become fused with the 'seeing' itself. Since it is the 'work of art as perceived' to which one responds emotionally, to which one directs his critical attention, and which one evaluates, this matter of perception is of great importance.

Turn to the picture that accompanies these pages. Don't hurry yourself in observing it. Then come back and read the next paragraph. . . .

Were you at all conscious of your eye movements and fixations? To what 'objects' did your eyes keep coming back time and time again? What sensations of line and shape did you later on give attention to that at first you overlooked? What areas of the picture did you neglect? Did you at first see the man climbing into the far side of the boat? . . . Are you at all conscious of what part context (your past experience of human forms, etc.) played in your complex perception? Did you give attention to the lower right corner of

Eugène Delacroix, THE BARQUE OF DANTE, Louvre, Paris

photo by Braun

the picture?[1] Did you perceive a pair of figures? Where is the head of the left-hand figure of the pair?... Whose hand is that in the very center of the picture? Go back to the picture for another period of observation before reading the next paragraph. . . .

As perception is the integration of sensory data with data from experience, what you 'see' when you observe a painting is partly dependent upon what you already know and what you think and feel at the moment, and only partly dependent upon the pattern of light reflected into the eye. If you know something about the *Commedia* written by Dante Alighieri (1265-1321), you may recognize the figure with upraised arm as representing Dante himself, the figure in the darker robe (it is red in color) as his guide Virgil. You may recall that, visiting Inferno (Hell), they were rowed across a Stygian marsh by one of the damned. Their way was obstructed by those souls who for their sins were doomed eternally to its stagnant waters, and their progress was threatened by one (a Florentine enemy of Dante) who seized the boat!

You might, with even this small amount of additional context, return for another observation of *The Barque of Dante* (sometimes called 'Dante and Virgil in Hell') by Eugène Delacroix (c. 1799-1863). The original, nearly six feet in height, is at the Louvre, Paris. (The City Art Museum of St. Louis, Missouri, has an interesting sketch that Delacroix made of this subject.) If you turn back to the picture now, it may actually look a bit different to you. . . .

The next page of illustrations reproduces two copies made of Delacroix' painting. The one, which is to be found at the Art Institute of Chicago, is a meticulously detailed copy by an unknown artist. The other, in the Metropolitan Museum in New York City, is by Edouard Manet (1832-1883). Give some attention to the differences in your sensory perception as you compare these two copies. . . .

4. *The visual process in reading*

The process of sensory perception in experiencing a poem, short story, or similar work of art is somewhat different from that involved in the observation of a painting. The visual process in reading brings the words on the page into focus at the fovea a few at a time so that they may be seen clearly enough to be discriminated and interpreted. The pattern of eye movements and fixations is such as to

---

[1]Herman F. Brandt has shown in his *Psychology of Seeing* that the observer tends to give more attention to the upper half of a picture than to the lower, and more to the left half than to the right.

Contemporary copy by unknown artist   Courtesy Art Inst. of Chicago

Copy by Edouard Manet   Courtesy Metropolitan Museum of Art, N. Y.

Two copies of THE BARQUE OF DANTE after Delacroix

take in these groups of words in a continuous sequence: *jerk* (pause) *jerk* (pause) *jerk* (pause), etc. But attention itself moves along smoothly from word to word, from sensation to sensation, the successive black configurations in the white field. And these sensory data are integrated with context (past experience of words and things) and are perceived as words, meaningful signs.

There are other eye movements besides the saccadic jumps along the lines of printing. Some of these, for instance when one comes to a poem in a book, are exploratory in nature, like the first kind described by Buswell. A number of early fixations at the top and bottom of the printed verses, to the left and right, etc., may 'take in' the typographical form of the poem. There may also be random eye movements when attention wanders from the poem, or when other sensations (from outside or internal stimuli) crowd in with their demands irrelevant to the reading sensations.

One difference between the sensory perception of a poem and of a picture is that the pattern of eye movements is radically different, and this is so because the pattern of attention is radically different. Because we know 'how to read,' context pulls our attention along; the expectancy that the successive word-sensations will organize with least effort and most interest keeps attention moving quite literally in the *right direction*; and the eyes make their saccadic adjustments under the demands of this dynamic attention. However, there is no conventional pattern of eye movements for looking at pictures; so, unless the observer is given specific directions, his attention is free to heed demands from any direction in any order.

Another difference between the sensory perception of a poem and of a picture is that in reading a poem the sensory data sent up from the retina are simpler and the context much more complex than is the case in looking at a picture. There are the same old configurations of black and white, the same old words—but in amazingly new combinations that are meaningless except as they are integrated with an organized past experience of words and thoughts and things and events, the verbal and vital context. The sensory data are but a series of shapes; they are perceived as symbolic signs, words that demand interpretation. In the sensory perception of a picture, the sensory data are much more complex: the varied sensations of intricate shapes, and the amazingly varied sensations of color in areas of divers hues, values, and saturations. But the sensory data are not symbolic in the way language is, and the observer may integrate the sensory data quite simply with the context readily at hand. You may really have had a meaningful perception of Delacroix' picture without knowing about Dante and the *Inferno*; but your perception of the Italian verses of the original poem would be utterly meaningless unless you had wide experience in reading Italian and perhaps also a considerable body of relevant theological and historical and biographical knowledge.

To further your understanding of the visual process of reading, observe your sensory perception of the following passages from Dante's *Commedia*, the *Inferno*. The concluding part of Canto VII is here given in a prose translation; the beginning of Canto VIII, in an earlier verse translation. Besides their relevance to Delacroix' painting, the selections will here serve to suggest the difference between the visual perception of prose and of verse.

from THE DIVINE COMEDY
by *Dante Alighieri*

from *Inferno*, Canto VII, translated by *Charles Eliot Norton*

We [Dante and Virgil] crossed the circle to the other bank, above a fount that bubbles up and pours out through a trench which proceeds from it. The water was far darker than perse; and we, in company with the dusky waves, entered down through a strange way. This dismal little stream, when it has descended to the foot of the malign gray slopes, makes a marsh that is named Styx. And I, who was standing intent to gaze, saw muddy people in that swamp, all naked and with look of hurt. They were smiting each other, not with hand only, but with the head, with the chest, and with the feet, mangling one another piecemeal with their teeth.

The Good Master [Virgil] said: "Son, now thou seest the souls of those whom anger overcame; and also I will that thou believe for certain that under the water are folk who sigh, and make this water bubble at the surface, as thine eye tells thee wherever it turns. Fixed in the slime, they say: 'Sullen were we in the sweet air that is gladdened by the Sun, bearing within ourselves the sluggish fume; now we are sullen in the black mire.' This hymn they gurgle in their throats, for they cannot speak with entire words."

Thus we circled a great arc of the foul fen, between the dry bank and the slough, with eyes turned on those who guzzle the mire. We came at length to the foot of a tower.

from *Inferno*, Canto VIII, translated by *Henry F. Carey*

My theme pursuing, I [Dante] relate, that ere
We reach'd the lofty turret's base, our eyes
Its height ascended, where we mark'd uphung
Two cressets [flares], and another saw from far

Return the signal, so remote, that scarce
The eye could catch its beam.
                          I, turning round
To the deep source of knowledge [Virgil], thus inquired:
"Say what this means; and what, that other light
In answer set: what agency doth this?"
    "There on the filthy waters," he replied,
"E'en now what next awaits us mayst thou see,
If the marsh-gendered fog conceal it not."
    Never was arrow from the cord dismiss'd
That ran its way so nimbly through the air,
As a small barque, that through the waves I spied
Toward us coming, under the sole sway
Of one that ferried it, who cried aloud,
"Art thou arrived, fell spirit?"—
                          "Phlegyas, Phlegyas,[1]
This time thou criest in vain," my lord replied;
"No longer shalt thou have us, but while o'er
The slimy pool we pass."
                          As one who hears
Of some great wrong he hath sustain'd, whereat
Inly he pines, so Phlegyas inly pined
In his fierce ire. My guide, descending, stepp'd
Into the skiff, and bade me enter next,
Close at his side; nor, till my entrance, seem'd
The vessel freighted. Soon as both embark'd,
Cutting the waves, goes on the ancient prow,
More deeply than with others is its wont.
    While we our course o'er the dead channel held,
One drench'd in mire before me came, and said,
"Who art thou, that thus comest ere thine hour?"
    I answer'd, "Though I come, I tarry not:
But who art thou, that art become so foul?"
    "One, as thou seest, who mourn," he straight replied.
    To which I thus: "In mourning and in woe,
Curst spirit! tarry thou. I know thee well,
E'en thus in filth disguised."
                          Then stretch'd he forth
Hands to the barque; whereof my teacher sage
Aware, thrusting him back: "Away! down there
To the other dogs!" then, with his arms my neck
Encircling, kiss'd my cheek, and spake: "Oh soul,
Justly disdainful! blest was she in whom

---

[1]Phlegyas was so incensed against Apollo, for having violated his daughter Coronis, that he set fire to the temple of that deity, by whose vengeance he was cast into Tartarus. See Virgil, *Aeneid*, vi, 618.

Thou wast conceived. He in the world was one
For arrogance noted: to his memory
No virtue lends its lustre; even so
Here is his shadow furious. There above,
How many now hold themselves mighty kings,
Who here like swine shall wallow in the mire,
Leaving behind them horrible dispraise."
    I then: "Master! him fain would I behold
Whelm'd in these dregs, before we quit the lake."
    He thus: "Or ever to thy view the shore
Be offer'd, satisfied shall be that wish,
Which well deserves completion."
                    Scarce his words
Were ended, when I saw the miry tribes
Set on him with such violence, that yet
For that render I thanks to God, and praise.
"To Filippo Argenti!"[2] cried they all:
And on himself the moody Florentine
Turn'd his avenging fangs. Him here we left,
Nor speak I of him more. . . .

    We earlier said that perception is the integration of sensory data
with data from experience. That is, in looking at Delacroix' picture
you did not experience mere visual sensations of dark and light
shapes, what we called 'sensory data'; but you 'saw' heads and arms,
boat and oar. That is, you perceived 'things.' Now, in reading the
passages from Dante's *Inferno* as translated above, you did not 'see'
merely small black shapes on a white field, but words—words made
up of letters, words grouped as phrases; words that had (or, in one
or two cases, did not have) meaning for you as your attention moved
forward in reading them. And this integration of sensory data and
experience in perception may suggest the point in art theory introduced as an example in the Foreword—the fusion of the formal and
representational aspects of a line to form a new thing. So 'b a r q u e'
is perceived, not as black marks of certain shapes, but as the word
'barque' meaning boat.
    So you saw the word 'barque.' But you may also have seen the
boat itself in your imagination as you read the passage. If so, you
are using the word 'see' in two somewhat different senses: you perceived the word; you imagined the boat. "Perception is the appre-

---

[2]Boccaccio tells us that Filippo Argenti "was a man remarkable for the
large proportions and extraordinary vigor of his bodily frame, and the extreme waywardness and irascibility of his temper."—*Decameron*, Giorn-
ix Nov. 8.

hension of immediately present objects and events," as Feldman and Weld put it. It is the printed matter that is immediately present to the senses, not the boat. "Its limitation to the present is what distinguishes perception from recollection and imagination." But, then, you'll add that in looking at Delacroix' picture, it was only the painting that was immediately present to the senses, not the boat itself. And that is very true; but, as a resemblative sign, the representation of the boat was perceived as a boat, whereas the symbolic sign 'barque' was perceived as a word, a word meaning boat. And it is true that you 'saw' the direct sense image of the *pictured boat* and *printed word*, and that you also 'saw' the purely mental *image of a boat* evoked by the meaning of the word.

Images of direct perception that result from immediate sensations, we shall call sense-imagery; they are the concern of this chapter. Images merely suggested, and not directly of present objects and events, we shall call free-imagery; they will be considered further in the next chapter. But now we must say something more about the visual process in reading.

The reading of music is similar to the reading of language as far as the process of sensory perception is concerned. The pattern of eye movements in the reading of a single staff (line) of music is not so very different from that for the reading of a line of type. But the pattern of eye movements in the reading of two staffs (as with piano music) and in reading or even following a symphonic score is much more complex, for attention will move from left to right horizontally, but also from staff to staff. As in the reading of language, the sensory data, the configuration of the black notes against a five-lined background, will be less complex than the context with which it is integrated in perception; for written music, like language, involves a complex symbol system.

A single isolated sensation, as represented by the accompanying note on a bit of staff, may serve to organize an amazing amount of data in a given musical context. It means F as the clef mark at the beginning of the line was treble. It means F$^\#$ for there is a sharp on the upper F line in the key signature, as indicated at the right. It means *ti* in the major scale, since the key is G major. It is an eighth note in relative duration as indicated by the single flag; but it is one beat, because the time signature is six-eight. It is unaccented, as it is the last eighth note in the measure. It is soft; the passage is marked *p*. It is second finger on the D string, as it is for violin. It is staccato; there is a dot under it. And so on. . . . The beginner will work hard to bring to bear all of the relevant contextual data. But the experienced

musician will integrate the core and context without conscious
thought. He will 'see' this one mark (here pointed out by an arrow)
as F#, second finger on D string, light down bow, integrating in a

flash a very considerable body of musical experience. No wonder it
takes more than ten easy lessons to astound your friends as a parlor
performer!

5. *Auditory sensation and perception*

The auditory process involved as one listens to music is quite different from the visual process either of reading or of looking at a
picture. First, what we have called the music-in-the-air, the complex
pattern of sound waves, comes directly into the ear; whereas, not the
picture itself, but only a pattern of light waves reflected from its surface comes into the eye. Second, there are no significant ear movements comparable to the eye movements, those adjustments to the
demands of attention that bring light waves reflected from one or another part of the picture into focus at the sensitive fovea. Third, although one can change his seat at a concert so as to improve one's
hearing of the music, this adjustment of position is like the changing
of one's point of view, not like the turning on of more light or light
of a different color or from a different angle. (However, both volume
and tone control are commonplaces of radio and record player.)

There is nothing much you can consciously do in adjusting the
ear for favorable reception of sound, except turning the head, stop-
ping an ear or cupping it with a hand, equalizing the air pressure of
the middle ear by swallowing, and perhaps a conscious alerting of
the ear by tensing certain muscles controlling the ear drum. Even
so, a brief description of the ear and its function may be of some
help in considering the auditory process of listening to music, oral
reading, dance, and theater art.

The ear consists of three parts: the outer ear, the middle ear, and
the inner ear.

The outer ear includes the actual ear on the outside of the head,
and the tube-like opening or canal into the head. This tube is closed
off at the inner end by the eardrum. The outer ear collects sound
waves and funnels them in, concentrating them and directing them
against the eardrum.

The middle ear is an open space back of the eardrum and within the bony structure of the head, with the Eustacian tube, usually collapsed, connecting it with the back of the throat. The eardrum itself is a taut membrane, like a delicate and sensitive drum head except that it is not round but oval and capable of responding to various wave lengths. Attached to the eardrum is the first of three tiny bones called the hammer, the anvil, and the stirrup. These three are linked together and connect the eardrum with the inner ear by way of an oval opening or window, which is closed by the so-called foot plate of the stirrup. As one swallows or yawns, the Eustacian tubes open to let air into or out of the middle ear so as to adjust the air pressure of the middle ear to atmospheric pressure, equalizing the air pressure upon the two sides of the delicate eardrum. It is within the middle ear that vibrations of the eardrum are conducted mechanically, by means of the three little bones, directly to the opening of the inner ear.

The inner ear is a yet more amazing structure, for it contains two distinct sense organs: first, the semicircular canals and the sense organs of equilibrium; and second, the cochlea and sense organs of hearing. It is easy indeed to become lost in the labyrinth of the ear! The cochlea is shaped like a snail shell; it is a tube about an inch and a half long, but coiled or rolled up from the small end. Within one of its long narrow canals (filled with liquid) is an arrangement of some 3000 hair cells, auditory nerve endings, each one sensitive to fluid waves of a certain frequency and intensity. The particular auditory nerve ending thus agitated transmits an impulse along its own nerve fiber which goes from the inner ear to the auditory center of the brain. The vibrations, transmitted mechanically to the inner ear by the stirrup bone, are transformed into waves in the liquid medium within the inner ear, and it is to these waves that the hair cells respond.

To summarize, then: the pattern of sound waves, what we have called the music-in-the-air, is conducted by the outer ear to the eardrum, which is set in complex vibration. These complex vibrations (of many different frequencies and amplitudes at once) are transmitted mechanically by the tiny linked bones of the middle ear to the window of the inner ear. Here the complex mechanical vibrations are transformed to a complex of waves in the fluid of the cochlea which certain of the thousands of minute hair cells respond to. In this way a pattern of sensory impulses is sent along the many-stranded auditory nerve to the adjoining brain.

The hearing, the actual sensations, are in the brain, a part of consciousness. As with visual stimuli and other nerve impulses, you will not 'hear' many of the sound waves that strike the ear. Of some of them you will have only a vague awareness. Others will demand your attention. To yet others you will wish to give your attention. One can, as it were, close his ears to music; that is, withhold attention or consciously attend to some other stimulus at the moment. Or one can just barely hear music; that is, with continuous but passive awareness of the auditory sensations in the field of consciousness. Or one can listen to music; that is, give active attention to it. For attention will shift about within the group of continually changing sensations, just as in looking at a picture attention will move from one to another of the sensations of shape and color brought into focus in successive fixations.

These auditory sensations, of which attention makes one sharply aware, come not singly but in groups, and they are integrated with one's past auditory and other sensory and ideational experiences into the complex perceptions of music. Again it must be said that what one perceives is not the sensory data but an organization of sensory data with past experiences. Certainly some listeners do not 'hear' the dissonances or discords that others hear.

For musical perceptions are complex and individual. A single perceived tone is the fusion of separable sensations of pitch, quality (overtone structure), loudness, and duration (length). But such simple perceptions are not 'the music.' Nor are the more complex perceptions of rhythm, melody, harmony, and counterpoint. In these and yet larger perceptions, as of musical form, more and more contextual data are integrated with the sensory data. These contextual data, the musical and other experience, differ widely from individual to individual; so, too, the matters of attention, for only certain sensations in the field of consciousness will come into sharp awareness. One listener will give his attention to the rhythm while another 'hears' only the melody.

Individual differences in listening to music are, then, largely matters of attention and context. Attention, is, at least in part, a matter of training; and context, a matter of experience. That is, one may learn how to listen to music more skillfully, and one may also develop a larger body of varied musical experiences. But there are some individual differences that result from the unique structure or neural deficiencies: the malformation or injury of some part of the ear may result in the impairment of hearing, partial or total deafness, or what is called tone-deafness (the inability to distinguish differences in pitch). But even among persons of normal hearing, there are differences in auditory acuity. As earlier quoted, Seashore said that, of two equally intelligent persons, one may have "more than a

from STRING QUARTET No. 39
by *Joseph Haydn*

Da Capo al Fine

hundred times as fine a sense of pitch, sense of rhythm, sense of time, or sense of timbre as the other." Some of these persons have what is called an ear for music. This includes an unusual capacity for discrimination in auditory sensations and sequences, an unusual capacity for integrating such sensory data with relevant contextual data from their musical experience.

Let us bring this section to a close by suggesting a musical illustration. It is impossible, as we have already noted, to get the music itself into a book; but the musical score for the second movement of Haydn's *String Quartet, No. 39*, opus 33, no. 3, is presented on a nearby pair of pages.

Joseph Haydn (1732-1809) was an Austrian composer who lived to a ripe old age and wrote a great deal of chamber music (for string quartet, trio, etc.) as well as many symphonies. A string quartet is a composition, usually in four movements, for two violins, viola, and violoncello. The viola is an alto violin; music for it is written in the alto clef with middle C on the middle line. If four instrumentalists are not available, you might sit down with three others at a piano and pick out the parts. Better yet, if the recording is at hand, play it for repeated listening, and follow the score. . . .

Have you given some thought to the process of sensory perception while listening to the music? If not, play it again and note the individual sensations and musical tones as perceived. Note the play of your shifting attention within the field of consciousness. In listening to it, try to follow the second violin part—sing or whistle it along with the playing to help in keeping your attention on it. Then notice how your attention shifts from one part to another. . . .

Now give brief attention to the larger perceptual units. Does it alter your perception (fusion of sensory data with contextual data) when you learn that this is often called 'The Bird' quartet? Listen to it once more. . . .

6. Compound sensory perception

Less space will be given here to those works of art that are perceived through two or more sensory systems.

In classifying art works briefly in the first chapter according to the mode of sensory perception an audiovisual category was set up. We noted earlier in the present chapter that music-on-the-page is perceived through the sense of sight alone, and we have just now concluded a discussion of music-in-the-air as perceived through the sense of hearing alone. Musical performance, of which something has been said in the immediately preceding chapters, is perceived by sight and hearing together. Indeed, all of the activity art works, as we called them, most of which result from performance as a sort of interpretative creative activity, are both auditory and visual in sense perception. This included not only musical performance, but the dance and stageplay as well.

In listening to a musical performance, watching a dance or attending a play, auditory sensations will be fused with visual sensations and together they will be integrated with contextual data. In each case the visual data will be more than the simple sensations of shapes and colors, but also the complex perceptions of movement. One does not have clear sensations of movement, but only sensations of blur between fixed points and of brief duration, which are fused in the perceived motion. It is true that the perception of a musical performance is primarily auditory, and that the perception of a dance is primarily visual. In the perception of a stageplay, however, sight and hearing are of relatively equal importance, but the sensory data are integrated with more elaborate contextual data, as the speech sounds call for interpretation as language symbols.

In experiencing a musical performance, dance, or stageplay, there is the further organizing of direct sensory data with induced kinesthetic data, faint muscular sensations that result from the beholder's empathic response to the bodily postures and movements of the performers. This matter of empathy will be considered further in the next chapter, for it is one of the more important of the naive responses. But it must at least be mentioned here: You tend to project your own consciousness into that which you behold, to identify yourself with the actions that you witness, to assume in the imagination the postures and forms that you perceive visually. This may even be accompanied by slight bodily movement and your consciousness of actual muscular tensions as well as your free imagery of such. And these induced actual kinesthetic sensations are integrated with the visual and auditory sensations in your perception of a musical performance, dance, or stageplay. The kinesthetic responses of rhythm, induced by music or speech or by the bodily movements of the performers, represent somewhat different muscular sensations, and they too become a very important part of the fusion.

A brief illustration or two may make this clear: When you are listening to a singer, you not only hear the sounds and see the facial expressions, bodily posture and gestures, evidences of muscular strain or relative ease, but you may tense your own abdomen, hold your own breath, raise your own chest and chin. And your experience of even one final note may include sensory data of these three sorts (auditory, visual, kinesthetic) integrated with various contextual data and perceived as high, dominant, concluding, crescendo, climactic, continuing, breath-taking!

At the end of *Pyramus and Thisbe* the actor who plays Bottom lies dead upon the stage as Pyramus. Following the Duke's comment that 'Moonshine and Lion are left to bury the dead,' Demetrius adds 'Ay, and Wall too.' At that moment your eye sends up visual data of blur followed by a changed pattern of light; your ears send in auditory data of certain sounds. You see that Bottom, no longer dead Pyramus, has sat bolt upright; you hear him speaking in his own voice. Having identified yourself with Bottom's playing of Pyramus, you may also have faint starting-up sensations from empathic muscular activity in your own back. You experience 'Bottom starting up and answering the Duke in his own person' as a complex perceptual unity.

The sensory perception of a musical performance, dance, or stageplay integrates a variety of sensory data with a wealth of contextual data. We shall call this compound sensory perception. Let us, as a final illustration take an art work of quite another kind that stimulates compound sensory perception somewhat different in sort. In the classification of art works according to the mode of sensory perception, there might well be a visual-tactile-kinesthetic category comprising those things, such as statues and vases, that invite the beholder to touch them or pick them up or otherwise sense their surface texture and mass. Works of architecture fall into this class.

The particular building that we shall take as an example—the *Nebraska State Capitol* at Lincoln, Nebraska—is well worth a closer study than can be given it in this place. A visiting Swedish architect named it and the Los Angeles Public Library among the three most distinguished examples of recent American architecture. Both of them are the work of Bertram Grosvenor Goodhue (1869-1924).

In 1919 the Nebraska State Legislature approved construction of a new capitol building and appointed a commission to undertake the project. A competition was announced, and the design submitted by Goodhue was selected by the judges. Working with Goodhue were his architectural associates, including Harry F. Cunningham, who developed the plan for the tower; Hartley Burr Alexander, the philosopher, who developed the symbolic scheme and inscriptions for the entire building; Lee Lawrie, the sculptor; Hildreth Meiere and Augustus V. Tack, painters who designed the various panels and murals. Ground was broken early in April 1922, and although certain state offices were occupied by the end of 1924, construction continued progressively through the rest of the decade.

The building is essentially a one-story block, more than four hun-

Bertram Grosvenor Goodhue, NEBRASKA STATE CAPITOL, Lincoln, Nebraska

dred feet square with a central tower rising four hundred feet into the air. Its brilliantly colored dome, topped by Lawrie's statue of The Sower, can be seen far and wide across the prairies. Its vast system of murals, mosaics, bas-relief and engaged statues are by no means mere decoration, but an integral part of the entire building. It is a flexible structure, housing the many state legislative and administrative functions. At the same time it is a monument to the many forces, primitive and pioneer and historic, that have shaped the State of Nebraska.

The accompanying illustration provides but scant basis for considering the complex sensory perception of a great building. For experiencing a building involves more than seeing one view of it from the distance. Every angle from which it is seen presents a new and different picture to the eye. As one approaches a building, the first simple perception is enriched by details observed from various distances, as the eyes are called from one focus of attention to another and the new sensory data are fused with additional contextual data.

The observation of a building or any three-dimensional work of art is further enriched by the interpretation of various depth cues. One but by no means the only one of these is the effect of binocular or two-eyed vision. That is, the observer's two eyes, though moving as a pair, send up ever-so-slightly different patterns of neural impulses, because, about $2\frac{1}{2}$ inches apart, they will see the building from slightly different angles. Although the two sets of visual impulses are normally fused into a single image, the fact that they are slightly different accounts in part for the perception of depth.

But experiencing a building is not merely a complex visual process. It is tactile and kinesthetic as well. There is the feel, even through thin-soled shoes, of the various floor surfaces—granite, mosaic, polished marble. There is the feel of polished handrails, the feel of cool hallways, and so on. There are, furthermore, the widely various muscular sensations in one's arched back and neck as he looks up at the great tower and dome, in one's leg muscles as he climbs the approaching steps.

The perception of an actual building, such as the Nebraska State Capitol, is a complex activity involving sensations of rich variety integrated with a wide assortment of contextual data. It is quite different from seeing a mere photograph reproduced in a book.

7. Some positive suggestions

Although the purpose of this chapter is merely to describe the first, the sensation-perception part of art experiences of various kinds, it will conclude with some positive suggestions. If you want to, you can improve your skill in looking at pictures and reading literature, your skill in listening to music and perceiving those art works that provide sensory data of several sorts. These pointers may prove helpful:

1. *Free yourself from conflicting stimuli.* Although it is true that competing stimuli may increase your concentration under some circumstances, they also distract your attention. Worse yet, they may crowd in irrelevant sensations that become fused into the perception of the work of art. Turn off the radio when reading works of literature; the music may provide the wrong background. Lay down the magazine when listening to good music; the narrative may suggest an inappropriate program story for the music. Shut off your companion's comments when visiting an art gallery; another person's pleasantries and gossip, preconceptions and opinions may quite upset your patterns of sensory perception.

2. *Be willing and curious to receive sensations.* This willingness takes time, of course, and energy. The eye movements, as we noted, are controlled by the demands of attention. Attention first calls for a general exploration of the picture or statue; then some persons move on to another work. Be willing to stay for a second period of closer observation, a more curious attention to details. It means not only seeing but looking at pictures. Willingness to attend, to become more clearly aware of various sensations within the field of attention, is also necessary if one is to increase his enjoyment of music. It means active listening, not just hearing. And for almost all works of art, not one sensory system, but two or more, will provide sensory data if the observer encourages them to do so. Be alert, then, to all relevant sensations.

3. *Rehearings, reseeings, rereadings provide richer integrations* of sensory data with contextual data. There is just so much that even a willing and curious attention to sensory data can do at one time. Fatigue enters in, and it is time to move on. But come back again. And again. Each time attention will have new demands, and fresh sensory data will have more past experiences with which to be fused into clearer perceptual patterns. You will see things in the picture that were not there before; you will hear things that you didn't note in earlier hearings.

4. *Back off for a full view and come up for a near look.* The approach to a work of architecture, seeing it first from a distance, is

very important to the perceptual integration of the parts that are then seen close to. A large picture must be seen from across the gallery as well as from a nearer position. In the reading of a story and in listening to music, one can, at least figuratively, back up to see the work as a whole in its broader outlines. And in this full view, attention to sensations that delimit the work of art and that mark off its larger masses may well precede as well as follow the closer attention to detail.

There are other suggestions that will be made later. These are concerned particularly with sensation, attention, and perception, the first general part of the responsive art experience.

Chapter 8. Naive Response to the Work of Art

> The artist speaks to our capacity for delight and wonder, to the sense of mystery surrounding our lives; to our sense of pity, and beauty, and pain.
>
> Joseph Conrad, Preface to *Narcissus*

> Without innocence no work of art can be created or enjoyed.
>
> Ludwig van Beethoven, *Conversation Books*

> I never heard the old song of Percy and Douglas that I found not my heart moved more than with a trumpet.
>
> Sir Philip Sidney, *An Apology for Poetry*

THE FIRST ASPECT of the responsive art experience is the sensory perception of the work of art, the immediate seeing in the mind of the picture as a public object or the hearing in the mind of the music. The second aspect, now to be considered, is the artee's naive response to the work of art.

The meaning of 'naive response' may be suggested by these phrases: immediate result, direct effect, natural evocation, unlearned reaction, unreflective interpretation. Such ingenuous and artless responses as here implied are often the subject of some belittlement. In *Art and the Social Order*, Gotshalk says, "Naive aesthetic experience perceives a work of art as if it were an everyday object elevated momentarily to the purely perceptual level . . . The naive percipient admires the cozy setting given a house in a painting. He relishes the sweetness of the melody played by an orchestra. He delights in the graceful posture of a sculptured figure. . . . But his experience is naive in a number of ways." And he observes that such experience is usually very limited; it reacts to represented objects as though they were real; it is very subjective; and it is unsustained, slipping from the aesthetic to the unaesthetic. "Naive as it is," he says, "the experience just described probably embraces a great majority of the usual experiences of works of art," but he adds that they are 'not to be confused with serious art' and that "Disciplined aesthetic experience is in most respects the exact opposite of naive aesthetic experience."

However, it is the view of this present book that naive responses to a work of art are one aspect, and a very important aspect, of a full art experience. In some ways they are more important than the disciplined (or, as we shall call it, critical) interpretation. For the scope of naive response, as herein considered, includes simple recognitions and imagery, empathy and the feeling for form, beauty and taste, mood and emotion, overt action and residual attitudes. To recall Upton's three-fold classification, these various naive responses are essentially affective as opposed to sensory qualifications, and are to be distinguished from the logical or rational responses that will be taken up in the next chapter.

Such naive responses, it will be recalled from the discussion early in the preceding chapter, are not direct reactions to the work of art outside the mind, to the public object. Rather, they are evoked by the work of art as perceived—the picture as actually seen by the mind, the music as heard in the brain, the poem as picked up by the eye. And, as we have noted, the seeing of a picture is by no means purely sensory, but an integration of sensory data with contextual data, part of which are often imagined and emotional. The very activity of perception, then, involves a certain amount of naive interpretation.

We do not really have separate responses, let us say, of mere seeing, but intimately interrelated sensory, affective, and logical responses to a work of art. Furthermore, one does not first see a picture, then turn away and enjoy it, and finally stop enjoying it so as to start thinking about it! Sensory perception keeps right on; and, as naive responses and critical interpretations control attention, new demands are made for fresh sensory data. The eyes jump off to fix upon hitherto neglected areas of the picture; the ears prick up, as it were, and attention isolates neglected strands in the auditory complex.

But, though sensory perceptions, naive responses, and critical interpretations are inseparably intertwined, it will be helpful to continue in our separate consideration of them. However, let us again say: it is the work of art as it is perceived, not the thing as it exists outside the mind, to which the observer makes further naive responses.

1. *Simple recognitions and imagery*

The first sort of naive response, to be considered in this section, is the perception and recognition of simple signs and their relationship in larger wholes. Discussion of this will take us back to Chapter 3 in our thinking. There we dealt with a work of art as a complex sign compounded of many simple signs, each of which is interpreted, each of which has meaning. It is impossible to tell where complex sensory perceptions leave off and simple recognitions or unreflective interpretations begin. It will be quite as impossible to decide exactly where these unreflective interpretations or simple recognitions merge into more complex recognitions or critical interpretations to be discussed in the next chapter. This section stands, then, on the boundary between this and the preceding chapter; and, strangely enough, it also stands on the boundary between this chapter and the next.

It does not require much critical thought or reflection to piece together the principal characters and sequence of events in the reading of a simple narrative. Popular fiction, at any rate, and the great and enduring masterpieces have usually allowed for such simple recognitions of the principal elements in their structure by persons who have the rudiments of the language, the symbol system involved. So the most unreflective could follow the story in the *Parable of the Sower*. And, in the same way, the reader of a poem, after perceiving the words as simple signs of meaning, will usually make some sort of sense of the statements as he reads, with simple recognition of common phrases and (at first) relatively unreflective interpretation of the larger units.

In listening to music, too, the more complex perceptions stand on the threshold of further naive interpretations—the simple recognition of thematic units, the bits of tune that occur and recur, the underpinning bass, the accompanying figures and even middle voices, the preparation for the closing phrase, and so on. We have already referred to the way music makes sense—or sometimes fails to make sense—in this way to the listener.

The unreflective interpretation of the resemblative signs perceived in a picture is a similar process. The more complex perceptions—hand, arm, head—are the basis for the simple recognition of 'a man.' And the interpretation proceeds by the organizing of all the simple recognitions into a system of relationships, leading to a more critical interpretation. This general interpretation, however naive or critical, is often pronounced as the subject of the picture.

In talking about the subject or subject matter or substance of a work of art, it is sometimes convenient to use the phrase 'active forms' to name. the more complex perceptual units. Torossian has said, "The *active forms* are the recognizable members in a representative work of art, or the functional or organic forms in an abstract pattern—the arms and legs of a figure statue; the characters in a story; the trees and animals in a landscape painting; the actors [-characters] and situations in a drama; the motifs or themes in an abstract visual [-wall paper] or auditory [-musical] pattern; the walls, roof, doors . . . of a building; the arms and back of a chair . . . " For different artees, of . course, these recognizable members, or perceptual units as we called them, may be quite different. One person will perceive head, body, arms, and legs as having separateness yet constituting the human figure. For another person, hand, forearm, upper arm, shoulder will be separate active forms. One listener will perceive melody and rhythmic accompaniment as active forms; another will also hear an alto voice and a separate bass beat with harmonic after-beat in the tenor. One man will see columns; another will perceive separate capitals, shafts, and bases. Not only will the active forms, which make up the total subject matter, be quite different for different persons, but the organization of these active forms also will be quite individual in the observer's naive response to the work of art.

To illustrate this matter, turn back to the Delacroix painting reproduced in the last chapter . . . What is its subject matter? Three men on a barque? . . . Drowning persons trying to save themselves? . . . Or, Dante and Virgil crossing the Stygian marsh? . . . Even the simple recognition of the subject matter of a painting or statue will often be quite various. And the organization of the active forms in a non-representational work of art will also differ from person to person.

Turn now to the first illustration for the present chapter. (There is no need to repeat that a print is a poor substitute for a statue. Many views are better than one, but even that does not allow for an entirely satisfactory sensory perception of the work.) Look at it for a little while before coming back to the text. . . .

As you looked at the reproductions of this statue, you were doubtless conscious of the active forms. What were they *for you?* Make a penciled list of them on a scrap of paper without going back to look at the print. . . . Then write down a suggested title for the statue, a title that will name (*for you*) its subject matter. . . . Now take another look at the picture. . . .

photo by Alinari

Unknown Pergamon sculptor, GAUL AND HIS WIFE, Terme Museum, Rome

Certainly the simple recognition of the two human figures, a man and a woman, will be the same with all observers. The list of active forms for some may be simply: man, woman. For others: man, sword, woman, dress. For yet others: the man's bent left leg, right leg back, right upraised arm, back-turned head, and so on.

Interpretation of this work of art may go no further for some persons than this unreflective simple recognition of subject matter. For other persons it may be considerably richer: 'I recognize at once that this man, supporting a fainting or dying woman, is about to kill himself.' That the man represented is a Gaul (rather than a Saxon, a Briton, or a Slav), that the woman represented is his wife (rather than sister, mistress, daughter), that it is the Roman soldiers who have cornered him (rather than Huns or wolves), that the woman is fainting from fatigue (rather than wounded or already dead), that the man prefers death by his own hand to slavery (rather than death from Roman hands, or torture in the arena)— these are certainly *not* naive responses, unreflective interpretations, simple recognitions; they involve critical thought and judgment, and fall outside the bounds of this chapter. Even the title of this statue, 'A Gaul and His Wife,' the deduction that it is by an unknown Hellenistic sculptor of the First Pergamon School, and the fact that the original is to be seen in the Terme Gallery in Rome, are critical rather than naive responses.

Without further consideration of the unreflective interpretations this statue may evoke, let us proceed to a consideration of the second kind of naive response, which we shall call *imagery*.

To begin with, there are three sorts of imagery: first, the sense-imagery already referred to in the preceding chapter, the direct image in the mind of the picture or words actually being seen on the page before you; second, tied-imagery, the sound of a word that is heard in the mind's ear when the printed word is seen; and third, free-imagery, the various pictures in the mind's-eye and sounds in the mind's-ear freely suggested and fleetingly evoked as naive response to works of art.

Free images are sensory events in the mind that are not the result of immediate sensory stimuli. If, when you listen to a musical performance, you become conscious of dream-like pictures of hills and trees in the mind's eye, they would be called free images, for they are not the result of the pattern of light falling upon the retina of the eye at that time. The actual image of the pianist, resulting from the stimulation of the retina by light waves, we shall call a sense image; for the 'seeing' of the pianist involves immediate sensory perception. Free images are also mind events, but they make use of recalled sensory data, and often an utterly new organization or integration of such data. If you happen to be a musician, you may, while listening to this performance, have strong kinesthetic (muscular) images evoked of the sensations you would have were you actually playing the composition. These would be called tied-imagery, and are comparable to the example cited in the paragraph above.

Free images are such stuff as dreams are made of. Not only the dreams from which one awakes at night or in the morning, but day-dreams, too. They represent the activity of the so-called imagination. But all free images are not visual, pictures in the mind's eye. There are, or may be, free images related to all of the various sensory systems. Auditory free-imagery is experienced by many people: they 'hear' the sound of a pounding surf in their mind's ear while looking at a picture of great waves, or they 'hear' ominous footfalls outside their door while reading a murder mystery. But, to a less notable extent, people also have free-imagery that is olfactory and gustatory, thermal and tactile. And the free images of muscular and equilibrial and various organic sensations are especially important in the art experience, and will be considered in the next section of this chapter.

These free images, which for some persons are a very important part of the art experience, are naive responses to the work of art as perceived. You will have comparatively little control over them; they do not come or go at will. They are not necessarily relevant; they are sometimes misleading; they sometimes get in the way of a fuller and more appropriate response. But irresponsible and fleeting as free-imagery may be, it is nevertheless important. Tidbits of it often become integrated with the sensory perceptions, and it is hard to say sometimes what you really see and what you only imagine that you see.

As you look at a picture of a horse, you may imagine that you feel the warm gloss of his coat, or that you smell the pungent odor of horse flesh, compounded of hair oil and dried perspiration, or that you can feel yourself seated in his saddle, or that you can feel the complex motions of his gallop, or that you can hear him snort or nicker—these would all be free images of one kind or another, a naive response to the sensory perception, the sense image of the picture. But you might also have visual free-imagery at the same time: fleeting images of your own favorite horse, of bridle trails, of other persons riding, of corral or stable or stall.

So, in looking at pictures and at statues, in reading literature and listening to music, one is likely to experience more or less free-imagery. It will be very different in amount and kind for different persons and for the same person as he experiences different works of art and works of the different arts.

For some persons, for instance, there will be comparatively less or very little free-imagery evoked during the performance of a stageplay in the theater. Because the theater provides such a rich variety of actual sensory data—visual sensations of scenery and actors in motion and continuous auditory sensations of the dialogue, and occasional background music and sound effects—the artee's attention is kept pretty busy with the complex of this sense-imagery. But the reading of a drama or playbook makes unusual demands upon the reader's imagination and usually stimulates a rich assortment of free images under more than usual control. On the other hand, the experiencing of a work of architecture is for many people almost without free-imagery as a part of the naive response.

As you read the following poem, your visual sense-imagery will consist of your seeing the whole poem on the pages of this book and your visual perception of the successive groups of words. If you read it silently, your 'hearing' the words themselves, the melodic flow of the words as if they were actually read aloud, is auditory tied-imagery. However, as you read and reread *The Black Panther*, give more particular attention to such visual and other free-imagery as may be evoked as a part of your naive response to this work of art.

THE BLACK PANTHER

by *John Hall Wheelock*

There is a panther caged within my breast,
But what his name, there is no breast shall know
Save mine, nor what it is that drives him so,
Backward and forward, in relentless quest—
That silent rage, baffled but unsuppressed,
The soft pad of those stealthy feet that go
Over my body's prison to and fro,
Trying the walls forever, without rest.

All day I feed him with my living heart,
But when the night puts forth her dreams and stars,
The inexorable frenzy re-awakes:
His wrath is hurled upon the trembling bars,
The eternal passion stretches me apart,
And I lie silent—but my body shakes.

As you think over your experience in reading *The Black Panther,* do you distinguish the three sorts of imagery: the actual seeing of the words of the poem, the hearing of the words in your mind's-ear, the mental picture of the panther in his cage? . . .

No special comment need be made on the sense image of the poem *The Black Panther* here on the page. The retinal image, resulting from the pattern of light that enters the eye, is seen as sense image in the brain. By means of a pattern of eye movements, successive groups of words are brought into clear focus that results in sharp enough sense images to allow for the discrimination of letters and words. But enough was said about this in the last chapter.

Let us now consider such auditory tied-imagery as you may have had in reading *The Black Panther.* The sound of the words in the mind's-ear as you read the poem silently (or the actual sound, if your reading was oral) constitutes the so-called music of poetry. The most conspicuous feature of this pattern of word sounds is the poetic rhythm. Although the general nature of rhythm will be taken up in the next section, it must here be defined as that particular feeling that may result from the awareness of recurring stressed syllables in the succession of auditory tied images. This undulating flow is like ripples on the surface of a stream. It is by no means a mechanical sequence of deDUMM deDUMM deDUMM de-DUMM deDUMMs, yet is more or less regular. The simple rec-ognition of the sense of the words suggests the underlying pattern of beats, which is most nearly regular in the line: 'His wrath is hurled upon the trembling bars.' But the plain sense of the words usually calls for some slight variation of this basic metrical pattern, as at the beginning of the first line. However, there are other fea-tures of the sound of this poem as heard in the mind's-ear that may have attracted your attention: for instance, the recurrence of rime words at the ends of adjacent lines, at times the relation of the sounds of words to their sense, and so on. There is no need to in-troduce here the technical language of poetics that would be useful in a more detailed consideration of the auditory tied-imagery of your silent reading of *The Black Panther.*

But it is the free-imagery, those fleeting pictures in the mind, and the similar counterfeits of sensation, that is of more particular interest to us here in considering your naive response to *The Black Panther.* Although the sense image of the poem on the page will be almost identical for most observers, and the tied-imagery of its music will be at least roughly similar, the free images that it evokes will certainly be highly individual for each and every reader. Each of us has had different experiences with zoos and circuses, panthers and similar cats. But your mind pictures will differ in yet other ways: some persons will see a fairly steady cage-panther-restless image throughout their reading of the poem; for others this will give way to some sort of an image of the restless 'I' of the poem. Some will experience panther and person images alternately or concurrently. And other persons, less visually minded, will simply see no mind-pictures at all.

It may be that other sorts of free-imagery were evoked as you read *The Black Panther.* You may have enjoyed the imagery of acrid zoo odors. You may have heard in your mind's-ear (along with the music of the poem) the 'soft pad' of the panther's 'stealthy feet'— you may have heard the impact when 'His wrath is hurled upon the trembling bars.' You may have experienced the strong imagery of muscular sensations: restless pacing, pushing against a wall, full bodied springing, the long stretch, and the body shaken.

It is this last kind, kinesthetic free-imagery, that brings us directly to the subject of the next section.

2. *Empathy and formal feelings*

In the discussion of sensory perception in the preceding chapter, it was said: You tend to project your own consciousness into that which you behold, to identify yourself with the actions that you witness, to assume in the imagination the postures and forms that you perceive visually. This may even be accompanied by slight bodily movement and your consciousness of actual muscular tensions as well as your free-imagery of such. Perhaps you are one of those persons who, when listening to a singer, may become conscious of his own abdominal tensing and held breath and laryngeal strain.

In discussing the various theories of beauty in Chapter 2, we quoted brief definitions of *empathy* by Theodor Lipps and Vernon Lee. Melvin Rader has said, "Empathy simply means the disappearance of the two-fold consciousness of self and object, and the enrichment of experience that results from this interpenetration. So completely is the self transported into the object that the contemplator of a statue, for example, may unconsciously imitate its posture and implied movement by definite muscular adjustments." The German word for this empathy is 'Einfühlung,' which may be literally translated as 'in-feeling.'

Without looking back to the illustration, try to answer these questions about *A Gaul and His Wife:* What is the position of his left leg? . . . of his left arm? . . . of his right arm? . . . of his right leg? . . . . of his head? . . . There is a strong probability that, in

trying to answer these questions, you will feel out in your own muscular system the posture of the Gaul. You may actually stand up
and assume the stance and posture. . . . By the by, which way is
he holding the sword, up or down? . . . and which way is his fist,
thumb side up or down? . . . You see, you may only be able to
tell by the feel of it. If your empathic response to this dramatic statue
was strong, you probably did more than merely imagine fleeting free
images of past muscular sensations, you probably experienced actual
muscular tensions such as those suggested by the posture of the Gaul.
If this occurred, you therefore experienced actual kinesthetic sensations that, as tied images, were fused into your complex perception
of the statue. So, when you tried to remember how the Gaul held
the sword, you may have been able to recall what your own sensations actually were, or you may have recalled some of them—the
shoulder strain with high elbow—and then proceeded to reconstruct
the rest of the sensory experience.

This empathic response to the *Gaul* is similar to that which you
may experience in watching a dance, stageplay, or musical performance, as suggested in the preceding chapter. The same is true
of the comparable responses to pictures and works of architecture.
Lipps says, "In viewing a large hall I feel an inner 'expansion,' my
heart 'expands;' I have this peculiar sense of what is happening
within me. Connected with it are muscle tensions, perhaps those
involved in the expansion of the chest." And these would all be in
the nature of actual induced sensations or tied images of muscular
sensation. They are therefore slightly different from the free images
of muscular sensations evoked by reading *The Black Panther,* though
these also may come under the general heading of empathy.

Such empathic muscular images and sensations are important
naive responses to works of art as perceived, for they engage the
body itself in the art experience. This phase of the total personality
response was neglected in the study of the arts until the present
century.

Let us turn, however, to a number of related bodily sensations
and feeling states that, long recognized, have not yet been adequately
explored. They are the physio-psychological basis for several of the
time-honored art principles, but we shall refer to them as the *formal
feelings* for want of a better name. Two of them will be considered
briefly at this time.

Balance is the most important of these art principles or formal
feelings. It would hardly seem necessary at this point to say that
balance does not exist in the work of art as a public object. But it

is very commonly said that the picture itself has or has not balance. Indeed, balance is frequently pointed out as being out there in the picture on the wall, though you may be too stupid to see it there! However, when balance is said to exist, it is really either a naive or a critical response to the work of art as perceived. In this chapter we shall only be concerned with the affective qualification of balance, not with the more critical or logical qualification one may have of it.

Another point must be cleared up: Balance, as a felt-response to a picture as perceived, is not visual but essentially equilibrial; that is, it is not something that you see or imagine that you see, but has to do with your feeling of uprightness, steadiness, or poise, or your feeling of being pulled off balance. It is not one of the data of visual sensation—shapes, colors, binocular differences, and visual sensations of motion. Balance is essentially a feeling-state. Therefore, you do not really 'see' that the picture is in balance or exhibits active forms that are in balance; you *feel* that the active forms are in balance.

The feeling of balance is a perceptual fusion of equilibrial and muscular sensations integrated with visual and/or other sensory data and a wide variety of contextual data. The equilibrial and kinesthetic sensations are the attentional focus in such a perception. And they are sometimes the actual sensations that accompany the tilting of the head to one side. When a landscape painting, for instance, isn't hanging straight on the wall, it is very upsetting to some observers, and they tip their heads so as to adjust their own horizon to that of the picture and the tilt of the frame. Or the observer's empathic response to the subject matter of a painting or statue may make him conscious of the muscular tensions of a posture that in turn calls up a free image of bodily equilibrium. Or he may perceive two active forms in viewing a work of architecture, doors to left and right of a main portal, and imagine himself weighing them in his two hands; but here, too, the equilibrial sensation is again imagined, for with unequal weights in the two hands one is pulled over to one side or is conscious of muscular tensions resisting such a pull.

Balance, of course, is the normal state; it is the feeling of imbalance that attracts attention, or the sensation of muscular tensions that come with the maintaining of equilibrium. Therefore it is unusual to have the feeling of balance itself as a naive response to a work of art. There is sometimes the sensation of imbalance, which is uncomfortable and disturbing, or the sensation of those muscular tensions that keep the body in a state of balance. These are not usually given separate attention; they are more frequently fused into more complex perceptions.

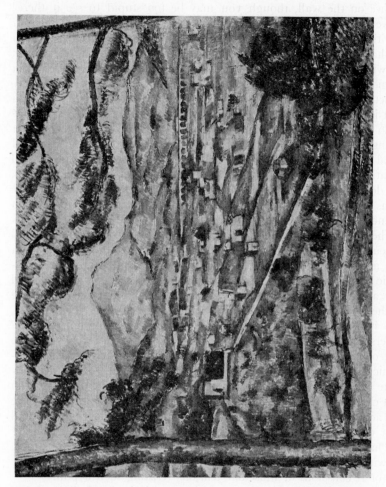

Paul Cézanne, MONT STE. VICTOIRE, Phillips Gallery, Washington, D. C.

Look again at the statue of *A Gaul and His Wife* and consider your feeling as regards balance. You are likely to observe that your attribution of balance to the Gaul is an empathic projection of your own consciousness into the posture in which you see him represented, and that your own muscular tied image or actual muscular tensions and your own equilibrial images or sensations are the basis for the general feeling of balance as a naive response.

For an example of a quite different sort turn to the accompanying reproduction of Cézanne's landscape, one of his several paintings of *Mont Ste. Victoire*. You may indeed have no very marked balance response to this picture, just as you may be unconscious of empathy. But a simple experiment may suggest that elements of such naive response are not entirely lacking. Take two 3 x 5 cards or half sheets of white paper, and use them as masks to alter the left and right margins of the picture. For instance, use them to frame a narrow, tall picture, the left quarter of the landscape. . . . Do you have any feeling response to this? . . . Now frame a narrow view with one of your cards running through the peak of the mountain. . . . Are you conscious of any difference in your naive response? . . . Try several other framings of separate parts of the whole . . . Then remove the cards so as to observe the entire picture. . . . Does the horizontal rectangle of the landscape evoke a different felt-response than the vertical rectangles that you framed in with your cards? . . .

This may bring us back to the bit of art theory introduced in the opening pages of this book: that we may have a certain feeling about lines irrespective of what they represent. This feeling is, at least in part, the result of empathy. We also have a certain feeling about the disposition of solids (as we perceive them) left and right of a felt center. Cézanne was especially conscious of such felt-responses. He said, "Treat nature by the cylinder, the sphere, the cone, everything in proper perspective so that each side of an object or a plane is directed toward a central point. Lines parallel to the horizon give breadth. . . . Lines perpendicular to this horizon give depth. But nature for us men is more depth than surface, whence the need of introducing into our light vibrations, represented by reds and yellows, a sufficient amount of blue to give the impression of air." But this further consideration of the naive responses to lines and forms and hues has taken us a bit beyond balance.

Balance is characteristic of one's naive response to spatial works of art, and is usually only a critical response in relation to temporal works. That is, the vague feeling of equilibrial adjustment and freedom from undue muscular strain (or the feeling of imbalance and of muscular strain to maintain balance) are commonly a response to such things as a building, a statue, a picture, also to the spatial aspects of a dance or stageplay. But, as we shall see in the next chapter, one can have critical 'thoughts about' balance in response to such temporal works as music or literature or the temporal aspects of dance or drama.

On the other hand, *rhythm*, the second of these art principles or formal feelings is essentially a naive response based upon muscular sensations induced by temporal works of art (music and literature), and only the temporal aspects of spatiotemporal works (dance and drama). But one can have critical 'thoughts about' rhythm in response to spatial works of art like a picture, statue, or building.

Rhythm is not one of the primary auditory sensations, nor is it essentially an auditory perception, though it is induced by auditory sensation and becomes fused into auditory perceptions. 'Rhythm' is here used to name the feeling that may accompany the awareness of repeated points of interest. And that particular feeling state is perhaps essentially muscular or visceral. It may be the result of, or it may result in, outward foot tapping or head nodding. It may be somehow related to such bodily functions as heart-beating and breathing and to such bodily motions as walking, running, skipping, dancing.

The feeling of rhythm is not the same as the consciousness of motion, either of oneself in motion or of something flowing by— gliding smoothly in a boat across a lake, or a river's flowing along. But it may involve this feeling of on-going movement. The feeling of rhythm is induced by the consciousness of recurrences or pulsations or undulations: the feeling of oar-pulls in a moving boat or the feeling induced by seeing surface ripples on a moving stream.

As one observes a dance, one may empathically feel out in his own muscular system the alternating steps, the recurrent postures and gestures, induced by the perceptual fusion of the sounds of the music and footfalls and the sight of successive motions of the dance. There may be actual kinesthetic sensations resulting from these induced muscular tensions; and these may give rise to a strongly rhythmic feeling, consciousness of some sort of organic pulsations. These kinesthetic and organic sensations will doubtless fuse with the auditory and visual data in the more complex perceptions.

As one listens to music the feeling of rhythm will be induced by the alternations in loudness, and to some extent pitch and quality, in the on-flowing continuum of sound. There may be a strongly empathic response to the observed motions of musical performers— down bowing, chord attacking, drum beating. Therefore, actual

muscular sensations may fuse in perception with the organic sensations of heart-beats and breathing. Head noddings, foot tappings,
and other slight bodily movements may evidence the listener's consciousness of the rhythm.

As we observed in regard to *The Black Panther*, the reader of a
poem—whether it is read aloud or silently with strong auditory tied-

THE HAPPY FARMER
by *Robert Schumann*

imagery—will usually become aware of a feeling of rhythm resulting from syllable accents and word stresses that become organized into a sequence of more or less regular recurrences. Sometimes the reader will also be conscious of articulatory activity of the lips, tongue, and throat (or tied images of such activity) in the process of reading the verses; and the kinesthetic sensations (or images) of articulation will be fused with the organic sensations of rhythmic recurrence.

Another illustration may well be introduced to conclude this section. Here is the musical notation for Robert Schumann's piano-pupil's classic, *The Happy Farmer*. You may be able to play it from childhood memory, or whistle it (once you get started) with the right-hand accompaniment ringing in your ears. In one way or another, alone or with necessary help, make some sort of music from the notes before reading further. . . .

Were you conscious of a strongly marked rhythm as you experienced this music? . . . Did you feel it moving in slow two beats to the bar? or in a steady four beats to the bar? or in a lively eight to the bar? . . . Were you conscious of the right-hand recurrences off the beat? . . . Did this give you a feeling of two concurrent rhythms out of step with each other? . . . Even without playing it, did you have any kinesthetic sensations of muscular tensions or activities? head noddings, foot tappings? in-breathings or out-breathings? alternating left-hand and right-hand sensations? Were you conscious of longer-time recurrences as the four-measure phrase was repeated?

Go back to *The Happy Farmer* for another look at it, another hearing of it. . . .

Were you conscious of any strongly marked feeling of balance as you experienced the music? Did you feel that the rising effect of the first two measures was balanced by the descending effect of the next two measures? Did you feel that the two measure phrase after the double bar served to balance what went before with what came after it? . . . Perhaps your answer is, 'Yes, now you mention it, I did have these feelings of balance.' Or perhaps your answer is, 'No, I didn't have any equilibrial sensations or related muscular sensations at all, but I know what you mean.' . . . Do you really?

Let us again say that balance is a naive felt-response to spatial works of art—pictures, statues, buildings—and to the spatial aspects of dances and stageplays. It is only by analogy that we impute balance to works of literature and music, which we have called time arts.

Balance and rhythm, two of the art principles, are what we have here called *formal feelings*. We have described their relation to empathy and to various kinesthetic, equilibrial, and organic sensations.

But there are other affective responses that are of comparable importance in the art experience: the feeling of order—and the disturbed feeling of disorder or chaos; the feeling of harmony—and the disturbed feeling of dissonance; the feeling of resolution and finality—and the unsatisfied feeling of expectancy and anticipation. Space does not permit inquiry into the physio-psychological bases of these other formal feelings. They are recognized as assuming a large place in many art theories. We might well have made 'form vs. substance' one of the pairs of contrasts in our discussion of art theories in Chapter 2, and you may recall that the second of the many definitions of the beautiful was 'anything . . . which has a specified form.'

In the Platonic dialog *Philebus*, Socrates says, "I do not now intend by beauty of shapes what most people would expect, but for purposes of my argument, I mean straight lines and curves and the surfaces or solid forms produced out of these by lathes and rules and squares, if you understand me. . . . And I mean colors of the same kind. . . . I mean that such sounds as are pure and smooth and yield a single pure tone are not beautiful relatively to anything else but in their own proper nature, and produce their proper pleasures." And we may well close this discussion of those affective responses that we have called the formal feelings by quoting William Mitchell of our own century: "Shapes and curves, as well as rhythms, are naturally gay or austere; and rhythms, like shapes, are smooth or rugged. These affective qualities of sound and sight are not borrowed from the associations in which we happen to have met them. We do not have to learn them, though their expressiveness develops with our experience."

3. *Beauty and affection*

This chapter opened with the discussion of simple recognition and free imagery, which are naive responses, all right, but not affective or felt responses. However, the second pair of naive responses, empathy and formal feelings, are certainly affective in character, as are the next two pairs: beauty and affection, mood and emotion.

The pair of affective naive responses indicated for this section have already been discussed at sufficient length in the earlier sections of this book. Some cross references and a simple definition are all that will be needed in this place.

Beauty as a felt response was considered in the opening section of Chapter 3, which was prepared for in final sections of Chapter 2.

For the purpose of this book the word *beauty* has been used to refer to those felt-responses of positive and terminal value attributed to a variety of things, and it was described as naive and intuitive in character.

The word *affection* is here used to name that second sort of value response, that intuitive liking, which is the basis of your individual taste. The matter of taste was introduced in the first section of Chapter 2 and was further developed in Interlude I 'On the Personal Cultivation of Taste.' You may recall that 'taste' was defined as the pattern of your likes and dislikes. It was described in terms of preference and aversion, and was characterized as intuitive and irrational. As here used, the word 'affection,' in the homely sense of fondness or just plain liking, is only one of the several different affective or felt responses. If affection is a naive response, we must not forget that dislike is a feeling state of a similar sort.

It is not necessary to enlarge upon the differences between beauty and affection as herein used. Beauty, as earlier described, is object centered; that is, the artee usually regards it as possessed by the work of art. Affection is subject centered; that is, the artee recognizes it as his own feeling about the work of art. Sometimes you like a thing that you do not feel is beautiful, and you may attribute beauty to a work of art without really wanting to possess it. But more often your affections and beauty responses go hand in hand and are causally interrelated: you like something because it is beautiful, or feel that it is beautiful because you like it. Both beauty and affection are value responses.

4. *Moods and emotions*

Some persons would say, as we saw in Chapter 2, that the emotions evoked by a work of art are by far the most important part of the entire responsive art experience, and that communication of emotion is the special function of art. Mere recognition of subject matter, fleeting and often irresponsible imagery, empathic responses, such feelings as balance and rhythm, beauty and personal affection are, in the view of these critics, of much less significance than those more intimately organized feeling states that we shall describe as the moods and emotions. However, there are others who prefer to think of the art experience as essentially unemotional and detached.

What are here called moods and emotions are the third pair of distinctly affective responses to works of art. They are similar in that they seem to engage the entire personality, but they are different in their intensity and dynamic character. Moods are pervasive but passive feeling states; emotions are consuming and active feeling states. We shall describe them separately in more detail.

A person's *mood* at a particular moment is his state of mind or disposition. A mood is the sort of feeling one has when he is in a good humor—or in a bad humor. It is closely related to organic states and general muscular tone, to good health or illness, to refreshment or fatigue. Certain such feeling states are well known as cheerfulness, melancholy, earnestness, cynicism, querulousness, sentimentality, awe, tolerance, and so on. They are very important indeed to a consideration of the art experience, and one or two general observations will be made about them.

First, the artee's mood when he comes to a work of art will, in a very considerable measure, determine the nature of his entire art experience. It will often affect his sensory perception, condition his naive responses, and guide his critical interpretation. A person in a perverse mood may actually 'see things wrong!' He may fail to make the usual recognitions and perhaps have especially irresponsible free images; unnatural empathic and other formal feelings may be evoked in him; and his other naive responses may be unexpected. If the artee approaches a work of art in such a perverse mood, he may enjoy making hypercritical and irrelevant interpretations, perhaps accompanied by prejudiced and offensive remarks! But the person who brings to a work of art a mood of eager anticipation and expectation will, as a result, enjoy a very different kind of responsive art experience.

Second, the artee's mood will very possibly change somewhat as he looks at a picture or listens to music. Coming to it in a depressed mood, he may be quite cheered up by it. Or, contrariwise, he may approach it eagerly, but find his mood changed to one of frustration. If the music or poem or painting suits his mood, he may have his original melancholy fortified, or he may find himself purged of his unhappy or confused feeling as a result of his experience. This is the sort of thing Dorothy Parker referred to in her Aristotelian definition, "Art is catharsis."

But moods, as here defined, are pervasive feeling states that are relatively static in nature, though we have noted some ways in which they may change as a part of the art experience.

By *emotion* we mean something different both in kind and degree from these.

The question of emotion is an unusually complex and controversial one in psychology. As with other naive responses and critical interpretations, it is difficult to make thoroughly objective studies of the emotions. But something about emotion will be said here even though it must be largely speculative. The common emotions of love and hate, fear and anger, joy and grief, admiration and disgust, and so on, are by no means merely the milder sort of moods or general feeling-states or states of mind, which were said to be static; neither are they simple likings or mere affection. Emotions are dynamic. They are dynamic organizations of various organic and external sensations together with the basic psychological drives of which we spoke in an earlier chapter.

Well over half a century ago the American psychologist, William James, and the Danish professor of anatomy, Carl Lange, pointed out the importance of internal sensations, muscular and organic, to an understanding of emotion. They described emotions in terms of the feeling of bodily sensations. Today we know from the work of endocrinologists how important glandular activity is to emotional states. Emotional responses, then, engage the entire personality and are potentially dynamic; they call for action, or accompany action, or result from action.

The emotion of fear is the feeling of those muscular and organic sensations that make for, or are made by, flight from something. Glandular and other organic changes (increased heart-beat, and so on) prepare for escape, though one may be momentarily frozen and speechless with fright. The emotion of joy is the feeling of the organic and muscular sensations that might include jumping for joy and the complex sensations of laughter (diaphragmatic spasms and pleasant facial contortions, etc.), organic sensations of well-being. The emotion of love is the feeling of the muscular and organic tensions, the visual and tactile sensations of love-making integrated with a complex of sentiments, and impelled by the sex drive. It may seem amusing to describe love in such terms. But certainly love is no mere affection, no mere mood of companionability, no merely vague state of being. Love is indeed dynamic.

But does the naive response to a work of art ever include such dynamic feeling-states as those here described as the emotions? Perhaps not usually; perhaps not such driving emotions as those here suggested; perhaps not in such violent degree. But emotions once experienced can be recalled from the vaults of memory. Emotions can be revived to be re-experienced, sometimes with much of their earlier poignancy, sometimes with a measure of detachment.

Some works of art call for more dynamic emotional responses than others. Who has not given way to the emotion of grief in witnessing some work of theater art? Who has not been tense with terror in watching a murder movie? Who has not been filled with overflowing joy in watching a dance routine of abandoned gayety? Who has not felt the deep emotions of love in reading one of the great love poems or novels or dramas? Who has not felt exalted and spiritually uplifted in experiencing a great cathedral or symphony?

Most art experiences may leave the artee relatively unmoved. Indeed a certain degree of psychical distance, as Edward Bullough calls it, is necessary and desirable. The artee usually maintains some measure of detachment in observing works of art. It is, fortunately, an extremely rare event for someone to stand up in the balcony and shoot the villain on the stage—though occasionally one does hear spectators who are moved to whisper advice to the endangered heroine *not* to open that closet door! For the most part, however, the artee's emotions do not run high enough to discharge themselves in action. A change in mood is all that may result for certain persons as a naive response to many or most works of art. And, often enough, the observer will remain as cool as a cucumber, quite unaffected. Some persons maintain that this is as it should be. But not all. For it has been said that the communication of emotion is the chief business of the arts.

Certainly it can be said that, only when the mood or emotion evoked in the artee is similar to the mood or emotion that the creative artist tried to give expression to, has the art process been effectively completed; for it is only then that mood or emotion has been communicated.

Let us look, now, at two or three previous illustrations of this chapter. First, *A Gaul and His Wife.* . . .

As you looked at the statue, recognizing the active forms and the two figures, you may have had free images of pursuing Roman soldiers, perhaps also of some physical obstruction that has cornered the fleeing Gaul and his wife. Such images may accompany the reflective thinking about the statue that we shall consider in the next chapter. Recognition of the Gaul's emotion of fear, and of desperate courage to take his own life rather than submit, may be a purely intellectual process. You might reason this out and remain utterly unmoved yourself; you might interpret the Gaul's posture as consisting of so many signs of the posture of flight and the emotion of fear.

But for many persons, as we have seen, there will be a more or less strong empathic response; they will feel out the posture in terms of their own muscular tensions, slight tendencies to assume the posture, and consequent kinesthetic and related organic sensations.

Since the emotion of fear is the feeling of the muscular and organic sensations of flight—since the emotion of courage is the feeling of the muscular and organic sensations of making a stand against opposition—*the observer* (in whom there are also the dynamics of bodily and egoistic self-preservation) *may actually experience a complex emotion* that is akin to that which the sculptor seems to have given expression to through his creative activity.

It is important to observe this relation of the mood or emotion to the empathic response through which the artee projects his consciousness into the very postures of persons represented or the abstract forms that he contemplates. For it serves as a logical explanation of the way in which a work of art—statue, picture, stage-play, dance, poem, story, and less obviously a building or musical composition—may arouse emotion in the beholder even without consideration of the subject matter represented. The postures and forms perceived evoke muscular and organic sensations that are the bodily concomitants of emotions previously experienced; and the bodily sensations, empathically realized, then evoke the emotion itself or a related mood.

Turn once again to John Hall Wheelock's *The Black Panther* and consider it in the light of what has been said about mood and emotion. . . .

It may seem unnecessary to comment upon the way in which recognition of the plain sense of the successive words and phrases serves to evoke (for most persons) a series of visual and auditory but, also and especially, kinesthetic images. Probably you not only see the caged panther in your mind's eye, but also image the muscular sensations of pacing up and down, springing upon the trembling bars, the sensations of being stretched and shaken. These kinesthetic images—this empathic response—may be indistinguishable from actual though faint muscular sensations. These are indeed the muscular and organic components of an emotion that you have doubtless yourself experienced, and serve to revive either the memory of such emotion or an appropriate mood or emotion itself.

Surely the affective response caused by Schumann's *The Happy Farmer* will be significantly different from this. We spoke of it earlier in relation to the formal feeling of rhythm. Now we shall suggest the mood or emotion that may be evoked by it. For many persons, it will be a jolly feeling, the kind of sheer delight that youngsters feel in their play. Certainly it has stirred generations of children far beyond the ecstasy of five-finger exercises! It is easy to see that the mood evoked is related to foot tappings and head noddings, silent whistlings and phrasal breathing, the whole complex of muscular and organic sensations of the musical performance.

The part that certain kinds of music play in evoking appropriate moods for various social activities is too well known to need more than mention: it induces the mood as well as the rhythm for social dancing; it provides the background and sets the mood for various kinds of teas, receptions, dinners, and parties; it evokes desired moods in relation to radio drama, cinema, and theater. And, for many persons, the great pleasure to be derived from listening to so-called classical music is to be found in the divers moods and emotions that are evoked by it.

5. *Attitudes and actions*

With the brief consideration of actions and attitudes in this section, we shall bring this discussion to a close. There are five pairs of naive responses in all—simple recognitions and images, empathy and formal feelings, beauty and affection, moods and emotions, attitudes and actions. The central three pairs are all affective responses, feeling and emotion of one kind or other. This final pair of naive responses are of a somewhat different sort, though certainly related to the preceding pair.

What is the final result of an art experience? Does anything really happen to a person as a result of looking at a picture, listening to music, reading a novel or poem? We have prepared the answer to such a question as this in Interlude II 'On the Human Need for Art.' There it was said that creative and responsive art experiences minister to various human needs. The satisfaction of such needs, then, is the end result. Human beings effect certain personality adjustments as a result of art experiences.

It is enough in this place to point out that such results may be of two related sorts: changed or reinforced attitudes and overt actions.

An attitude is simply the readiness to respond in a particular way. We all have innumerable attitudes toward all manner of things. These are predispositions to act in a certain way when occasion arises. We are inclined to suspect a particular person, or we are ready to overlook his faults. We are all set for a fight, or tend to see certain things in a favorable light. Each of us, then, is a bundle of such attitudes; and when something does stimulate us to act, we move off in the direction already established by these attitudes. But many events do not stimulate us to overt action; however, they may effect an alteration or reinforcement of certain of our attitudes. We are constantly being affected in this way, our complex systems of attitudes —predispositions, prejudices, preconceptions—are being changed or fortified. And among the life events great and small that are influencing us in this way are our various responsive art experiences.

It is perhaps characteristic of works of art that they do not usually stimulate overt action as a part of the total response. You are unlikely to rush up to the statue of the Gaul to stay his hand. It is probably seldom that crime fiction actually leads to criminal activity. Rarely does the spectator at a play really talk back to the actors on the stage. Hardly ever does the auditor at a concert sing out lustily with the trumpets. And yet there may indeed be tendencies in this direction. Furthermore, certain forms of overt action in response to works of art have become part of our social conventions. This is especially so in those arts that involve performance before an audience. In the theater there may be hissing as well as laughter, boos as well as tears, and there is almost always applause. This applause serves as a means of release for energy and tension that may be built up during the dramatic performance—built up because overt action, except for outbursts of laughter, is not usually appropriate during the course of the play. Much the same is true of music and the dance; but the solitary experiencing of a painting or statue, building or novel is unlikely to result in activity—other than the respondent's talking about it as soon as he finds someone to listen.

No, the responsive art experience is, for the most part, a passive sort of art activity; that is, the activity is psychological rather than overt. Except for the public manifestations of audience response to performances, the final results of art experiences are most characteristically to be found in the human attitudes that are evoked, reinforced, or changed. And it is very hard indeed to put one's finger on these. It may be that, as a result of experiencing *A Gaul and His Wife*, you have a new appreciation of the desperate plight of individual free people hounded and cornered by the forces of tyranny. It may be that in consequence of *The Black Panther* you have developed a new understanding of your own psychological conflicts. It may be that now after contemplating Cézanne's *Mont Ste. Victoire* you are inclined to see natural scenes with a fuller realization of their possible effects upon your bodily postures and moods. It may be that *The Happy Farmer* experience has predisposed you to listen for a wider range of rhythmic stimuli. But this is at best guesswork: except for such overt activity as may result, the final effects of art experiences are indeed likely to be lost to view in the complexity of our everchanging attitudes.

6. *Some positive suggestions*

This chapter, like the last one, should conclude with some positive suggestions. For, just as one can improve his skill at the level of sensory perception in looking at pictures, listening to music, and reading literature, so one can also effect a change in his naive responses to art things as they are perceived.

1. *Relax and free yourself from inhibitions.* That is suggested by the very word 'naive'—just be yourself, and with confidence. There is no need to reproach yourself for not really knowing anything about art. And there is some danger of pride if you think you know all the answers. In experiencing a work of art, just take it easy, and don't work too hard at it. Many persons are self-conscious or have a feeling of inferiority about one or another of the arts, or about their ignorance of aesthetics, or about the homes they live in or the families they come from or the limited training they have had. But remember that you are really in the same boat with the rest of humanity. Your honest and forthright naive responses are not only important to you individually, for they are an expression of your personality, closer to you than breath itself; but they are essential data for any intelligent art theory. Don't fool yourself: it does matter what your feeling responses are to this or that work of art!

2. *Take time to look, listen, or read.* You will remember the suggestions in the preceding chapter. Again let us say: Free yourself from conflicting stimuli. Be willing and curious to receive sensations. Come back time and again for repeated seeing, hearing, and reading so as to allow for a fuller response. Back off for the full view and come up for the near look. Indeed, it is only upon the basis of an adequate sensory perception that you will enjoy rich and appropriate naive responses that may be part of your art experience. From simple recognitions to final resultant attitudes these responses are interrelated. It is unreasonable to expect that such a rich complex of effects can be evoked in the fleeting moment of a hasty reading or a single inattentive hearing or casual glance.

3. *Hold off on critical interpretations and evaluations.* Of course you can't help using your head; you can't avoid proceeding from sensory perceptions and simple recognitions to more critical interpretations. But make no special effort to answer all the questions

that arise. You don't need to ask the source of this or that image or why you have the formal feeling of balance or imbalance, to rationalize your beauty response or affection, to analyze your mood or emotion. At this stage it is quite enough to recognize and imagine, to empathize and respond to form, to enjoy beauty and preference, to sense a mood or feel the emotion, to laugh or realize an attitude. It is time enough later on to proceed with critical interpretation and evaluation.

4. *Reach out toward the work of art.* This is not meant quite literally, though you may well reach out for tactile exploration of works of sculpture. But it really is important to be willing and eager, to meet the artist halfway. That halfway point is, of course, the work of art itself. Be alert and responsive to it as you perceive it. First you were told to relax, now you are asked to reach out or lean toward the work of art. The ideas are not contradictory. One kind of relaxation is flabby and passive; but another involves a certain muscular tonus that takes the slack out of muscles in preparation for action. The suggestion, then, is: be relaxed but ready. You'll have stronger empathic and emotional responses if your mind and body are in a willing and receptive attitude, eager to engage in the art experience, eager to respond fully to the work of art as perceived.

Chapter 9. Critical Interpretation of the Work of Art

The work of art is . . . a whole system of signs, or structure of signs, serving a specific aesthetic purpose.

René Wellek, *Theory of Literature.*

Every work of art without exception must have much read into it.

J. F. Herbart, *Encyclopedia of Philosophy.*

People complain that music may be construed in so many ways, and that no one knows how really to interpret it, while words are easily comprehended. But the opposite holds true with me.

S. Hensel, *Die Familie Mendelssohn.*

IT WAS SUGGESTED that you try to hold off the more thoughtful consideration of the work of art as perceived until you had given yourself full opportunity to respond naively. But it was pointed out at the same time that you cannot really refrain from using your head. 'Don't think' is one of the strangest orders that can be given, and least likely to be obeyed. Yet it is worth while to make an effort to hold off critical interpretation so as to allow for full and unrestricted sensory perceptions and for uninhibited recognitions and images, empathic and formal feelings, beauty and affection, mood and emotion, and even appropriate actions and resultant attitudes.

Now it is time, however, to turn our attention to the more critical thoughts that may be evoked. Critical thoughts may be directed at any or all of the points in the whole art process: the artist himself, the art activity that created the work of art, the work of art itself as a public object, any one or all of the three aspects of the responsive art experience, or even the personality of the artee in relation to the work of art. This, indeed, has been the sort of thing we have tried to do in this book. But we must now give our attention to what we have called critical interpretation of the work of art—that system of closely controlled thoughts about its meaning, its form, its relation to the artist, to the times—and, we might add, to its type, theme, style. This will call for a high degree of self-consciousness, a more purposeful use of contextual data, and an awareness of the artee's art theory.

The first of the four sorts of critical interpretation to be touched on in this chapter will take us back to a consideration of meaning.

1. *Semantic interpretation*

By semantic interpretation we shall mean simply the artee's thoughts evoked by the work of art as 'a whole system of signs, or structure of signs,' to use Wellek's phrase. Our own definition of art in terms of beauty and meaning responses led us, in Chapter 3, to the general problem of meaning in art. There is marked divergence of opinion, you will recall, for some critics would say that art is really meaningless. Some believe that works of art have meaning of a sort that cannot be explained, or, as others say, can only be explained by the experts. Yet other critics, however, believe that works of art are not only meaningful but generally understandable. It was this view, of course, that encouraged us to move forward to the discussion of art works as signs of meaning.

It may be worth while to glance over those paragraphs and to revive and review the elaborate diagram based upon the two triangles one below the other. You will recall that the framed work of art, a complex of signs, was at the left; the two worlds of the artist's and artee's experiences, the referents of their several thoughts, at the right; the artist's head at the bottom, the artee's at the top. It was observed that, as no line connects the mind of the artee directly with the mind of the artist, the only route from mind to mind is via signs. Furthermore. the work of art and the world of things are only linked by the minds of artist and artee. Now, interpretation is the process of reading signs. Interpretation is the process of bridging the gaps from the artee's mind to the artist's, and from the work of art to the world of things.

We have already noted that perception itself is interpretative, that in the integration of sensory data and contextual data we tend to see things or hear things that, in the light of our experience, make sense. And we have already considered, as a form of naive response, those simple recognitions which indeed are also interpretations of an unreflective sort. Now we shall be concerned with those more self-conscious or critical interpretations of meaning—shrewder guesses of what the work of art may stand for in the world of things and experiences, more calculated surmises of what the artist may have had in mind.

The meaning of a work of art may be very complex indeed, and a work of art may be a very complex sign. For instance, the words of a poem are first of all symbolic signs: they are words in a language system whose conventions condition the thoughts that are evoked and the referents they stand for in the world of experience. But these words may also evoke non-referential effects, as we pointed out in Chapter 3. And we saw, in the opening Foreword, that a given line in a picture may mean not only 'curved shape' but also 'shoulder.' In the same way a musical phrase may serve not only as a natural but as a resemblative sign, and even occasionally, as we observed, as a symbolic sign of meaning.

The analysis of a complex meaning may be simplified by adopting a classification developed by I. A. Richards and C. K. Ogden in *The Meaning of Meaning* in regard to language and extended by Richards in his studies of literature and the arts, *Principles of Literary Criticism* and *Practical Criticism*. What are therein called the several functions of language will here be called *four phases of meaning*. The meaning of a single sign or of a complex work of art may have as many as four phases: the plain sense of it, the artist's intention, the tone or attitude, and the feeling or emotion. The first of these, the sense, is the referential phase of meaning. The intention, tone, and feeling may be called non-referential or emotive phases of meaning.

The *sense phase* of meaning is usually the most obvious. It is clear enough, for instance, what we mean by the mere sense of the words of a poem. It is most easily revealed by the process of paraphrase, which attempts to put the literal meaning of the verses into other words. This was commented on in the earlier discussion of *The Parable of the Sower* and the consideration of simple recognition or unreflective interpretation (Chapter 8). As stated in those earlier sections, the recognition of the various active forms in a picture or statue—the simple interpretation of the resemblative signs: 'That's a head . . . that's a face . . . that's a nose . . . that's a neck'—is equivalent to the literal meaning of a poem. In the same way, the recognition of musical phrase and theme, tune and bass, repeat and development, cadence and coda —this is the plain sense of a musical composition.

So, too, a chair makes sense in that the functional character of its active forms—seat and legs, arms and back—is recognized at a glance. A work of architecture makes sense in that certain openings are interpreted as doors, others as windows; some forms are steps, others are balustrades. A stageplay makes sense as the plain sense of the actors' words and of their gestures and movements reveals the chief characters and their principal relations and actions. So, too, in the interpretation of an abstract pattern, such as a rug pattern or nonrepresentational dance, the active forms make sense in the same way that the elements of absolute music make sense—various bits of pattern are perceived as component parts in certain relations to each other, repeated and varied, beginning and ending, dominant and subordinate, and so on.

Making sense of a work of art is the interpreter's running-fire sequence of thoughts of the things that the signs stand for, whether those signs are word symbols, resemblative forms, or abstract forms. In reading a poem or novel, listening to music, attending a stage-play or dance, this process of making sense of it continues throughout the time of reading, hearing, or performance. In looking at a picture, statue, building, chair, or rug, the stream of thoughts that makes sense of it may be compressed into the first fleeting moments of the responsive art experience—unless, for some reason, the work of art doesn't readily make sense to the beholder. If, with a certain minimum of effort, the work of art doesn't make sense, the artee is likely to give up with a shrug or in disgust, or he may stay with it in stubborn confusion. Sometimes he goes to work in a patient effort to make sense of it. *Modern art is often distressing to those who believe that a work of art should make sense to them at first glance.*

But, important as the plain sense is as one phase of the full meaning, the non-referential or emotive phases of meaning are often of yet greater importance in critical interpretation.

The second phase of meaning may be called *intention.* The artee's thoughts about the artist's purpose in creating the work of art, about his underlying motive, and about his intention—this will call for that shrewd sort of guessing that makes use of all manner of available clues. Such thoughts come to the interpreter when he asks himself, 'What is the artist really trying to do?' It is the close attention to this second phase of meaning that alerts the reader to go beyond the mere sense of the line: 'There is a panther caged within my breast.' Indeed the literal sense of those words fails to make sense as a direct statement of possible fact, and the search for sense suggests some special intention, which leads to the critical interpretation of the statement as metaphor. But the *Mont Ste. Victoire,* which makes sense enough as direct statement, still invites critical interpretation of the artist's intention, and you may be led to reflect upon Cézanne's statement, 'treat nature by the cylinder, the sphere, the cone,' quoted in the last chapter. Surely your critical thoughts about Schumann's intention in writing *The Happy Farmer* will hardly impute to him motives very different from these: the composition of a good left-hand folk tune with a muscular right-hand rhythm, a boisterous exercise for inclusion in his *Album for the Young.* To look for profound or subtle meaning here would be as much of a mistake in critical interpretation as to overlook Cézanne's formal intentions or Wheelock's metaphorical intention in *The Black Panther*.

Tone, the third phase of meaning, suggests the relationship between artist and artee. In listening to a speaker, we are quick to catch the cynical or sarcastic tone, the pleading or ingratiating tone, the tone of open-eyed wonder or of earnest reflection. Sometimes a careful consideration of tone will be a clue as to the artist's intention; it may alter the plain sense of it. Irony is a special sort of tone that reveals the intention to communicate a meaning directly the opposite of the apparent sense. Taken by and large, artists are pretty serious; it's therefore easy to overlook the interpretation of this phase of meaning. For whom was the artist creating his work of art? For me and those like me? or for others? And what was his attitude toward them? Surely the tone of *The Happy Farmer*—Schumann's unpatronizing recognition that children love a strong rhythm and a simple tune—is very different from the tone of the *Mont Ste. Victoire*. Indeed Cézanne once said, "Art addresses itself to an excessively small number of individuals. The artist must scorn all judgment that is not based on an intelligent observation of character. He must beware of the literary spirit which so often causes painting to deviate from its true path—the concrete study of nature—to lose itself all too long in intangible speculations."

The fourth is the *feeling* phase of meaning, the artee's thoughts about the artist's feelings and emotions. Again it is important to distinguish 'thoughts about' emotion from the actual experiencing of emotion. In the preceding chapter we considered the mood or emotion that may be evoked in the artee as a part of his naive response to a work of art. You may have experienced a strong mood or emotion in reading *The Black Panther*. This stirring of your own feelings is quite different from your 'thoughts about' your own emotion or your 'thoughts about' the emotion that the poet may have experienced and to which he gave expression in the poem. To put into so many words the thoughts evoked by human moods and emotions is difficult indeed. For our language is poor in words that discriminate the more complex human feelings, and a normal reticence restrains the candid effort to name and describe intimate feeling states. So the feeling phase of the meaning of Wheelock's poem and even of Cézanne's painting is difficult to isolate and discuss, although the bounce and good humor of *The Happy Farmer* is perhaps obvious enough as a phase of its meaning.

In the semantic interpretation of a work of art these four interacting phases of meaning may well be kept in mind. It is not enough to let the running-fire thoughts of the literal sense dominate the stream of critical consciousness. Continual reference must be made to the artist's possible intention, to his apparent attitude, to his probable feelings—the emotive non-referential phases of meaning, to surmise which the artee will inevitably refer to his own naive response, the images and feeling states, moods and emotions evoked in him by the work of art. So the questions, muttered under the interpreter's breath, 'What's the artist's intention? ... what's his attitude? ... what's his feeling?' must proceed hand in hand with the insistent search for the plain sense of it.

The phrase 'the plain sense of it' suggests that the semantic interpretation of a work of art may well go forward at *several levels* at one and the same time. This was illustrated in the earlier consideration of *The Parable of the Sower,* which evoked, in those who had ears to hear, two parallel streams of thought, the literal sense of the sower scattering his seed upon ground of varied fertility and the metaphorical sense of (let us say) Jesus preaching his truths to people of varied understanding. The critical idea of several levels of meaning is helpful in considering the general problem of interpretation, but there is no fixed number of such levels. In certain earlier periods of literature, all literature, for instance, was looked upon as having several well-marked levels of meaning including not only the allegorical but also the anagogical (spiritual or mystical). So in the Middle Ages most literary works were interpreted as allegory, and all students of English Renaissance Literature are aware of the various allegorical levels of meaning in *The Faerie Queene.*

In the interpretation of most works of art, no more than two or three levels need be considered. The *first* level, the literal meaning has been sufficiently dealt with—the plain sense of it, etc., as above described. The *second*—the level of symbol, metaphor, parable, allegory, and music program—is by no means always to be found. It is a critical mistake to read into works of art meanings of this kind that are not intended, but it is just as much a mistake to overlook meanings at this level. The *third* level is the over-all meaning, the intended meaning of the work as a whole, whether in the form of an implied generalization or the illustration of some broad theme or truth. Perhaps a *fourth* level of meaning may be conceived in somewhat different terms: the meaning in the sense of the importance or value of the work of art to the individual who experiences it. At the other end of these successive levels, as a kind of basement below the literal meaning, there is the mere recognition that the work of art is a sign of meaning.

It is about the second of these levels of meaning that something more should be said: symbol, metaphor, parable, allegory, and the programmatic element in music. The word 'symbol' is here used in a special sense related to our previous use of it to name a sign (such as a word or number) which has a conventional or arbitrary relation to its referent. In the same way the American flag is a symbol, established by custom and indeed by law as meaning the Government of the United States of America. The rose is recognized in many contexts as symbolizing love. The sounds that we recognize as 'Taps' are also symbolic, in certain situations, of Death. Symbols of this kind, to be found in all of the arts, are upon this second level of meaning. And so, too, are metaphors which are confined to literature and the other language arts. In a metaphor—'There is a panther caged within my breast'—words from one universe of discourse (or field of experience) are used to convey a meaning in another universe of discourse. 'Panther caged . . .' is from the zoo universe; but the beast driven to pace 'Backward and forward in relentless quest' is used to convey the idea of terrific emotion in the psychological universe. In a metaphor such as this one, the second level of meaning may be expressed in proportional terms, thus—

panther : cage :: pent up emotions : human body

That is, the panther is to his cage as the emotions are to the body. The relevant relation, common to the two halves of the proportion, is that the one is confined within or frustrated by the other.

This second level of meaning was well illustrated in the parable, with the two meanings running parallel to each other, the one in the agricultural universe of discourse, the other in the religious universe of discourse. Allegories are of the same general kind, though they are usually extended narratives and sometimes they evoke more than two parallel streams of thought. Somewhat similar, also, is so-called program music. In such music the motifs and themes, the bass and accompanying figure, middle voices and counterpoint, the repetitions and development—these make sense in musical terms, as we have said, at the first level of meaning. But when they serve not only as natural signs of such musical meanings but as somewhat resemblative or even symbolic signs at the same time, then the characters and events that they suggest, or the natural scene or atmosphere that they bring to mind, may be said to be at this second level of meaning. It must be remembered that not all works of art invite interpretation at this second level.

The third level, as we said, is the over-all meaning. It is a dangerous simplification to say that the theme of *Macbeth* is ambition, of *Othello,* jealousy. But it is true that we tend to generalize, consider the work of art as a complex sign, and attribute to it a single broad meaning. So we mentioned several possible interpretations of the over-all meaning of *The Parable of the Sower,* such as 'environment determines growth' or 'the readiness is all,' etc. For one person the broad meaning of *The Black Panther* might be this: 'No one knows what emotional conflicts may be locked up within a person.' To another: 'Man can restrain the beast within him.' Another: 'It is at night that frenzy seizes one.' In the same way *A Gaul and His Wife* may also suggest an over-all meaning such as 'Death rather than chains,' and even Cézanne's *Mont Ste. Victoire* may have meaning at this level for some persons. It is in interpretation at this third level that it is all too easy to do violence to the intention of the artist, and the warning must be given to heed all available clues relative to the non-referential phases of meaning.

As an illustration of a sort, but more to allow the reader a chance to apply for himself the foregoing discussion of semantic interpretation, the following poem is presented in its original setting:

from THROUGH THE LOOKING GLASS
by *'Lewis Carroll'*

There was a book lying near Alice on the table, and while she sat watching the White King (for she was still a little anxious about him, and had the ink all ready to throw over him, in case he fainted again), she turned over the leaves to find some part that she could read—"for it's all in some language I don't know," she said to herself.

It was like this:

ЈАВВЕЯWOCKY

'Twas brillig, and the slithy toves
Did gyre and gimble in the wabe;
All mimsy were the borogoves,
And the mome raths outgrabe.

(shown in mirror-reversed text)

She puzzled over this for some time, but at last a bright thought struck her. "Why, it's a Looking-glass book, of course! And if I hold it up to a glass, the words will all go the right way again."

JABBERWOCKY

'Twas brillig, and the slithy toves
Did gyre and gimble in the wabe;

> All mimsy were the borogoves,
>   And the mome raths outgrabe.
>
> "Beware the Jabberwock, my son!
>   The jaws that bite, the claws that catch!
> Beware the Jubjub bird, and shun
>   The frumious Bandersnatch!"
>
> He took his vorpal sword in hand:
>   Long time the manxome foe he sought—
> So rested he by the Tumtum tree,
>   And stood awhile in thought.
>
> And as in uffish thought he stood,
>   The Jabberwock, with eyes of flame,
> Came whiffling through the tulgey wood,
>   And burbled as it came!
>
> One, two! One, two! And through and through
>   The vorpal blade went snicker-snack!
> He left it dead, and with its head
>   He went galumphing back.
>
> "And hast thou slain the Jabberwock?
>   Come to my arms, my beamish boy!
> O frabjous day! Callooh! Callay!"
>   He chortled in his joy.
>
> 'Twas brillig, and the slithy toves
>   Did gyre and gimble in the wabe;
> All mimsy were the borogoves,
>   And the mome raths outgrabe.

"It seems very pretty," she said when she had finished it; "but it's *rather* hard to understand!" (You see she didn't like to confess, even to herself, that she couldn't make it out at all.) "Somehow it seems to fill my head with ideas—only I don't exactly know what they are! However, *somebody* killed *something;* that's clear, at any rate —

"But oh!" thought Alice, suddenly jumping up, "if I don't make haste I shall have to go back through the Looking Glass before I've seen what the rest of the house is like!..."

(In a note Charles L. Dodgson, Lewis Carroll's real name, explains: "Pronounce 'slithy' as if it were the two words 'sly, the': make the 'g' *hard* in 'gyre' and 'gimble': and pronounce 'rath' to rhyme with 'bath'.")

Perhaps you are with Alice in having some difficulty in interpreting the plain sense of these verses; but if you will remember what was said in Chapter 3 about context, you will doubtless make out a satisfactory interpretation of this phase of the meaning. But the artist's intention, tone, and feeling as other separable phases of the full meaning should also claim your attention before you turn to a consideration of the several levels of meaning. You will notice that for Alice the marks in the book at first had meaning at only basement level: she recognized that they were words, but in a language she didn't know; but the mirror set that right—at least in part.

Later in the book Alice looks to Humpty Dumpty for some help.

"You seem very clever at explaining words, sir," said Alice. "Would you kindly tell me the meaning of the poem called 'Jabberwocky'?"

"Let's hear it," said Humpty Dumpty. "I can explain all the poems that ever were invented—and a good many that haven't been invented just yet."

Th·s sounded very hopeful, so Alice repeated the first verse:

" 'Twas brillig, and the slithy toves
    Did gyre and gimble in the wabe;
All mimsy were the borogoves,
    And the mome raths outgrabe."

"That's enough to begin with," Humpty Dumpty interrupted; there are plenty of hard words there. '*Brillig*' means four o'clock in the afternoon—the time when you begin *broiling* things for dinner."

"That'll do very well," said Alice. "And '*slithy*'?"

"Well, '*slithy*' means 'lithe and slimy.' 'Lithe' is the same as 'active.' You see, it's like a portmanteau—there are two meanings packed up in one word."

"I see it now," Alice remarked thoughtfully. "And what are 'toves'?"

"Well, '*toves*' are something like badgers—they're something like lizards—and they're something like cork-screws."

"They must be very curious-looking creatures."

"They are that," said Humpty Dumpty, "also they make their nests under sundials—also they live on cheese."

"And what's to '*gyre*' and to '*gimble*'?"

"To '*gyre*' is to go round and round like a gyroscope. To '*gimble*' is to make a hole like a gimlet."

"And 'the wabe' is the grass-plot round a sundial, I suppose?" said Alice, surprised at her own ingenuity.

"Of course it is. It's called '*wabe*,' you know, because it goes a long way before it, and a long way behind it."

"And a long way beyond it on each side," Alice added.

"Exactly so. Well, then, *'mimsy'* is flimsy and miserable (there's another portmanteau for you). And a *'borogove'* is a thin, shabby-looking bird with its feathers sticking out all round—something like a live mop."

"And then *'mome raths'*?" said Alice. "I'm afraid I'm giving you a great deal of trouble."

"Well, a 'rath' is a sort of green pig: but *'mome'* I'm not certain about. I think it's short for 'from home'—meaning that they'd lost their way, you know."

"And what does *'outgrabe'* mean?"

"Well, *'outgribing'* is something between bellowing and whistling. with a kind of sneeze in the middle; however, you'll hear it done, maybe—down in the wood yonder—and when you've once heard it you'll be quite content. Who's been repeating all that hard stuff to you?"

"I read it in a book," said Alice.

2. *Formal interpretation*

The Foreword statement about 'the fusion of the two aspects of a line—its purely formal value with its representational quality' may well serve as a transition from semantic interpretation to formal interpretation. As it was there said, a line may be perceived merely as a curved form or as a sign meaning shoulder. But as Rhys Carpenter pointed out, it is the fusion of these two aspects of the line that is characteristic of the art experience. From this perceptual fusion, he says, "arises a new thing which I call the aesthetic or artistic emotion. This new thing, which may be surprisingly intense and vivid, is *not discoverable either in the represented object* per se *or in the mere formal value of the lines used*." And he adds later, "The forms of art, considered in and for themselves, are nearly always trivial and irrelevant."

In *Theory of Literature,* written with Warren, Wellek rejects "the old dichotomy of 'content versus form' which cuts a work of art into two halves: a crude content and a superimposed, purely external form. Clearly, the aesthetic effect of a work of art does not reside in what is commonly called its content." So Carpenter, who is speaking of space arts, wherein form is often thought of as most important, pronounces 'the forms of art' to be in themselves 'trivial and irrelevant.' And Wellek, speaking of literature, wherein content ('the ideas and emotions conveyed') is often considered paramount, says that the aesthetic effect is certainly not to be found in mere content: "There are few works of art which are not ridiculous or meaningless in synopsis."

Our separate discussion of the semantic and formal aspects of the art experience should not obscure the fact that in the total response, meaning and structure, content and form, are fused. There are certain advantages, however, in taking them up separately as we have undertaken to do in these first two sections of the present chapter.

Semantic interpretation, as we have seen, is concerned with the meaning of a work of art as perceived, the system of thoughts evoked by the signs of which it is composed. Formal interpretation also consists of a sequence of thoughts, not of the meaning of the active forms, but of the various formal feelings evoked by those forms. We have prepared the way for our present discussion by the section on 'Empathy and formal feelings' in the last chapter. There some consideration was given to balance as a naive response to such spatial art works as pictures and statues; and rhythm was noted as a naive response to such temporal art works as poems and music. In both cases the response was a fusion of muscular and organic sensations induced by seeing the picture or hearing the music. Perhaps it need not be repeated that the balance and rhythm are not *in* the work of art as a public object.

Balance and rhythm were named as two of the art principles. It is important to note that these principles are not restricted to art; they are inherent in man as a living organism. D. W. Gotshalk has written: "Good artistic form harmonizes in a very marked degree with man's basic biophysical organization. Man's muscular, vascular, and neural systems are governed in a very fundamental way by the principles of balance, rhythm, and dynamic equilibrium, and the larger processes of man's biophysical being are connected in an organic unity." *Balance, rhythm, organic unity, harmony, etc., are art principles simply because they are life principles* deeply rooted in man's biophysical structure, in his physiological and psychological processes.

There is no general agreement among artists and critics as regards just what these formal principles are, how many of them should be listed, or what names to assign to them. Therefore it may be wise, for our present purpose, simply to refer to our previous discussion of balance and rhythm, to discuss briefly and illustrate three or four other formal principles, and to name yet others that would merit discussion if space permitted.

Unity, for instance, often tops the list of art principles. It certainly bears some relation to man's organic unity as a human being. He is but one alone, though given birth and giving life. We are conscious of ourselves as relatively complete and independent, even self-sufficient individuals, units perhaps in the larger whole of family and society, yet organic entities. We have a feeling of oneness about ourselves, no unnecessary limbs or organs. With what contempt we consider tonsils and appendix, and with what distress a tumor or foreign growth! This formal feeling of biological unity is, let us assume, the basis for that comparable feeling that may be evoked by a work of art—the feeling that everything is there that should be and nothing that shouldn't be, that this is indeed a complete and independent unit. And indeed it is natural for the artist and critic —and you and me—to generalize an art principle: works of art, as we have experienced them, evoke this feeling of unity. Indeed, you may agree with those who say that a work of art *must* observe this principle!

It is a natural step to consider next the idea of *organization*. Man recognizes not only that all his bodily parts form a unity, but that each has its functional relation to the others. Indeed, when man is in good health, he feels himself to be a tightly knit organization of bone, muscle, viscera, nerve fibers, and brain. And a comparable formal feeling may be evoked as he looks at a picture, listens to music, reads a novel—a satisfied feeling that each active form is in place, doing its job, co-operating in the whole organic function. This feeling may lead to a critical generalization, the statement of an art principle—even to the pronouncement of a rule or law.

Let us consider briefly a second pair of formal principles: *uniformity* and *variety*. Man has become accustomed to a relative sameness in his own life and environment. There is something comfortable about the familiar and unvarying scene of home town and people; it can be counted on and gives one a feeling of security. But variety is the spice of life, murders make headlines, redecoration of the front room is pleasantly different, and out-of-town strangers are the topic of conversation. So, whether you think of them as uniformity and variety or as harmony and contrast, the artee is likely to have certain formal feelings evoked by a picture, a musical composition, or a novel. There's the feeling of expectancy that all will be similar, and the feeling of pleasant surprise at the deviations from the routine. Again, repeated experiences lead to the abstraction of art principles.

It is not necessary here to discuss such other formal principles as may be suggested by the following words: theme and development, center of interest and diversity, dominance and subordination, movement and dynamics, order and complexity, universality and uniqueness.

These formal principles are at work whether the artee realizes it or not, as we noted in our discussion of empathy. They will shape and condition his total response simply because, as a human being, his structure includes semicircular canals and a pulsing heart, eyes with a certain visual span, a brain that perceives sensations in patterns, and so on. Even when unity, organization, harmony, variety, balance, rhythm, etc., rise to the level of consciousness, they will be essentially naive responses, those formal feelings of which we have spoken. It is only the 'thoughts about' the formal feeling of balance, 'thoughts about' the feeling of rhythm, 'thoughts about' unity in a painting or poem or musical composition that are involved in formal interpretation. This distinction between affective and logical qualifications is most important to keep in mind. The present chapter is concerned primarily with the latter.

Formal interpretation is simply the process of thinking systematically about the formal feelings evoked by the active forms or perceptual units as a part of the total response to a work of art. It may go beyond that and consider what one ought to feel or probably does feel! As such it may be a very active part of one's art theory. There is a tendency for the theory developed in connection with the space arts, where the physical form of a work of art stays put, to dominate the thinking of many persons, but this danger is overcome by the repeated insistence that the only forms that really count with an individual artee are the forms that he perceives and responds to.

To illustrate this discussion of formal interpretation, let us turn back to works of art in the preceding section and chapter. It will be easiest to start with the picture.

Cézanne's *Mont Ste. Victoire* as a work of art may evoke in you a feeling of completeness and self-sufficiency, a satisfying unity, and at once you may sense the organization of the lines and shapes and colors into a coherent pattern and composition. The artist is faced with a twofold problem. He creates a pattern of colored shapes on a two-dimensional surface, the picture plane. He also, in most pictures, creates the illusion of three-dimensional space in which he composes the apparently solid objects that he represents. So Cézanne organized flat shapes (like bits of colored paper) in a surface pattern; but he also organized solid shapes in the outdoor space that he depicted, broad as the valley, tall as the tree and sky itself, far as from hillside under foot to the distant mountain top. Cézanne was conscious, as our earlier quotation indicates, that he was organizing solid shapes according to the optical laws of perspective with the horizon line perhaps a third of the way up the mountain, a little lower than the middle of the picture. The cool pastel tints of most of this picture are relatively uniform in value (degree of darkness or lightness), but with accents and outlines as you may note by squinting your eyes. But there is a subtle variety in the hues and in the blue-gray that gives the atmospheric effect of distance. In sharp contrast to the harmonious valley, far mountain, and depth beyond it, there are the sharp outlines of the tree forms in the foreground. We might go on to consider the horizontal-vertical contrast as the possible theme of this landscape and the development given it throughout the surface pattern and the composition in depth. Here are the tall tree and horizontal branches; there is the flat floor of the valley with Mont Ste. Victoire rising beyond it. But we shall not go on with our formal interpretation except to say, as we did in opening this section, that form and meaning are really inseparable.

Our formal interpretation of *The Happy Farmer* will take a somewhat different turn. Here the perceptual elements are not lines, shapes, solids, colors, but sound groups and sequences, rhythmic units and phrases, themes and accompaniment. The effect of the whole is, to your ear doubtless as to mine, a unity. We feel that it all belongs together and that nothing is lacking. The organization is easy to grasp: the theme (A) is stated boldly in the first four measures by the left hand; it (A) is then repeated; there follows a two-measure subordinate theme (B) in the same key and rhythmic pattern, which leads back to (A) the main theme now emphasized by both hands; again (B) the subordinate theme; and once more (A) the dominant theme. Its organization may be summarized: AABABA. It is the 4/4 time-scheme, the continuum of eighth notes, the four-measure phrases that provide the underlying uniformity. Such devices as the pick-up notes in the melody, the afterbeats in the accompaniment, and the two-measure subordinate theme supply variety. Formal analysis might go further, considering such matters as its being in the key of F major and the relation of the melodic line to the major diatonic scale and the several harmonic chords. Again the separation of form and content is arbitrary, for the active forms are the perceptual units, the musical phrases and ideas.

In making a formal interpretation of the *Jabberwocky* it is worth noting that, though it has a unity of its own, it is really a part of the larger unity of *Through the Looking Glass*. However, in the larger context it is declared to be a poem, and it is set off on the page by narrower margins and, in some editions, smaller type, which give it a certain unity to the eye. Without any reference to meaning, the lines of type are seen to be organized in four-line groups, stanzas; and, even without reading it, the first and last stanzas may be observed to be identical. It is impossible, of course, to read these verses aloud without any thought of their possible meaning, but a fairly unreflective interpretation will serve to turn these words into sound. When read or listened to as nonsense verse, the most noticeable feature is the poetic rhythm. This rhythmic feeling is based upon a metrical pattern as rigid as the 4/4 time of the above music and may be described technically as (iambic) aba^4 b^3—or demonstrated more objectively by the following:

deDUMM deDUMM deDUMM deDOVES,
deDUMM deDUMM deDUMM deDABE;
deDUMM deDUMM deDUMM deDOVES,
deDUMM deDUMM deDABE.

But this underlying uniformity for each stanza is given subtle variety as the stressed syllables and accented words deviate from the expectancy, once it is established. But our formal interpretation of this work might go on to consider the recurrence of various vowel and consonant sounds that evoke, at least in part, its special and unique effect. Then we should turn to the structure of the story itself—impossible, of course, except in terms of the sense of the words: the setting described, the father's admonition, the son's going forth, the approach of the dread creature, the triumphant conflict and return, the father's praise, the setting reaffirmed.

So much, then, for this brief excursion in formal interpretation, which should close, as it opened, with the warning that neither content alone nor form alone is enough in a work of art. There can be no meanings without signs, no signs without form. Indeed, such forms as are perceived are likely to be signs of one kind or another and therefore have some sort of meaning. F. R. O'Neill has written, "The *raison d'être* of 'FORM' in a work of art is the attainment of perfect expression and communication," and he uses the word 'form' "to denote an organization of the effects of a work of art, . . . the effects that are produced by shapes, lines, colors, textures, proportions, etc." He regards form "as a means to an end, not as an end in itself, . . . the means by which an artist gives order and 'pattern' *to our responses* to his work. . ." And the form of a work of art, he insists, "is intimately connected with the artist's meaning."

3. *Intrinsic and extrinsic interpretation*

The two sorts of critical interpretation considered so far, semantic and formal, have consisted of the close reading of the signs and close attention to the active forms comprising the work of art as perceived.

In such interpretation the artee's thoughts are upon the interrelationship of signs and forms within the framework of the picture, poem, or piece. Of course, the work of art is not considered in a vacuum, for the interpreter's world of experience does provide a context that gives the signs their meaning and the perceptual elements their form. But this kind of interpretation, which we shall call *intrinsic*, is essentially a pursuit of the work of art itself without conscious regard to its relation to other works of art, to the personality of the artist who created it, to the history of culture, to the art sub-types or genres, to the schools or styles.

Interpretation that studies the work of art as an expression of the artist's mind or life, that places the work against the background of its times, that involves comparison with other works of the same subtype, that views the work as embodying one or another of the historic or contemporary styles such as romanticism or surrealism— interpretation of this general kind we shall call *extrinsic*. It is not so much interested in the individual work of art as such, the complex inner relation of its signs and forms, as it is in something else: the mind and art of the artist, the culture of a certain period, the art type and subtype to which it belongs, the literary theme that it develops, the historic style that it illustrates.

Although the two kinds of critical interpretation seem to take contrary directions, one inward and the other outward, they really cannot proceed independently of one another. The full exploration of the meaning and form of a work of art cannot be made without reference to the extrinsic factors; and an adequate illumination of the artist, culture, art type, or style cannot be achieved without continued attention to the meaning and relationship of the signs and active forms.

Before introducing two or three of these extrinsic sorts of critical interpretation, let us pause to consider another work of art.

Turn to the first of the accompanying illustrations; examine it as closely as this print will permit. Allow yourself time for adequate sensory perception and for full naive response. Next put your mind to it, and interpret all the signs and active forms as you perceive them. Then, and not until then, come back to the text and read further. . . .

Now, if you have really gone forward as suggested with your independent critical interpretation, you may find it of interest to answer these questions: How many persons are represented? how many women? how many attacking men? . . . Did you read the legend at the bottom of the print? What does 'sack' here mean? Who are the

Brygos, RED-FIGURED KYLIX, Louvre, Paris
Exterior, depicting the Sack of Troy, Side A

Brygos, RED-FIGURED KYLIX, Louvre, Paris
Profile and Exterior, Side B

armed warriors? Why are the Trojans without shields or helmets? Have they other arms? What has the right-hand woman raised above her head, and what is she doing? Who is the extreme right-hand figure and what is he doing?. . . . Why would this be a suitable subject for decorating a Greek artifact? What are the intention, tone, and feeling phases of the meaning as you interpret it?. . . . Are these figures just any Trojans, or do you interpret them as representing particular Trojans? Can you guess whom?. . . What sorts of information might be provided by the various inscriptions on the kylix if you could interpret them?. . .

What do you interpret 'red-figured' to mean? What is a kylix? What does 'exterior' convey to you? Why is the design semicircular in shape?. . . What is the significance of the central circular area in the design? What are the two large odd shapes, lower right and left? What is the strange shape along the bottom edge just to the left of the double white line?. . . What is the function of the leaf-like design to the right, the one partly covered by the youth's foot?. . . Do your naive formal responses give rise to any relevant thoughts relative to unity and organization? uniformity and variety? balance and rhythm? If so, what?. . .

It is, of course, easier to ask these questions than it will be for the reader to answer them, particularly if his world of experience doesn't include adequate referents for 'kylix' and 'sack of Troy.' But the effort to explore the meaning and form of this work of art has, perhaps, served well to illustrate semantic and formal interpretation, the two intrinsic sorts of critical interpretation.

We shall only suggest briefly the general direction that the extrinsic sorts of critical interpretation would take in considering this red-figured kylix. Again we shall proceed by asking questions. Answers to the above questions could, for the most part, be found by giving close attention to the work of art itself. But answering these next questions would involve a very considerable research in libraries and museums, part of which would be a fruitless search for data that are not available. There is no need for the reader to try to find answers. It will be enough to follow the direction of the questions.

Who was the artist? Where does the phrase 'Brygos Painter' come from? What does it mean?. . . Is there anything known about the artist's birthplace, parents, upbringing, apprenticeship, training, other creative work, other life activities, success, reputation?. . . Are there other comparable works, such as decorated urns or vases or cups, attributed to him? If so, do they evidence similarities in subject matter and treatment, form and style?. . . What seem to be the interrelations of the artist's personality and this work of art?. . .

When and where was this kylix created? what is the basis for assigning it to the 5th century B.C.? . . . What political, social, and cultural factors were important at this time and place? Why would this subject have been suitable or of timely interest? What relation does the depiction bear to current or legendary modes of dress, accoutrement, social customs, war? . . . When did the sack of Troy take place, or did it? What are the chief records of it? Who were the chief characters involved? Who are the characters depicted on the kylix? . . . What is the history of this kylix? What kind of person probably owned it? Where was it found? Where is it now? What is its reputation as a work of its kind? . . .

Does this kylix belong to one of the major arts? If so, what one? If not, to what minor art would you assign it? . . . Into what division of ceramic art does it fall? What, again, is a kylix? What was it used for? Was this sort of kylix for daily use or for social occasions? . . . By what process was it made? What materials were used? What is its shape? How was it formed? How was the pigment applied? When in the process was it fired? . . . Is this a representative kylix? a good example of the type? unusual either in shape or subject matter? . . .

What is the relation of this kylix to other works depicting the same general theme? . . . Is the Sack of Troy depicted in the *Odyssey* or *Iliad*? Where in later epic poetry do you find an account of it? Which ones of the Greek dramas treat this theme? Is it treated elsewhere in Greek literature? . . . Are there other graphic representations of the Sack of Troy? Any depictions in sculpture? . . . What are the main events of the story? the principal elements of the theme? . . . What relation does the Sack of Troy bear to comparable themes in the traditions of other peoples? . . .

Which one of the historic styles does this kylix exemplify? What are the characteristics of its style of representation? . . . What effort is made to represent depth as a dimension of space? What depth cues are employed? What effort is made to make the legs appear solid? Are any of the limbs foreshortened? Why are the faces all shown in profile? . . . What means are used to represent action? How do you reconstruct what has just happened? How do you anticipate what is about to happen? . . . How does the artist suggest the texture of the various materials represented? flesh and blood? various metals and qualities of cloth? . . . What seem to have been his guiding principles of design? . . . What is the relation of these considerations to the historic style that the work exemplifies? . . .

Even asking these questions without attempting to answer them has been of value as pointing the directions that extrinsic interpretation of various kinds would go. For in each case the inquiry went out from the work of art itself to study its meaningful relations to the artist, the period, the art type, the literary theme, and the historic style.

But let us consider further, largely by means of illustrations, two of these extrinsic kinds of critical interpretation.

4. *Biographical interpretation*

Semantic interpretation calls for close attention to the interrelated signs comprising the work of art, thoughtful consideration of all four phases of meaning. One of these is the artist's intention. This will usually be surmised by taking account of such subtle clues as may be discovered within the work of art as perceived. But sometimes extrinsic evidence of the artist's intention may be discovered by diligent search in the artist's biography, his memoirs or letters. Usually such a statement will merely verify the artee's independent interpretation of the artist's intention in creating the work of art, but occasionally it will throw an entirely new light upon the over-all meaning of the work.

Biographical interpretation brings the relevant data of the artist's life to bear in developing a fuller understanding of a work of art. Such data provide a special enrichment of the artee's world of experience. Sometimes such factual data are indeed an essential part of the context necessary to evoke an adequate meaning response.

Every work of art reveals, in some measure, the personality of its creator as well as his specific intention. The artist's inherited structure and temperament, the environment and social forces that shaped him, the training that developed his special skills, the particular events that may have stimulated his creation of this work of art— these factors may all be of interest and may be of some importance in the critical interpretation. That *Jabberwocky* was written by a mathematician and by a man who loved children are relevant data for a full interpretation of it. The numerous incidents and incidental comments on the nature and meaning of words to be found in Lewis Carroll's pair of adult children's books reveal semantic insights that are understandable in the light of his mathematical knowledge; he well knew the nature of signs and symbols from his study of mathematics. And his love for children, especially Alice Pleasance Lidell, gave him those insights into fantasy and play and make-believe that explain *Jabberwocky's* wide-eyed charm. The facts of Charles L. Dodgson's biography serve for a fuller understanding of 'Lewis Carroll's' books. But biographical interpretation cuts two ways: a thoughtful interpretation of *Alice in Wonderland* and *Through the Looking Glass* serve, in their turn, to illuminate the author's life.

There are two difficulties that beset the artee when he wishes to pursue this kind of extrinsic interpretation. The relevant biographical data are often most difficult to find. Or, indeed, as we observed about the Brygos Painter, there simply are no data available. There is a considerable body of anonymous literature, many pictures are by Artist Unknown, and some music is of folk origin. Moreover, there is another group of art works that are of collaborative origin. A good number of dramas, several of Shakespeare's, were written by two or more playwrights; many master paintings are partly the work of apprentices; a certain amount of music also combines the creative work of two artists. Furthermore, it is often hard to tell whether such data as one does find are reliable. Biographers often draw their deductions about the artist's life and character from his works of art. Such deductions cannot then be relevant data for a further understanding of the works. It is indeed difficult to find adequate biographical material for use in the fuller interpretation of works of art.

A second difficulty is in using such material. It is easy to warp one's understanding of a work of art by misapplying biographical data. The creative process is very complex, and it is impossible to find all the causes or explanations for particular works of art. Therefore there is a temptation to oversimplify, and to read too much meaning into particular biographical data or to attribute too much meaning to particular signs in a work of art.

As an illustration of biographical interpretation, let us consider the so-called *New World Symphony* and its composer Antonín Dvorák. Of course it will be necessary to hear and respond to a performance of this musical composition before undertaking a critical interpretation of it. Furthermore, intrinsic interpretation, both semantic and formal, should go hand in hand with the extrinsic interpretation that we propose to make. Recordings of this work are readily obtainable. The following musical notation may be of some help in discriminating and considering the various active forms. . . .

Of course, if you know nothing at all about Antonín (or Anton) Dvorák, you will not be able to make any sort of biographical interpretation at all unless you first acquire some relevant biographical data. You may deduce from his name that he is or was a foreigner, and therefore may not have known the New World at first hand; but, of course, you may be mistaken.

Thematic Notes for
SYMPHONY NO. 5 IN E MINOR
"From the New World"
by *Antonín Dvorák*

Opus 95

First Movement (Allegro)

Second Movement (Largo)

Third Movement (Scherzo)

Fourth Movement (Allegro)

On the other hand, if you know anything at all about Dvorák, you will naturally bring this information, however scanty, to bear. If you only know that he was a Czech, lived recently, and wrote the *Humoresque* that your sister plays on the piano, then these will be the contextual data that you will use in such slight biographical interpretation as you can make. But you may choose to go further. The main facts of Dvorák's life are readily available in standard reference works, though items of special interest regarding this *Fifth Symphony* are still coming to light.

We shall do no more than summarize: Antonín Dvořák (1841-1904) was born near Prague, the son of a Bohemian butcher and innkeeper. He gave early evidence of musical talent, was helped with his training by local musicians, went to Prague at sixteen, earned his living on the side, and had his first success and recognition at thirty-two. By the time he was fifty he had received international honors, a doctorate at Cambridge University, and had been appointed professor of composition at the Conservatory of Music at Prague. He loved his native Bohemia, was an ardent Czech nationalist (Bohemia was under Austrian rule), but was decorated by the Austrian government.

In the summer of 1891, Dvořák was invited to become the director of the National Conservatory in New York City, and in September, 1892, he assumed his duties. Shortly after his arrival, James Huneker, teacher of piano at the school, editor and critic as well, called Dvořák's attention to an article on 'Negro Melodies' and raised the question whether a distinctive American music might not be developed from them. At first noncommittal, Dvořák became interested in some of the 'Plantation Songs.' Not long after, when interviewed by a journalist about the prospects for American music, Dvořák said that American composers should study the Negro folk songs and 'construe their themes in the idiom of them.' A controversy ensued. In published replies and rejoinders many of the contemporary European composers, Brahms excepted, ridiculed the idea. After reading their responses, Dvořák is reported to have said, "Well, we shall see!"

His interest in American folk music led him to run a special notice in the New York papers welcoming Negro students to his classes. He asked them to sing their spirituals for him. One youth, Harry Burleigh, who had an especially fine mind and rich voice, sang for him evening after evening. From the music critic Krehbiel, who had made a special study of American folk music, Dvořák borrowed manuscript copies of Negro songs. In turn, he showed Krehbiel his own compositions before they were performed. Dvořák's interest led him to visit many cities and the prairie country. He spent his summer vacations at Spillville, Iowa, a Czech community in which he felt very much at home and played the organ on Sundays. He loved the American countryside, and he also came to love the poems of Longfellow. Indeed he made some musical notes toward writing an opera on the theme of Hiawatha.

He made many sketches for the composition of *Symphony No. 5 in E Minor*, to which he gave the subtitle "From the New World." One of these musical sketches is dated 'Morning, Dec. 19, 1892.' The theme that later became the famous slow movement (Largo) is entitled 'Legenda' in this notebook, and it has been said that he wrote it after reading Longfellow's account of the courtship of Hiawatha and Minnehaha. The Scherzo was completed on Jan. 31, 1893, and the Finale on May 24th or 25th, before his departure for Spillville in June. It is there that he carried on much of the instrumentation. Meanwhile the controversy about the destiny of American music continued in the press. On May 25, 1893, the New York *Herald*, whose enterprising interview had touched off the discussion, carried a statement by Dvořák in which he stated his conviction "that future American music will and must be based on the so-called Plantation Songs, 'which he called "typically American." ' " Among those who doubted this was Dvořák's friend Anton Seidl, conductor of the New York Philharmonic, who said as much in a lengthy article.

Dvořák prepared a piano arrangement of the symphony for Krehbiel, who saw the completed score of the symphony before its performance. The New York Philharmonic agreed to perform this new work, and the score was delivered to Anton Seidl who, after studying it, confided to Kovarik, Dvořák's pupil and assistant, "You know, the symphony is Indian throughout!" It was performed in December 1893, with great success, and Dvořák seemed to have won the first round with his detractors.

But, ever since, critic and layman alike have listened to the symphony 'From the New World' intent upon catching the echoes of tunes actually borrowed from American folk music. When Krehbiel returned the MS to Dvořák he called his attention to the resemblance between a subordinate theme in the Fourth Movement (it is No. 6 in our notes, the last half of the bottom line) and 'Yankee Doodle.' The composer said that it was simply "the principal theme in diminution"—that is, speeded up. "But," asked the critic, "isn't the principal theme 'Yankee Doodle' in augmentation and the minor mode?" —that is, slowed down and changed from the cheerful to the mournful mode. In 1900, when this symphony was about to be performed in Berlin, Dvořák asked the conductor to omit from the program "that nonsense about my having made use of 'Indian' and 'American' themes —that is a lie. I tried to write only in the spirit of those national American melodies." However, the resemblance of the third theme of the First Movement to *Swing Low, Sweet Chariot* (reprinted in Chapter 1) has been frequently noted. Sigmund Spaeth observes that the opening theme of the last movement may have been suggested by the American folk song 'Peter Gray.' And even 'Three Blind Mice' seems to appear as a subordinate theme (No. 5) in the Fourth Movement.

But the defense by Dvořák and later of his sons was that he did not steal American folk tunes—as though that would have mattered—but developed his own themes in the spirit of American song. His success in doing this may be judged by reference to the famous Second Movement. Apparently this original melody was inspired by Longfellow's Indian epic, but it suggests the Negro spirituals to many ears. In fact, in the form of 'Goin' Home,' with words by William Arms Fisher, it is often mistaken for a genuine folk song. More recently the same tune reappeared as the briefly popular 'Wagon Wheels.'

However much this symphony 'From the New World' may owe to Dvořák's comparatively brief stay in the United States, it is still essentially a European work by a late nineteenth century romantic nationalist, who was proud of his Czech folk and their dances and music. Steeped in the tradition of Beethoven and Schubert, Schumann and Mendelssohn, he was a friend not alone of Smetana but of Brahms. It is a mistake to think of *The New World Symphony*, as it is usually called, as American music, though it was written in America. It is more like a musical letter written home 'From the New World,' giving the impressions made upon a talented and observant visitor by the American scene, its people and its song.

A biographical interpretation of Dvořák's *Fifth Symphony* would not end here, but enough has been said to illustrate this kind of extrinsic interpretation and to suggest its special problems.

5. *Historical interpretation*

There are a number of quite different things that might be meant by 'historical interpretation.' As biography is sometimes looked upon as a branch of history, the sort of interpretation we have called biographical might be called historical, and indeed we did review chronologically the chief facts about the conception, development, and performance of Dvořák's *Fifth Symphony*. But our interest was not so much in events as in the interrelations of the work of art and the artist's life and personality. By a slightly different use of the phrase 'historical interpretation,' we might mean the study of this symphony subsequent to its completion—the record of its various performances, the criticism that it evoked and reputation it established, the influence it had upon the work of other composers, its place in the history of music. But there is still another sort of historical interpretation, which studies the relation of the work of art to the environment of its creation. A work of art may have important and meaningful relations to various social, economic, cultural, and political factors in the time when it was made. Historical interpretation, in this third sense, will be concerned with such factors and relations.

It is true that a work of art is the result of the artist's creative activity; but the work of art is also shaped and formed by the society of a certain time and place. The artist himself, of course, is a creature of his period as well as a child of his parents. So we should be prepared to discover a complex relation. As you glance back over the discussion of Dvořák's creation of his *Fifth Symphony*, you will observe this interplay of personality and environment. Indeed, historical and biographical interpretations may be but opposite sides of the same coin, the one interested in the external social and cultural forces and events that shaped the work of art (through the artist, of course), and the other interested in the personal creative activity and expression of the artist (challenged by his environment, of course).

The same sorts of difficulties beset the artee in making an historical interpretation as were mentioned in relation to biographical interpretation. The truly relevant social and economic, cultural and political data are hard to come by, and there is at times the tendency to make too much of the scattered facts that do come to hand. If the psychological make-up of the artist is complex and his motivations usually obscure, certainly the sociological make-up of the artist's environment is complex and we cannot hope to see, through the dim pages of record, all the forces that seethe beneath the surface of society.

But there is a special difficulty—perhaps we should say danger—in all such extrinsic interpretation. The background facts of one kind or another may be so interesting in themselves that the interpreter loses sight of his objective, the better understanding of the work of art. While it is true that works of art may serve as social and cultural documents, illustrative and shedding important light upon the history of ideas and social institutions, interpretation of works of art with this end in view is surely contrary to the intentions of the artist. It is therefore desirable to keep historical interpretation in focus as but one of the kinds of critical interpretation, which in turn is but one of the three aspects of the responsive art experience.

To illustrate the sort of critical interpretation that we have called historical, we shall turn to *The Immaculate Conception*, one of the best known and most important paintings by Bartolomé Estéban Murillo (1618-1682), a Spanish artist. It may be well, first of all, to give close attention to the picture as here reproduced. In so far as you can, make use of the four suggestions, earlier given, that were intended to insure an adequate sensory perception of the work of art. Then allow yourself to respond naively, without inhibition and the intrusion of critical thought and with a willingness to enjoy and be moved by this picture as the artist hoped you would be. . . .

It is unfortunate, of course, that you cannot stand before the original of this picture, not artificially hung in an art gallery, but appropriately placed in the St. Francis Chapel in the Mission Inn at Riverside, California. For surely the environment surrounding a work of art—be it music, literature, or painting—will notably affect the artee's various naive responses.

A closer look at this painting of *The Immaculate Conception* should now result in such intrinsic interpretations, semantic and formal, as you may be led to make. This picture for you is a complex of perceptual elements, active forms, many of which are signs of one kind or another. Their meaning for you will depend upon the relevant contextual data in the private world of your experience.

What is the meaning of the title of this work of art? . . . Who is depicted? and what is the significance of her attitude? her costume? her surroundings? . . . What is represented as under foot? What are possible meanings that it may have? . . . What is the meaning of the light behind her? . . . . What are the heads in the upper corners? What is peculiar about them? . . . Who are the babies below her? What does each bear? What is the meaning of these objects? . . . What is the over-all meaning of the picture? . . .

The mistake is sometimes made of confusing the doctrine of the Immaculate Conception with the doctrine of the Virgin Birth. The former is concerned with the birth of Mary, the latter with the birth of Jesus. Mary was born the daughter of Anne and Joachim. It may indeed be looked upon as miraculous that Anne, who had been long married but barren, should conceive a child by her husband, but that Joachim was the natural father of the infant is not in question. Destined to grow up and in due time become the mother of Jesus, the Mother of God, Mary "in the first instant of her conception by a singular privilege and grace granted by God, was preserved free from all stain of original sin." The immaculateness (purity) does not refer to the physical conception of Mary within the womb of her mother, for Joachim was her father; it refers rather to the creation of her soul in purity at the moment of its infusion into her body.

The painting does not represent St. Anne, but Mary herself who had been conceived without sin. The various active forms are not only natural and resemblative signs, they are also symbolic. Forty years before Murillo's birth, the Spaniard Pacheco set down certain

photo by Field Studios

Murillo, THE IMMACULATE CONCEPTION, Mission Inn,
Riverside, California

rules, the symbolism prescribed by the Church, to be followed in depicting the Immaculate Conception, and these were for the most part followed. The apocalyptic vision (Revelation 12:1) of "a great wonder in heaven; a woman clothed with the sun, and the moon under her feet, and upon her head a crown of twelve stars," was the basis for the rules, which indicated that Mary should be shown as a maiden of twelve or thirteen, with 'grave sweet eyes, golden hair,' features 'with all the beauty painting can express,' hands folded in prayer. She should be shown in a flood of sunlight, the crescent moon under foot with points turned down. Twelve stars should crown her head. She should be shown in a spotless white robe, with mantle or scarf of blue, and a cord of St. Francis about her waist. Cherubim should be shown bearing roses, palms, and lilies, and the bruised head of the vanquished dragon should be under foot (Rev. 12: 3-13).

Murillo did not follow the prescribed symbolism exactly in this picture. The clouds symbolic of the Assumption replace the dragon's head; the points of the crescent point up; roses, lilies, and palms are supplemented by a mirror. (Each of these, of course, has its special meaning.) But he followed most of Pacheco's points, though this representation of the Virgin Mary may get her dark hair from Murillo's own daughter, Francisca, who sometimes served as her father's model. However, he painted the subject of the Immaculate Conception more than twenty-five times, and all the surviving pictures differ somewhat in their details. Some of them still remain in cathedrals, churches, chapels in Spain; others have found their way into museums in Madrid and Seville. A good number are in private collections and museums in England, France, Russia, and the United States. For a fine example, now in the Louvre, the French government paid $177,000 in 1852. Another fine example, the one included in this book, was originally painted in 1670 for the Convent of the Barefoot Carmelite Nuns at Madrid. It was taken to France after the Napoleonic Wars, sold later to a London banker. The example at the Walters Gallery in Baltimore shows the Virgin Mary with upturned eyes, head surrounded by twelve stars, standing upon a full moon. Another, with her hands not in prayer but holding her mantle to her breast, is to be seen at the William Rockhill Nelson Gallery in Kansas City, Missouri.

It is of interest that Murillo first achieved recognition because of his three years of work decorating the cloister of the convent of St. Francis in Seville, for the doctrine of the Immaculate Conception was especially close to the hearts of the Franciscans, the first of the orders to accept it. The doctrine itself, however, goes back to the *Protevangelium of James*, a second century apocryphal writing; and the Feast of the Conception of Mary—or of the Conception of St. Anne, as the Greek Orthodox Church celebrated it—is indeed very ancient. At first the Feast celebrated the miraculous birth of Mary, but by the 12th or 13th century its purpose had been changed to celebrate the 'exemption of Mary from the law of original sin.' There was a gradual development of the doctrine in the writings of the Fathers, and its special advocates were at first found among the English monks. There seems to have been wide popular belief in it, and the Franciscans led for its official adoption in opposition to the Dominican order. Most of the 14th century pictures of this subject were painted for the Franciscans, and the first papal decree relative to it was made by Pope Sixtus IV who had been a Franciscan Friar. Throughout the Middle Ages and the Renaissance disputation and argument surrounded this doctrine.

During the seventeenth century, the central two-thirds of which was spanned by Murillo's life, the Church in Spain was particularly strong in its advocacy of the Immaculate Conception as an essential belief. Its inclusion as an article of faith became an issue in the Catholic world. Even the Spanish crown threw itself into the controversy and sought (at that time vainly) a papal declaration in favor of the doctrine. That Murillo was so frequently commissioned to paint this subject—and there were many copies of his treatments of it by lesser artists—is indicative of a growing interest that spread even to the New World. To the far off Franciscan Mission of San Diego—on the Mexican coast of Alta California—was carried one of these paintings, whether original or copied, which was saved from destruction and is now hanging in the restored mission church. But the popular and clerical enthusiasm for this doctrine did not win its full recognition in Murillo's century. It was not until 1854 that Pope Pius IX proclaimed it as dogma, declaring it an article of belief.

Certainly, as you study Murillo's painting *The Immaculate Conception*, an historical interpretation, including the relevant data of theological controversy and Spanish partisanship, adds materially to your total understanding of the meaning of the work.

There are other kinds of extrinsic interpretation, in addition to the biographical and historical, three of which were suggested in the series of questions asked about the Greek kylix, *The Sack of Troy*. One of these is concerned with the relation of the work of art to similar works; this involves the study of the major art types and subtypes. A second of these is interested in the relation of the work of art to works of similar meaning; this involves the study of the chief literary themes. A third of these gives its attention to the relation of

the work of art to works that reveal similar basic attitud
volves the study of the principal historic styles. These oth
extrinsic interpretation—of type, theme, and style—are indeed important, particularly to the historian of the arts. But they are also
valuable in achieving a full understanding of the individual work of
art. However, a detailed discussion and illustration of them falls
outside the scope of this book.

6. *Some positive suggestions*

Let us conclude this chapter on 'Critical Interpretation of the
Work of Art' and this third part of the book, 'The Responsive Art
Experience,' by again making several positive suggestions. The body
of these chapters has been more or less descriptive, considering the
sorts of things that actually go on or may go on while you are looking at a picture, listening to music, or reading a book. These suggestions are intended to indicate what you can do about it, what you
can consciously do to increase the richness of your responsive art experiences, to increase your sensory enjoyment, naive appreciation,
and critical understanding of individual works of art.

1. *Lay aside your critical preconceptions.* When you have had
sufficient opportunity to respond naively, and the time therefore
comes for the more definitely thoughtful consideration, then by all
means see to it that the ground is properly cleared for thoughtful
action. Remember that the artist is a person other than yourself, different in temperament and life experience. It is ridiculous to expect him to have created the work of art that you yourself might
have created on the same subject. Do not let your preconception of
how you think it ought to have been done stand in the way of your
thoughtful interpretation of what the artist actually has done. Of
course you will bring your own art theory to bear; you cannot help
this even if it were well to try. However, if you have a narrow and
dogmatic view of art, you may not be able to hold your ravenous
preconceptions at bay! But try to.

2. *Alert self-questioning should lead the way in critical interpretation.* Now that the time for thinking has come, alert your Art Intelligence. Let your left lobe ask the right: What's the artist aiming
at? What's his purpose? There is no use trying to wring from the
work of art something that was certainly not intended to be there.
If the work is apparently representational, what is the subject matter? the active forms? the over-all meaning?... But go on from
here: Is the meaning as important in this work as the formal de-

sign? Ask yourself about your formal feeling-states? and what formal principles are involved? and what in the work of art seems to cause your formal responses? . . . Then what is the relation of the work to the artist's life and personality? the relation of the work to the time and place of creation? to the art types, the literary themes, the historic styles? . . . And so, the observer should go on keeping his wits about him in the process of alert self-interrogation.

3. *Self-answering should use all available data.* Not to be outwitted by his own alert questions, the observer must make use of the full range of his past experience—from life as well as art, experience at first hand as well as second-hand through reading. The more complex perceptions, the simple recognitions, the interpretation of meaning in each and all of its phases and over-all, the answering of critical questions—these all depend upon the ready and full use of contextual data, relevant tidbits of stored experience. And certainly as the questions present themselves to be answered, the observer will go back to the work of art time and time again for fresh sensory data. By listening attentively to the music once more, by looking closely at the picture yet another time, by rereading the poem with a new question in mind, the critical interpreter will doubtless gather in fresh data for meaningful fusion with relevant contextual data that may answer the question of the moment. But the relevant contextual data may be lacking.

4. *Then go forth to learn what you lack.* You will discover yourself wanting during this process of self-interrogation and self-answering. Some, perhaps much, of the contextual data that you will want simply are not in your head. They're not there, perhaps because they were never put there, perhaps because they have been thrown down into the trash heap of the unconscious. But many of the bits of information that you may want will be readily available in libraries. Dictionaries and encyclopedias, general works on the particular art and special studies of the artist may prove useful in filling the blank spots of your present knowledge. Space does not permit an enumeration here of the bibliographical aids and reference works useful in each of the several arts. They are well-known, of course, to those kindly guides to the bewildered and benighted, those Virgils of the Stacks, the librarians. And this final suggestion, then, is: Go forth to learn what you lack, so that you may more fully answer the alert questionings of your own mind during the critical interpretation of a work of art.

POSTLUDE

On Art Appreciation and Criticism

Although the art of all races and of all times has a common value—human, universal—each new cycle must work for itself, must create, must yield its own production—its individual share to the common good.

Orozco, *New World, New Races, and New Art*

WHEN ALICE was in Wonderland "she was a little startled by see-ing the Cheshire Cat sitting on a bough of a tree a few yards off.

"The Cat only grinned when it saw Alice."

Presently Alice asked, " 'Would you tell me, please, which way I ought to walk from here?'

" 'That depends a good deal on where you want to get to,' said the Cat.

" 'I don't much care where,' said Alice.

" 'Then it doesn't matter which way you walk,' said the Cat.

" '—so long as I get *somewhere*,' Alice added as an explanation.

" 'Oh, you're sure to do that,' said the Cat, 'if only you walk long enough!' "

In the Wonderland of Art, many an Alice has asked, Where do we go from here? For, as Michelangelo has said, "An infinite number of things still remain unsaid which might be urged in favor of these arts."

The general function of this Postlude is to bring this book to a close. But it must also point a direction—a direction in which the reader may go if he wishes to carry on his self-cultivation. One of the purposes of this volume has been to help you clarify and develop your art theory. Another has been to present a number of works of art to you in such a way as to evoke enriched responsive art expe-riences. Yet another purpose has been to help you establish a worthy goal for the personal cultivation of your taste and to encourage your liking of a wider range of art works. It has been a further purpose to

312

give you some understanding of the creative process and to increase your awareness of the many sorts of sensory, affective, and logical factors that make up a complex responsive art experience. Again, it has been the added purpose to suggest that art is not a luxury but a necessity in human life. Certainly these several objectives have not been fully achieved. But it is hoped that you have made some progress, and will now carry on this clarification of your art theory, this enrichment of your experience, this broadening of your taste, this development of your understanding, and this balancing of your mental life by further adventuring in the World of Art.

There is, however, a further purpose that this book should have: to help you establish for yourself some standards of value in the arts. And this will be the special function of this Postlude 'On Art Appreciation and Criticism.'

1. *Two enigmatic smiles*

One peculiarity of the Cheshire Cat, besides its mad logic, was that it could vanish and reappear time and again, and one time "it vanished quite slowly, beginning with the end of its tail, and ending with the grin, which remained some time after the rest of it had gone.

" 'Well! I've often seen a cat without a grin,' thought Alice; 'but a grin without a cat! It's the most curious thing I ever saw in my life!' "

It may seem a far cry from the vanishing Cat with the haunting grin to the famous portrait of *Mona Lisa* by Leonardo da Vinci. But the picture did vanish from that wonderland the Louvre in a real-life mystery in 1911 (though later recovered), and its smile lingers as the subject of countless discussions.

Leonardo da Vinci (1452-1519) was one of the great men of the Italian Renaissance, painter and inventor. Born near Florence, he studied as a youth with Verrocchio. Leonardo did much of his work in that city, but later in Milan and in Rome, and even in France.

If *The Last Supper,* the mural in a refectory in Milan, is his most famous work, certainly *Mona Lisa* is his most controversial. Mona Lisa Gherardini became the wife of the Florentine Francesco del Giocondo at about eighteen, and was in her early twenties when she sat for this portrait. Leonardo is said by Vasari to have worked off and on for four years on this small painting, which measures only twenty by thirty inches; and the artist, it is said, never felt he had finished it. According to Vasari, often given to romancing in his famous *Lives* (1550), Leonardo wanted so to rival Nature in his

Leonardo da Vinci, **MONA LISA**, Louvre, **Paris**

portrait that the very soul of Mona Lisa should be mirrored in her smile; and directed that music be played, songs sung, and poetry recited while she posed. On one occasion he even called in mountebanks to amuse her, to cause her continual smile. Whatever the facts about Leonardo's creative activity, this now-dulling painting on a wood panel became the pride and pleasure of kings, a puzzle and problem for critics. King Francis I is said to have paid 4000 gold crowns for it. It was a prized possession at Fontainebleau; Louis XIV had it in his collection at Versailles; it hung in Napoleon's bedroom in the Tuileries. Now in the Louvre, it has been reproduced and copied countless times.

And much has been written about it. Before reading the following interpretation of it by Walter Pater (1835-1894)—it is part of a longer essay *Leonardo da Vinci,* from his volume *The Renaissance* —you may do well to turn to the picture itself, as here reproduced, for a thoughtful experience of it . . .

from LEONARDO DA VINCI
by *Walter Pater*

. . . We all know the face and hands of the figure, set in its marble chair, in that cirque of fantastic rocks, as in some faint light under sea. Perhaps of all ancient pictures time has chilled it least.* As often happens with works in which invention seems to reach its limit, there is an element in it given to, not invented by, the master. In that inestimable folio of drawings, once in the possession of Vasari, were certain designs by Verrocchio, faces of such impressive beauty that Leonardo in his boyhood copied them many times. It is hard not to connect with these designs of the elder, by-past master, as with its germinal principle, the unfathomable smile, always with a touch of something sinister in it, which plays over all Leonardo's work. Besides, the picture is a portrait. From childhood we see this image defining itself on the fabric of his dreams; and but for express historical testimony, we might fancy that this was but his ideal lady, embodied and beheld at last. What was the relationship of a living Florentine to this creature of his thought? By means of what strange affinities had the person and the dream grown up thus apart, and yet so closely together? Present from the first incorporeally in Leonardo's thought, dimly traced in the designs of Verrocchio, she is found present at last in *Il Giocondo's* house. That there is much of mere portraiture in the picture is attested by the legend that by artificial means, the presence of mimes and fluteplayers, that subtle expression was protracted on the face. Again, was

---

* Yet for Vasari there was some further magic of crimson in the lips and cheeks, lost for us.

it in four years and by renewed labour never really completed, or in four months and as by stroke of magic, that the image was projected?

The presence that thus rose so strangely beside the waters, is expressive of what in the ways of a thousand years men had come to desire. Hers is the head upon which all "the ends of the world are come," and the eyelids are a little weary. It is a beauty wrought out from within upon the flesh, the deposit, little cell by cell, of strange thoughts and fantastic reveries and exquisite passions. Set it for a moment beside one of those white Greek goddesses or beautiful women of antiquity, and how would they be troubled by this beauty, into which the soul with all its maladies has passed! All the thoughts and experience of the world have etched and moulded there, in that which they have of power to refine and make expressive the outward form, the animalism of Greece, the lust of Rome, the reverie of the middle age with its spiritual ambition and imaginative loves, the return of the Pagan world, the sins of the Borgias. She is older than the rocks among which she sits; like the vampire, she has been dead many times, and learned the secrets of the grave; and has been a diver in deep seas, and keeps their fallen day about her; and trafficked for strange webs with Eastern merchants; and, as Leda, was the mother of Helen of Troy, and, as Saint Anne, the mother of Mary; and all this has been to her but as the sound of lyres and flutes, and lives only in the delicacy with which it has moulded the changing lineaments, and tinged the eyelids and the hands. The fancy of a perpetual life, sweeping together ten thousand experiences, is an old one; and modern thought has conceived the idea of humanity as wrought upon by, and summing up in itself, all modes of thought and life. Certainly Lady Lisa might stand as the embodiment of the old fancy, the symbol of the modern idea.

In a recent book on Leonardo (1934), M. Raymond Boyer is quoted as saying: "The mystery of La Gioconda is her half-smile—by which I mean an attenuated smile, composed of the interplay of several disconnected and discrepant smiles. If we apply the method of eclipse to that world-famous face, covering first one portion of it, then another, we make an interesting discovery. It is a nicely adjusted correlation—a visual counterpoint—of *competing* aspects that gives the face its psychic ambiguity." Whatever that means!

In a yet more recent essay on 'The Problem of Criticism,' in *The Enjoyment of the Arts*, George Boas writes: "The Mona Lisa has up to very recent times been universally admired, but the critics of the sixteenth century admired it for its fidelity to 'nature,' those of the nineteenth century—following Gautier and Pater—saw it as a symbol of 'enigmatic womanhood.' If you ask which was right, you are asking a foolish question. For no one in the sixteenth century could have seen it as a symbol of enigmatic womanhood for the simple reason that woman did not become enigmatic until a certain form of romanticism had become popular." It may be added that the smile of Mona Lisa has, in our own day, been subjected to a Freudian interpretation. And the end is not yet.

However, the smile of Mona Lisa, whatever the intention of Leonardo or the secret thoughts masked in the mind of La Gioconda, may be accepted as a symbol. For us it may well stand for the riddle of art, those meanings that one almost but not quite grasps, those values that one intuits but cannot express in words or communicate to another.

2. *Evaluation and art judgment*

Although we described the World of Art in broadest terms in the Prelude, it was necessary at once to mark out some boundaries for this world by the process of definition, and this we proceeded to do in Chapter 1. We put a three-strand fence around our grazing range and posted it: *This is Art*. In doing so we introduced 'beauty,' a value word. We explored some of its meanings in Chapter 2, and developed a working definition in Chapter 3. In Interlude I, 'On the Personal Cultivation of Taste,' a second sort of value was introduced, intuitive liking, which we later referred to, in Chapter 8, as naive affection. You will recall that beauty was said to be object centered; that is, the artee regards it as possessed by the work of art. However, naive affection was said to be subject or ego centered; that is, the artee recognizes the liking as his own feeling about the work of art. In Interlude II, 'On the Human Need for Art,' a third and somewhat different value was implicit in the discussion of art therapy; for works of art are of value in so far as they serve human needs. But some of these human needs are satisfied by works of art without regard to the possible attribution of beauty, and some of these human needs are satisfied without the artee's developing any affection for the work of art. Satisfaction, then, the fulfillment of psychological needs, is a different value from beauty and affection, though certain interrelations may at times be noted.

In any consideration of THE ARTS AND HUMANITY, then, there is no avoiding the insistent question of value. "The arts are our storehouse of recorded values," writes I. A. Richards in *Principles of Literary Criticism,* a penetrating study not of one alone but of all the arts. "They spring from and perpetuate hours in the lives of exceptional people, when their control and command of experience is at its highest, hours when the varying possibilities of experience are most clearly seen and the different activities which may arise are most exquisitely reconciled, hours when habitual narrowness of interests or confused bewilderment are replaced by an intricately wrought composure. Both in the genesis of a work of art, in the creative moment, and in its aspects as a vehicle of communication, reasons can be found for giving to the arts a very important place in the theory of Value. They record the most important judgments we possess as to the values of experience."

The phrase 'important judgments' suggests not only the artist's evaluation of his experiences, but also the artee's critical evaluation of the work of art.

Art judgment, which was mentioned briefly in Chapter 2, will be the fourth, then, in our list of art values—beauty, affection, satisfaction, and value judgment. These statements, then, refer to somewhat different values: (1) 'The picture is beautiful,' (2) 'I like it a lot,' (3) 'It does something for me, helps me,' (4) 'I think it's a very good painting.' The fourth of these, like the first, is object centered; it attributes a certain value to the work of art. But, unlike all of the first three, it is not a naive response, it is a critical judgment; it is thought out. Art judgment might well have been discussed in the preceding chapter on 'Critical Interpretation,' except that it is not concerned with understanding works of art but with estimating their worth.

The title of this Postlude 'On Art Appreciation and Criticism' serves to emphasize these two sorts of evaluation: the naive felt-responses of beauty, liking, and satisfaction; and the critical, logical, or rational response of art judgment. The aim of art appreciation might well be to gain some acquaintanceship with works of art, to enrich one's art experiences, to develop some understanding of art processes, to cultivate personal taste. These indeed are among the purposes of this book. The aim of art criticism might well be to analyze the creative process and the responsive experience, to improve techniques of interpretation, to discriminate various modes of evaluation, to develop standards of art value and skill in art judgment. In some measure, these too have been purposes for this book.

This contrast of art appreciation and criticism raises some important questions: Are not works of art intended to be enjoyed rather than judged? This is the kind of question often asked with an exclamation point and carrying its own answer. The answer is, of course, Yes, art is intended to be enjoyed, not judged. D. W. Prall has said, "The aesthetician would remind us, with relation to art, judging of relative merit is for the most part irrelevant."

But is it irrelevant? Whether works of art are intended to be judged or not—and whether the merit of a particular work relative to some other work or abstract standard is relevant to your experience of that work—still, each one of us is bound to ask of art experiences whether they are worth while, whether they represent a good expenditure of time and energy, whether they are more valuable or less valuable than other human experiences competing for our attention. Works of art, then, will inevitably be evaluated even though intended to be enjoyed.

There is a second question: Shouldn't works of art be enjoyed first and judged afterward? The answer, again, is, Yes. At any rate works of art must be experienced fully, whether such experience is pleasurable or not, before they are subjected to final rational judgment. This is only logical: a work of art cannot be judged in its entirety until it has been read through or heard through or examined throughout. We have enlarged upon the necessity of repeated sensory experiences, ample time and willingness for naive response, the various directions of critical interpretation. Surely it is not fair to pronounce final judgment on a work of art without giving it a chance to testify fully in court.

Works of art are not prisoners at the bar, however, and you are not jury. You are not obliged to remain in the courtroom to hear out their testimony if you consider it to be indecent or vulgar, shallow or boring, dogmatic or bombastic. So, too, you may lay down the book that does not hold your attention or stimulate your interest, move on from the picture that fails to make sense or evoke other effects of value, or turn off the radio or record player if the music doesn't seem worth while. It is inevitable that, upon the basis of preliminary judgment, you may at times wish to disqualify yourself as judge without enjoying further trial. However, if you do give a final judgment, certainly your evaluation should not be made until the work of art has been fully realized—perceived, responded to, interpreted.

The judicial analogy should not, however, be carried too far. There is no generally accepted body of Art Law or trial procedure. However, several observations may be made about the practice of art criticism as distinguished from art appreciation. For instance, art criticism is assumed to be objective. It seeks consistency through the establishment or utilization of some sorts of standards. It is essentially rational in character. However, its effort to proceed in this way has sometimes led to the mistaken assumption that the values are somehow *in* the work of art as a public object. It has sometimes generalized formal rules and art principles that have had, at best, but limited applicability to works of art falling within a prescribed circle or a single culture. It has at times tried to utilize inappropriately the scientific techniques of exact measurement. Yet man does seek, and should seek, for standards of value for the thoughtful evaluation of works of art.

If art principles are to be found, it is the contention of this book that they will grow out of psychology, the science of human behavior conditioned by man's biological structure and function. Laboratory studies, such as Guy Buswell's *How People Look at Pictures,* and analytical studies of human responses to art works, such as I. A. Richards' *Practical Criticism,* are part of the modern effort to establish the basis for criticism.

As yet there is no simple list of objective art standards that will serve the layman as a handy yardstick for judicial criticism. Nevertheless, as we asserted in the Foreword, everyone does have some general notions of what is art and what isn't, of what he considers good, mediocre, and bad. This art theory, however vague and fragmentary and inconsistent, includes abstractions that do serve, for weal or woe, as a yardstick for the evaluation of particular works of art.

It is well to remember, however, that another kind of measuring device is ready at hand. Comparative criticism simply measures one work of art against another. The only necessity is that the two works be comparable; that is, they must fall into the same category in one or several classifications. For instance, Leonardo's *Mona Lisa* and Holbein's *Edward* might be compared as portraits; Delacroix' *Barque of Dante* and Dante's poetic description, as representative of the same scene; Barber's *Adagio for Strings* and Haydn's *String Quartet.* It might be difficult, however, to find an adequate basis for comparative study of Pater's interpretation of *Mona Lisa* and Schumann's *The Happy Farmer.* Upon the basis of some perceived similarity, then, the two works are examined as to their differences. This may be a purely descriptive comparison, or the discriminated differences may be evaluated one by one. That is, you may decide that the *Edward* is better than the *Mona Lisa* in regard to this or that point of comparison. Your decision may in each case be purely intuitive— you simply like the color composition better, let us say; or it may be a critical judgment involving standards generalized in your art theory. In any case, comparative studies and comparative criticism do have the advantage of greater objectivity, for both works of art do exist as public objects. It must be remembered, however, that it is only works of art as perceived that can be compared.

For those who wish their system of evaluation to help them in picking out those works of art that are 'really and truly good,' comparative criticism itself is not of much help. Whatever its faults, judicial criticism at least attempts to establish standards and absolutes. Comparative criticism presented with two comparable mediocre works can do no more than choose the less bad. But there is a special form of comparative criticism that may be of great service. In it works of widely recognized value but of many different kinds are selected to be used as touchstones in measuring the worth of such new things as are to be judged. This method was devised by Matthew Arnold and was given its classic expression in his essay sometimes called 'The Study of Poetry.' Carrying about in his mind chosen bits of poetry which, the work of the great masters, have the true ring of highest poetic quality, the reader may have some confidence in his ability to match untried work against these eternal samples. This method is an advance over comparative description (which has no standards at all) and comparative criticism which falls back upon mere preference or upon vague absolutes. However, there are two disadvantages: the huge and complicated systems of touchstones necessary to evaluate the many different aspects of art works of all sorts, and the temptation to judge a work of art solely by bits and not as a whole. But there is another difficulty inherent in the touchstone method, which seems more objective than it is: no new works of art are likely to shine with a lustre comparable to those well-worn and beloved touchstones.

It is but a step from this method to the similar use of art masterpieces as the basis for criticism. Herein the yardstick is not to be found in various tidbits of unparalleled excellence, but in complete works of all the established types and subtypes. Earlier, we said that classical taste would be a false goal for self cultivation, because, in idealizing the achievements of the great past, we may ignore contemporary culture. However, we were then talking about liking; we are now talking about judging. One should indeed develop a magnanimous taste—contemporary, classical, and catholic—and set oneself the ideal of liking all good things of all cultures and countries, classical and contemporary. But, in the chaos of art in our day and at a time when art works are coming to us from far places but dimly understood, a treasury of art masterpieces may indeed serve as a rock in the shifting sands of fashion.

Bases, then, for your critical evaluation of art works will be found in your gradually developing art theory, in your judicious comparison of pairs of art works, in your acquisition of touchstones of high excellence, and in your growing understanding and appreciation of those undoubted masterpieces in all the arts that have withstood the test of time, providing generations of persons with worthwhile art experiences.

3. Art and democratic idealism

Many things indeed remain to be said about the arts and humanity. In the Interlude II 'On the Human Need for Art,' emphasis was placed upon the arts as serving individual human needs. But the arts also serve group needs. We saw how paintings of *The Immaculate Conception* served the Church in Spain. The Nebraska State Capitol at Lincoln, Nebraska, serves a definite governmental need. Mozart's Overture to *Figaro* and the American spiritual *Swing Low, Sweet Chariot* also served, somewhat differently, social purposes. We live in a time when in some parts of the world the arts are coerced to serve the state. But in other lands artists perform willing service to their cultural idealism.

The *Lincoln Portrait* by Aaron Copland will be the final work of art presented in this book. It will illustrate the above paragraph; it will also provide an opportunity for applying the discussion of evaluation from which we have just now turned.

Aaron Copland is a modern American composer, Brooklyn born in 1900, whose compositions include music for two ballets, *Appalachian Song* and *Billy the Kid*, and various works for piano and for orchestra. At the beginning of World War II, Andre Kostelanetz suggested to Copland, and to two other composers, the idea of writing the musical portrait of a great American. After toying with the idea of using Walt Whitman as his subject, Copland chose Abraham Lincoln. He decided to embody some of Lincoln's great utterances on human freedom, and searched the Lincoln letters as well as the famous speeches for material. He made sketches for the musical work in February 1942, completed the score on April 16, and Kostelanetz conducted the première performance with the Cincinnati Symphony Orchestra on May 14.

Copland says of the *Lincoln Portrait*: "The composition is roughly divided into three main sections. In the opening section I wanted to suggest something of the mysterious sense of fatality that surrounds Lincoln's personality. Also, near the end of this section, something of his gentleness and simplicity of spirit. The quick middle section briefly sketches the background of the times he lived in. This merges into the concluding section, where my sole purpose was to draw a simple but impressive frame about the words of Lincoln himself."

Many performances of this work have been given both in this country and abroad. Two recordings are available: one, by the

Boston Symphony Orchestra, Serge Koussevitzky conducting and Melvyn Douglas, outstanding liberal actor, as narrator; the other, by the New York Philharmonic, Artur Rodzinski conducting and Kenneth Spencer, prominent Negro baritone, as narrator.

In listening to The *Lincoln Portrait* you may hear the echoes of such different Americana as the old hymn 'Rock of Ages' and bugle calls such as 'Taps.' Copland made conscious use of two tunes of the Civil War period: 'Springfield Mountain' (or 'The Pesky Sarpent') and 'The Camptown Races.' The musical notation of the principal themes (with bar numbers) and the narrator's words may be helpful in your study of this work of art.

Thematic Outline and Text
LINCOLN PORTRAIT
by *Aaron Copland*

(The following selections from "Lincoln Portrait," copyright 1943, reprinted by permission of Boosey & Hawkes.)

The first section, of which Copland spoke, opens with a slow rhythmic and harmonic figure that leads directly to the first theme beginning with the eighth measure and developed through bar 37. Then comes the second theme, stated 'with simple expression' by the solo clarinet, as called for in the score, and restated by a muted trumpet. The horns echo the first theme to close this first section.

The second section opens with a quick but simple accompaniment figure at measure 57, and almost at once the third theme, a bright tune by the oboe; this figure is repeated and then the tune again. Then comes its companion theme at 73 in the flutes. The accompanying figure now leads to a simple descending motif in thirds by the violins at bar 81. The complex and exciting development of these musical ideas leads to a noisy climax at bar 244 that brings this section to a close.

The third section opens with the second theme in augmentation, that is, at half its original speed, accompanied by unobtrusive echoes of the third theme; and this leads directly to Lincoln's words. The music that accompanies the speaking of the lines makes use of the themes already stated and developed musically. It underscores and comments upon the meaning of the words, which are here reprinted.

"Fellow citizens, we cannot escape history."

That is what he said,
That is what Abraham Lincoln said:

"Fellow citizens, we cannot escape history. We of this Congress and this administration will be remembered in spite of ourselves. No personal significance or insignificance can spare one or another of us. The fiery trial through which we pass will light us down, in honor or dishonor, to the latest generation. We—even we here—hold the power and bear the responsibility."

He was born in Kentucky, raised in Indiana, and lived in Illinois.
And this is what he said:
This is what Abe Lincoln said:

"The dogmas of the quiet past are inadequate to the stormy present. The occasion is piled high with difficulty, and we must rise with the occasion. As our case is new, so we must think anew and act anew. We must disenthrall ourselves, and then we shall save our country."

When standing erect he was six feet four inches tall.
And this is what he said:
He said:

"It is the eternal struggle between two principles—right and wrong —throughout the world ... It is the same spirit that says, 'You toil and work and earn bread—and I'll eat it.' No matter in what

shape it comes, whether from the mouth of a king who seeks to
bestride the people of his own nation and live by the fruit of
their labor, or from one race of men as an apology for enslaving
another race, it is the same tyrannical principle!"

Lincoln was a quiet man.
Abe Lincoln was a quiet and a melancholy man.
But when he spoke of democracy,
This is what he said:

He said:

"As I would not be a slave, so I would not be a master. This
expresses my idea of democracy. Whatever differs from this, to
the extent of the difference, is no democracy."

Abraham Lincoln, sixteenth President of these United States, is
everlasting in the memory of his countrymen,
For on the battleground at Gettysburg, this is what he said:

He said:

". . . that from these honored dead we take increased devotion to
that cause for which they gave the last full measure of devotion:
that we here highly resolve that these dead shall not have died
in vain; that this nation, under God, shall have a new birth of
freedom; and that government of the people, by the people,
and for the people, shall not perish from the earth."

It may seem an impertinence to suggest that this *Lincoln Portrait*
may not only be interpreted critically but also critically evaluated.
There are some persons, at least, who will ask: Is this a good work
of art? Is it perhaps great art? It is too recent in origin to assert
with confidence that it will survive the generations, though it bids
fair to last well beyond its decade. If one were to seek comparison
of *Lincoln Portrait* with recognized masterpieces, classics of the subtype of music to which it belongs, then one faces an immediate difficulty: there is nothing quite like it. It is not absolute music; it is
not purely a tone poem, though it is in part that; it is not music
for the ballet, dramatic, or operatic theaters; it is neither cantata
nor oratorio. But it is, certainly, program music, and may therefore
be compared with the classic examples of that type both as a whole
and in its parts.

A somewhat different comparison suggests itself, with *The New
World Symphony*. Both are symphonic works written in this country
within a half century of each other; both make use of native musical

themes and ideas; both have something to say about American life and idealism.

Such comparative study may indeed lead to critical evaluation; it is almost certain to lead to critical understanding, and this, in turn, to a realization of some of the art values already considered— beauty responses, naive affection, and the satisfaction of individual and social needs.

4. *In conclusion—pointing a direction*

This Postlude, we said, should bring this book to a conclusion and also point the reader on his further way. This will be done now, briefly, by formulating a final foursome of positive suggestions. The preceding three chapters have ended with four suggestions each. It is hoped that they will make your responsive art experiences more vivid in perception, more fully realized in naive response, and more meaningful. They have been directions for getting the most out of those things that you come across in your World of Art. But it is not enough to be a passive or even an active recipient of the good things that come your way. You should reach out for good things near at hand and move out toward the perhaps better things at present beyond the horizon.

Early in the book it was said that you can only start off from where you now are. Shortly thereafter a goal was suggested toward which you might well move—magnanimous taste—and a course was roughly plotted toward that end. And a further goal was introduced: the well-adjusted personal life and enriched understanding of human experience. Now we have, in this Postlude, proposed the gradual acquisition of standards and touchstones and masterpieces as the bases for critical evaluation. As a means of progressing from where you now are to where you may well wish to be, these final suggestions are made:

1. *Welcome the art experiences that are within your reach.* There has never been a time when the materials for self-cultivation have been so ready at hand. The Great Books are on every news stand in pocket editions. The classics and modern music and opera are weekly if not daily features on the radio and are increasingly available as inexpensive recordings. The masterpieces of painting and contemporary works of interest are reproduced in color in many of our magazines. Public libraries, concert series, and art galleries are civic enterprises in even our smaller cities. Public and private schools, through all age levels from kindergarten to university and

adult education, provide courses and cultural opportunities in the fine arts and humanities. For almost all persons, right at hand, are the opportunities for further art experiences. Welcome them, make use of them, as one means for attaining the abundant life.

2. *Build purposefully upon what you already know and like.* Now you know the names of certain works of art that are to your taste. Seek out other works by the same artists or of the same type or on similar themes. Proceed from what you know and like to other works of art that give promise of similar pleasure and profit. But remember that you are building up a body of meaningful and valuable experiences, not simply adding to it, so remember to make use of ladders or habituation series that will serve to cultivate gradually a taste for art works that may now seem strange and new. Reading and record lists, program and gallery notes, may help you to decide what to try next in the purposeful enlargement of your art experience to include more and more of the world masterpieces and significant contemporary works.

3. *Discriminate consciously while in process of experiencing.* If you are alert to mark the difference in the various items of your experience, far from becoming hypercritical or destroying your pleasure by cold analysis, you will actually increase your enjoyment of works of art. Noting similarities and differences is the basis of all knowledge: definition, classification, generalization are all dependent upon it. The pleasures of novelty and variation, repetition and contrast, come as a result of discrimination. We earlier suggested that you free yourself from inhibitions, that you allow yourself ample opportunity for naive response while holding off critical interpretation and evaluation. However, we then pointed out that you can't quite do this. And we have said in this Postlude that you should indeed lay down the book or turn from the picture or shut off the music that *when given half a chance* really bores you or fails to evoke a meaningful and valuable response. But a mind with some notion of the complexity of the responsive art experience will find ample opportunity for making a wide variety of discriminations. An alert mind with breadth of interests is unlikely to be bored.

4. *Evaluate your art experiences while still enjoying them.* We have said seriously that art comes to you, not to be judged, but to be enjoyed. There is a very real danger that, for some persons, the kind of close scrutiny of works of art proposed in this book—the analysis of various responses and the search for their meanings—may actually destroy the work of art for them, rendering it a problem to be solved rather than a pleasure to be secured. " 'Tis murder to

dissect," wrote Wordsworth, and Shelley could think of nothing worse than "to cast a violet into a crucible."

But works of art do not come full-blown as living things into the consciousness of man. A work of art as perceived is, rather, a synthesis. What unity it possesses in perception is the result of the fusion of various sensory data with contextual data. What unity it possesses in full experience is the result of a further fusion of the work of art as perceived with all manner of naive responses and critical interpretations. The work of art, as you know it and perhaps love it, is pieced together within your mind. To examine its amazing complexity is not to destroy it. To evaluate a work of art—by beauty response and affection, by noting human satisfactions and comparing it with standards or masterpieces—is but to enhance one's enjoyment of it.

INDEX

color, 161, 227; 'color,' 156, 159, 164, 166, 175-7.
color blindness, 46.
communication, 109; c. of emotion, 271.
companionship, 213.
conception of creative idea, 138, 145, 151, 185-6.
conflicting stimuli, 275.
Confucius, 72.
Conrad, Joseph, 250.
Constable, John, 62.
content, 287.
context, contextual data, 96, 226, 229, 233, 237, 240, 244-5, 247, 248, 278, 311.
COPLAND, AARON, 322, 323-5.
creative art activity, 33, 123ff, 154, 178ff, 206-8.
creative idea, conception of, 138, 145, 151, 185-6.
creative process, 137ff., 185ff.
critical evaluation, criticism, 275, 312, 318-21, 326.
critical interpretation, 94, 252, 275, 277, 292-3, 310.
Croce, Benedetto, 207.

Dance, 37, 165-6, 197, 244-5, 260.
Dancing Peasants, frontispiece, 3-5, 7, 28.
DANTE, 231, 234-236.
Da Ponte, Lorenzo, 8.
DA VINCI, LEONARDO, 57, 313, 314, 315-7.
DEBUSSY, CLAUDE, 106,
definition, 20-21, 28, 34.
DELACROIX, EUGENE, 63, 230, 231.
de Medici, Cosimo, 142.
Denis, Maurice, 153.
development of creative idea, 138-40, 141, 146, 151, 185-6.
Dewey, John, 62, 213.
Diana and Acteon, 110, 111.
Discus Thrower, 188, 189, 190.
Divine Comedy, 234-36.
Dobrée, Bonamy, 61, 87.
Dobson, Austin, 70.
DODGSON, CHARLES L., 285, 298.
DORE, GUSTAVE, 194, 195.
Ducasse, Curt, 62, 72.
DVORAK, ANTONIN, 299, 300-1, 302-6.

ear, 238-9.
Edward, 103, 104, 105-6.
Einfühlung, 259.
emotion, 61, 71, 268-73.

empathy, 72, 244, 259-60, 263, 264, 269, 271-2, 288.
enrichment, 212.
equilibrial data, 261; e. adjustment, 263; e. imagery, 256.
Erlking, The, 179, 180-3, 184, 188.
Erskine, John, 215.
escape, 211.
evaluation, see critical e.
EVANS, RUDULPH, 66, 67.
evocations, 94-6.
execution of creative idea, 140-1, 146, 152.
experimentation, 60.
expression, 57, 71.
extrinsic interpretation, 293, 297.
eye, 226-7.

Fall Plowing, 158, 161.
feeling phase of meaning, 281.
figurine, 20.
Fine Arts, vii, 37, 208.
form, 69, 156, 159, 161, 166, 263, 267, 287, 292.
formal feelings, 260-7, 269, 288-90.
formal interpretation, 287-92.
FRANCE, ANATOLE, 13-16.
free-imagery, 255-60, 269.
French, Daniel Chester, 176.
Fry, Roger, 69, 72.
functional, 40.
funding, 229.

Gaul and His Wife, 254, 255, 259-60, 271, 274, 284.
Gerard, Sanford, E., 52, 115.
Géricault, Théodore, 123.
Gestalten, 226.
Girl Before a Mirror, 121.
GOETHE, J. W. VON, 180, 181-3.
GOODHUE, BERTRAM GROSVENOR, 245, 246.
Gotshalk, D. W., 44, 73, 81, 250, 288.
GRANDVILLE, J. J., 194-5, 196.
Grave in the Foothills, 134-5, 135-41.
Great Lover, The, 76, 86.
Greene, Theodore M., 32, 69.
Groos, Karl, 71, 211.

Hambridge, Jay, 69.
HAMMOND, ARTHUR, 41.
Hanslick, Edouard, 87, 150, 153.
Happy Farmer, The, 265, 266, 272, 274, 280-1, 291.
harmony, 140, 240, 288.
HAYDN, JOSEPH, 241-2, 243.

responsive art experience, 3-5, 33-4, 47, 154, 206-8, 219ff., 250, 271, 273-4.
Reynolds, Sir Joshua, 59, 112, 116.
rhythm, 214, 240, 243, 264-6, 267, 272-3, 288, 291-2.
Richards, I. A., viii, 68, 72, 89, 153, 213, 279, 317, 320.
Rivals, The, 113-115.
Roosevelt, Franklin D., 215.
Ross, William D., 73.
Rotunda, 66.
Ruskin, John, 19, 44, 52.

Sack of Troy, 294-5, 296-7.
Santayana, George, 44, 71, 81, 85.
scale, diatonic, 173-4; tempered, 174.
Schiller, J. C. F. von, 71, 72, 211.
Schopenhauer, Arthur, 211.
SCHUBERT, FRANZ, 179-81, *182-3,* 184-6, 304.
SCHUMANN, ROBERT, 178, *265,* 266, 304.
sculptor, 176.
Sculpture, 24, 37-8, 66, 110, 143-4, 156, 189, 245, 253, 254.
Seashore, Carl, 46, 240.
semantic interpretation, 278-84, 288.
sensation, 225, 237, 239, 248.
sense-imagery, 237, 258.
sense, phase of meaning, 279-80, 282; makes sense, 252, 319.
sensory classification, 38; s. data, 229, 233, 236-7, 248; s. perception, 155, 224ff., 226ff., 231ff., 238ff., 243ff., 251, 269.
SHAKESPEARE, WILLIAM, 81, 179, 197-8, *199-203,* 299.
Shelley, Percy B., 178, 326.
SHERIDAN, RICHARD B., *113-115,* 215.
Sidney, Sir Philip, 62, 250.
sign, signs of meaning, 89-109, 160, 252, 271, 278-9, 283, 292; four sorts of s., 96-9.
significance, *see* meaning, value.
significant form, 72.
Sistine Chapel, ceiling of, *129.*
social and cultural forces, 305.
Socrates, 85, 267.
'sound,' sound waves, 166-8, 171-4, 238ff.
sources of the artist's materials, 133-7.
Spaeth, Sigmund, 303.
spatial, spatiotemporal, 38, 155, 165.
spiritual, anonymous American, *42-3,* 302-4.
stageplay, 166-7, 197, 244-5, 260.

STEELE, SIR RICHARD, 192, *193*
Stevens, Wallace, 215.
stimulus, 145, 150-1, 186-7.
Stites, Raymond S., 73.
string quartet, 243.
String Quartet, No. 39, 241-2, 243.
styles, 293, 310.
subject matter, 159, 252-3.
sublime, 73, 82.
substance, 156, 159, 161, 164, 165, 171.
Sullivan, Louis, 139.
Sunflowers, 21, 22, *25,* 27, 37, 40.
Swing Low, Sweet Chariot, 42-3, 44, 303, 322.
symbols, symbolic signs, 39, 96, 162, 196, 279, 283.
Symphony No. 5 in E Minor, 300-1.
synaesthesis, 72-3.

Table Lamp, *26, 27,* 37.
tactile data, 245, 247.
tangible, 37.
taste, 51-2, 115-6, 268; cultivation of, 112; 'good t.,' 118 magnanimous t., 119, 321.
technique, 62, 127, 138ff.
temporal, 38.
tensions, 214.
terminal value, 40, 81.
tertiary qualities, 80.
Theater Art, 10-11, 37-8, 113f., 166-7, 199ff., 221-4, 257.
themes, 309.
therapy, 209, 214.
Thomas Jefferson, 66.
Through the Looking Glass, 284-5, 286-7, 299.
tied-imagery, 255-8, 260.
time-space arts, 38.
Tolstoy, Leo, 59, 63, 87, 213.
tone, phase of meaning, 281.
Torossian, Aram, 253.
total personality response, 220-1, 224, 260, 274.
touchstones, 321.
translation, translators, 179, 184, 188-94, 196.
Truman, Harry S., 215.
TUDHOPE, WILLIAM, *191.*
types of art, 309.

unity, 139, 288-9, 326.
Upton, Albert W., viii, 81, 94, 251.